11,0973

With Signs Following

The Story of the Pentecostal Revival

in the Twentieth Century

011303

Revised Edition

By

Stanley Howard Frodsham

GOSPEL PUBLISHING HOUSE
Springfield, Missouri 65802

02-0635

Foreword

Many godly men have foreseen that in the last days God would graciously send an outpouring of the Spirit like to that which was seen in the first days of the church.

In the excellent commentary on the whole Bible produced by Jamieson, Fausset and Brown, we read this word on "until he (or it) received the early and latter rain" (James 5:7): "The receiving of the early and latter rains is not to be understood as the object of his hope, but the *harvest* for which these rains are the necessary preliminary. The early rain fell at sowing time, about November or December; the latter rain about March or April, to mature the grain for the harvest. *The latter rain that shall precede the coming spiritual harvest will probably be another Pentecost-like effusion of the Holy Ghost.*"

This word was a true forecast. The latter rain has come and this revival has indeed been "another Pentecost-like effusion of the Holy Ghost."

The author of this book has sought to tell some of the things he has seen and heard during the past four decades. It has been his privilege to meet many evangelists, pastors, and missionaries who have told him how graciously the Lord Jesus has confirmed the preaching of His Word with signs following. He has received hundreds of letters and many publications from all over the world, all telling the same story of the latter-rain outpouring of the Holy Spirit, accompanied by the same signs that were manifest in the days of the Acts of the Apostles.

The Gospel Publishing House in 1916 issued a book entitled "The Apostolic Faith Restored," by B. F. Lawrence. In writing the introduction to this book, J. W. Welch said: "If the Lord should tarry, it is hoped and expected that this book will be followed by another in which it will be possible to give a fuller and more accurate account of the greatest revival the world has seen since the early church period."

In 1926 the larger book entitled "With Signs Following" was published. A second edition with some revisions was published in 1928, but has long been out of print. The author now offers the third edition of "With Signs Following," adding to it much material that did not appear in the former editions.

This new edition goes forth with the prayer that our gracious Lord will make it a blessing to everyone who reads it.

S. H. F.

CONTENTS

CONTENTS

CHAPTER I

Gracious Showers of Blessing in the 19th Century

WHEN the writer was a young Christian, and a member of a large Congregational church, he was often troubled with the thought— Why do we not see miracles today as of old? The Lord Jesus went about doing good, and healing all that were oppressed of the devil. His apostles did the same. Why are we not having a like ministry today?

One day in the year 1908 a paper came into his hands. It told of the Spirit's being poured out in Los Angeles, Calif., just as at Pentecost. Many remarkable healings were described. As he read of this revival there came a strong witness to his spirit that this was of God. Later other papers came from Canada, England, India, South Africa, and different parts of the United States, and his eyes were opened to the fact that God was once more pouring out His Spirit in many places even as at Pentecost, that the Lord was truly with His people and confirming His Word today as He did in the beginning of this church age.

This same year, the Lord filled the writer with the Spirit, making no difference between him and those at the beginning. He was soon awakened to the fact that he was one of a large, world-wide fellowship. There were Baptists, Methodists, Presbyterians, Congregationalists, Episcopalians, Holiness people, Christians from every denomination and from no denomination, who had received a like experience. He noticed that all these Spirit-filled ones made very much of the precious blood of Jesus Christ, and that the cross of Christ had been made very real to all of them through the power of the Holy Ghost. He found that all that he came in contact with believed that the Lord healed today just as of old, and that many of them had had marvelous healings themselves. They were one and all looking eagerly for the soon coming of Christ. Everyone of them honored the Word of God, believing in every part of it, and they were all seeking to be not only hearers but doers of the Word.

He was made to realize that we are indeed now living in the last of the last days foretold by the prophet Joel, "It shall come to pass in the last days, saith God, I will pour out of My Spirit upon all flesh," and that the Lord Jesus Himself, exalted at the right hand of the Father, was the One who "hath shed forth this, which ye now see and hear." Acts 2:33.

He will never forget the first Pentecostal convention he attended. There was a newly baptized Dutch minister who preached several times, and he was so overflowing with the joy of the Lord that he made everyone covet to receive what he possessed. At the first meeting the writer noticed a young man come in and sit at the back of the building. His face was pale and emaciated, for he was far gone with tuberculosis. At the close of that morning's service this young man began to seek the Lord, and again after the afternoon session. Between this service and the one in the evening, this young man was eating a lunch with some of the workers when he suddenly felt the power of God coming upon him. He got on his knees and in one moment he was speaking in other tongues as the Spirit gave utterance. Then thumping his lungs, he declared, "I believe God has healed me." He felt in his body that he was healed of his plague. A few days later he had a complete medical check-up, and the doctor found that both his lungs that had been affected were now perfect. This young man, whose name was Frank Trevitt, became a remarkable soul winner and later went as a missionary to China, where God gave him a blessed ministry.

As the news of this "Latter Rain" outpouring began to spread abroad, it was found that spiritual showers had been falling for a number of years in various parts of the world, gradually increasing in volume.

Some years ago, V. P. Simmons of Frostproof, Florida, wrote a tract in which he told of many gracious manifestations of the Spirit that he had seen in New England. He stated, "In A. D. 1854 Elder S. G. Mathewson spoke in tongues and Elder Edwin Burnham interpreted the same. The writer knew both of these men of God well, and had often sat under their preaching. They were large men physically, mentally and spiritually." He witnessed a revival in New England in 1873, and stated: "The talking in tongues, accompanied largely with the gift of healing, was manifested." Their most noted leader was Elder Doughty, a man whom, all things considered, he regarded as "having the strongest faith and power in prayer of any person with whom I ever became acquainted." These saints had faith to see the gifts of the Spirit in operation, and God graciously gave them according to their expectation.

In the year 1873 Dwight L. Moody and Ira Sankey went to England. The story of their visit is recorded in a book entitled "Moody and Sankey in Great Britain," by Robert Boyd, published in 1875.

The two workers from America did not receive a very good reception at the beginning. They were invited to Sunderland, but their presence there aroused a good deal of opposition from unsympathetic ministers. A delegation of young men waited on Mr. Moody and asked him to speak at the Y.M.C.A. He consented. The Lord began to send a gracious awakening. Mr. Boyd described what he himself witnessed at one meeting. "When I got to the rooms of the Y.M.C.A. I found the meeting on fire. The young men were speaking in tongues, and prophesying. What on earth did it all mean? Only that Moody had been addressing them that afternoon. Many of the clergy were so opposed to the movement that they turned their backs upon our poor innocent Y.M.C.A., for the part we took in the work; but afterward, when the floodgates of divine grace were opened, Sunderland was taken by storm. . . . The people of Sunderland warmly supported the movement, in spite of their spiritual advisers. There was a tremendous work of grace." The same story was also published in "Moody and His Work" by W. H. Daniels, published in 1876 by the American Pub. Co., Hartford.

Thirty-four years later there was a similar visitation in Sunderland, not this time in the Y.M.C.A., but in an Episcopal church. On this latter occasion Christian leaders made their way to Sunderland from all parts of England. They were filled with the Spirit as on the day of Pentecost with the similar evidence of speaking in tongues. As they returned to their own assemblies the fire spread and many received a like experience.

A Pentecostal outpouring in Providence, Rhode Island, is described by R. B. Swan, a pastor in that city, who testified: "In the year 1875 our Lord began to pour out upon us His Spirit; my wife and I, with a few others, began to utter a few words in the 'unknown tongue.' I report one incident at this time. A sister was wrought upon by the Spirit to speak. She did not want this gift and kept her lips closed. We labored with her to yield to the Spirit, and when she did, she broke forth in a volume of words in an unknown tongue which continued for quite a time. Her name was Amanda Doughty. Her husband is an elder in my assembly.

"In the year 1874-1875, while we were seeking, there came among us several who had received the Baptism and the gift of tongues a number of years before this, and they were very helpful to us." (He mentions six people who came from five different states in New England.) These saints were known as the "Gift People." They were greatly despised, and many thought it was a disgrace to attend their meetings.

A young woman who was a confirmed invalid and a hunchback, heard of the healings that were taking place among them and asked her father to take her to one of the meetings. This he refused to do. Her sister, who was a wild, high-spirited girl, when she saw that her father refused, promised that she would herself take her at the first opportunity. One Sunday morning, when the old folks went to the regular place of worship, she went out and got a rig ready, carried her sister out to it and drove her to the "Gift" meeting.

When they arrived, they saw a man who had had his limb broken, who was carried into the meeting. The people went to prayer, and presently one from among them arose, went to the man with the broken limb, laid hands on him, and in the name of Jesus bade him arise and walk. He did so, much to the astonishment of the visitors. Then, turning to the invalid sister that had the hunchback, he laid hands upon her, and bade her to be straight in the name of Jesus. She was instantly healed. This wrought such conviction upon the heart of the girl who had brought her there that she fell prostrate under the hand of God, and when she arose she had yielded her heart to God. It was the custom of these people to pray over the new converts. They laid hands on her according to Scripture, and she spoke in tongues as the Spirit gave utterance.

In the year 1879, a young man in Arkansas, W. Jethro Walthall, received a mighty enduement from on high. He testified: "At the time I was filled with the Spirit, I could not say what I did, but I was carried out of myself for the time being. Sometimes in the services and sometimes when alone in prayer, I would fall prostrate under God's mighty power. Once, under a great spiritual agitation, I spoke in tongues.

I knew nothing of the Bible teaching about the Baptism
or speaking in tongues, and thought nothing of what
had happened in my experience."

He became a Baptist minister but says, "I knew the
light I had received was not countenanced by the
Baptist ministry, and it finally led to my being expelled
from the church for heresy.   The charges specified
against me were my belief in the Holy Spirit Baptism,
Bible Holiness, and Divine Healing."

Brother Walthall became a member of a movement
known as "Holiness Baptists."   He testifies: "We continued to press our way into a full gospel ministry,
looking for the restoration of the supernatural, when
the Spirit's downpour came in 1906.   Almost simultaneously with the great spiritual outpour, speaking
in tongues began among us.   With it came wonderful
healings, among them two advanced cases of cancer,
consumption, paralysis, etc., etc.

Later Brother Walthall joined the fellowship known
as the Assemblies of God, and for many years was
superintendent of the Arkansas District Council of that
church.

About the same time that Brother Walthall was
filled with the Holy Ghost, there lived in a village in
Switzerland a girl whose name was Maria Gerber, who
had a special visitation of the Spirit.   Filled with the
joy of the Lord, she would go out into the fields singing
in ecstatic worship in a tongue she did not understand.   To her it was no amazing thing.   She only
knew that she was yielding her once unruly heart to
the Spirit, and as she did so, He caused her to sing
psalms, hymns, and spiritual songs in a language she
had never learned.

Some years later she came to the United States to
attend the Christian and Missionary Alliance Bible
School.   She was unacquainted with the English
language and purposed to give herself entirely to the
study of English during the first few months of her
visit to America.

She was met by her brother in New York, who said to her, "Maria, I want you to go with me and visit a sick friend of mine. You have been marvelously healed of the Lord yourself, and I believe if you will go to this friend, God will give you the prayer of faith for him."

But she protested, "The first thing I am going to do is to learn English. I have made up my mind not to do any visiting until I have a working knowledge of the English language. So please understand that."

Her brother was disappointed, and departed, but he left behind him the address of the sick friend. After he had gone, the Lord dealt with her and said, "You did not ask *Me* if I wanted you to go and see this sick man. You made your own decision not to go. But I want you to visit him."

Here she was, a young Swiss girl, alone in New York City, knowing no tongue but German, for she came from that part of Switzerland where German is spoken. But she purposed in her heart to find that sick man. She started out and showed the address to the first policeman she met. She did not understand a word the policeman said, but she noticed the direction in which he pointed. Scores of policemen that day had that card to read, and she turned the way they pointed, until at last she arrived at the desired address.

She was taken to the bed of the sick man. She saw an English Bible by the bedside, picked it up and began to read. Then she prayed—not in her usual German language—but in perfect English. The power of the Lord fell on that sick man and he received immediate healing. And Maria Gerber herself received the gift of the English language. She later went to Armenia as a missionary where she labored for many years.

The following story was told the writer by a godly Scotch Presbyterian minister named John Telfer: "I had a nervous breakdown and my physician recommended that I take a vacation in Canada. I took his counsel, and thanks to the splendid and invigorating climate, I was soon restored to health. As I was leaving Montreal I found I had some time to wait, and I looked around the railroad station to see if there was anyone with whom I could have an hour of fellowship. I noticed a man in the uniform of the Salvation Army and thought, 'I guess that man is well saved. I shall get in touch with him.' So I approached him and we were soon enjoying a delightful time of fellowship in the things of God.

"As my train arrived I was compelled to leave my new friend and I said to him, 'Excuse me, but what part of England did you come from? I have never heard any one speak such pure English in my life.'

My Scotch friend continued, "The brother looked at me curiously for a moment and then said, 'I think I can tell you. I am not English but French. I was born in Quebec and knew nothing but the French language. I was a very great sinner and a terrible drunkard. However, I heard the gospel in a Salvation Army meeting in Quebec, and God saved my soul. Later I joined the Army and became an officer and for some while was in charge of French corps in different parts of the province of Quebec. One day orders came from headquarters for me to take charge of an English-speaking corps. I protested that I knew no English. Despite my protests I was instructed to go and take charge of this corps. I went, and cried mightily to the Lord for help. The following Sunday when I arose in meeting I was enabled to address my comrades in perfect English, and from that time I have had free use of this language.'

"And to confirm what he said," said my Scotch friend, "his brother came along just at that time and he introduced him. I found that his brother could hardly speak a word of English, and to make himself clearly understood he had to speak in French."

There were many who received the supernatural speaking in tongues toward the close of the last century.

Most of them did not associate the phenomenon with the Baptism in the Spirit received at Pentecost. They considered it one of the signs promised by the Lord in Mark 16, or one of the gifts of the Spirit referred to in the 12th chapter of first Corinthians.

In the year 1889 Daniel Awrey, of Delaware, Ohio, was converted. Nine months after his conversion, on the last night of 1889, while he was reading a spiritual book, he was led into deep communion with the Lord. As the bells were ringing the old year out and the new year in, the Holy Spirit spoke to his heart assuring him that God had for him a new and better experience.

That night (January 1, 1890) he attended a prayer meeting. His faith rose and he claimed an immediate fulfillment of the promise given in the midnight hour. Suddenly the Spirit fell upon him and he began to pray in an unknown tongue. His wife received a similar experience ten years later.

In 1899 the Awreys were living at Benah, Tennessee. At that time about a dozen received the Holy Spirit and spoke in tongues as the Spirit of God gave utterance. Later when Daniel Awrey came in touch with people who had received a similar experience he fell in line with them and had a very beautiful ministry in many parts of the world. He loved to visit missionaries to encourage them. It was when he was paying a visit to the Liberian field in 1913 that he was taken to be with Christ.

Henry H. Ness of Seattle, Wash., writes in a booklet entitled "Demonstrations of the Holy Spirit," of a Pentecostal outpouring in the Swedish Mission Church, Fourth Ave. and Tenth St., N. Moorehead, Minn., where John Thompson was pastor: "This spiritual revival began in 1892 and continued many years. There were many remarkable healings, and very often as Pastor Thompson was preaching, the power of God would fall, people dropping to the floor and speaking in other tongues as the Spirit gave them utterance. One sister in particular, Miss Augusta Johnson, received a mighty Baptism with the Holy Spirit, spoke in other tongues, prophesied, and had many wonderful visions. The Lord gave her a definite call to go to Africa, where she has labored as a missionary more than thirty years.

"Not only in Moorehead was the Spirit poured out at that time, but also at Lake Eunice, Evansville, and Tordenskjold, Minn. Both Mr. Thompson and many of the saints who were witnesses to those great manifestations of the power of God, are still active in the Lord's service. Another remarkable outpouring of the Spirit took place at Greenfield, S. Dak., in the First Methodist Church where Rasmus Kristensen was pastor. This was in 1896. As Brother Kristensen was preaching the power would fall, the people being filled with the Holy Ghost and speaking in other tongues; and many other wonderful manifestations of God being witnessed."

Pastor C. M. Hanson, of Dalton, Minnesota, testifies: "In 1895, while holding meetings and preaching the full gospel, a person came clear through and spoke in tongues as in Acts 2:4. Two years later I prayed with another soul for the Baptism in the Holy Spirit. Shortly after, the Spirit came on her and she leaped, shouted, praised God, sang, prophesied, and spoke in other tongues. Two years after this, I was led to get alone with the Lord. All at once, like a mighty rushing wind, the spiritual atmosphere was cleared up and my whole inward soul was enlightened. The atoning blood of Christ, justifying me before God, made everything clear. The Holy Spirit then, as a person, took possession of His temple, speaking in other tongues, while I realized myself a listener and an instrument in the hand of the Almighty." Brother Hanson today is a minister of the Assemblies of God, still preaching the full gospel.

In 1896 a revival meeting was started in the Shearer Schoolhouse in Cherokee County, North Carolina. Prayer meetings were held here by William F. Bryant, a leading man of that community. The power of

God fell and quite a number received the Baptism in the Spirit with the speaking in tongues. There were many remarkable miracles of healing in this revival, and numbers of hard-hearted sinners were converted.

In the year 1900 there was an outpouring of the Spirit in North Carolina where a number of people had withdrawn from the Baptist Church because of their stand on the doctrine of personal holiness. One night while meetings were in progress, a woman began to pray and presently broke into speaking in another tongue. Two ministers who were present went to Tennessee, and there some forty or so were baptized in the Spirit. One of these was Sarah A. Smith, who went to Egypt as a missionary. She was with Lillian Trasher in the early days of Miss Trasher's great orphanage work.

CHAPTER II

At the Beginning of This Century

 AN THE fall of 1900 a Bible school was opened at Topeka, Kansas. About forty came together with the one purpose of studying the Word of God. No textbook but the Bible was used in this school. One subject studied was the Baptism in the Holy Ghost. The students were given time for an exhaustive search of the Scriptures and then were asked, "What is the Bible evidence of the Baptism in the Holy Ghost?" They were unanimous in their answer, "Speaking in other tongues as the Spirit gives utterance."

One room in this Bible school was dedicated to the Lord as a Prayer Tower. The students resorted to this room for three-hour watches. Sometimes whole nights were spent in the Prayer Tower. Day and night, ceaseless intercession ascended to God.

The ministry of evangelism was not neglected, and meetings were held every night in the city of Topeka. We will let one of the students, Mrs. Agnes N. O. LaBerge, formerly Miss Agnes N. Ozman, who was the first to receive the Baptism in the Holy Ghost in the school, tell her story:

"I had been a Bible student for some years and had attended T. C. Horton's Bible School at St. Paul, Minnesota, and Dr. A. B. Simpson's Bible School in New York. In October 1900 I went to this Topeka school, which was known as Bethel College. We studied the Bible by day and did much work down-

19

town at night. Much time was spent in prayer every day and all the time.

"Like some others, I thought I had received the Baptism in the Holy Ghost at the time of consecration, but when I learned that the Holy Spirit was yet to be poured out in greater fullness, my heart became hungry. At times I longed more for the Holy Spirit to come in than for my necessary food. We were admonished to honor the blood of Jesus Christ and to let it do its work in our hearts, and this brought great peace and victory.

"On watchnight we had a blessed service, praying that God's blessing might rest upon us as the new year came in. During the first day of 1901 the presence of the Lord was with us in a marked way, stilling our hearts to wait upon Him for greater things. A spirit of prayer was upon us in the evening. It was nearly eleven o'clock on this first of January that it came into my heart to ask that hands be laid upon me that I might receive the gift of the Holy Ghost. As hands were laid upon my head the Holy Spirit fell upon me, and I began to speak in tongues, glorifying God. I talked several languages. It was as though rivers of living water were proceeding from my innermost being.

"On January 2, some of us went down to Topeka to a mission. As we worshiped the Lord I offered prayer in English and then prayed in another language, in tongues. A Bohemian, who was present, said I spoke his language and he understood what I said. Some months later, when at a schoolhouse with others, holding a meeting, I spoke in tongues under the power of the Spirit and another Bohemian understood me. Since then, others have understood other languages that I have spoken.

"The hearts of other students were made hungry for the Holy Spirit, and they continued to tarry before the Lord. On January 3, some of the students went to the mission and others gathered in prayer at the Bible school. God answered their prayers by pouring out His Spirit, and one after another began speaking in tongues and some were given interpretation."

Miss Lillian Thistlewaite writes of this heavenly visitation: "An upper room had been set aside for tarrying before the Lord. We would spend every spare moment in audible or silent prayer, in song or in just waiting upon Him. The presence of the Lord was very real and there were definite heart searchings.

"Through the Spirit I received this message, 'Praise the Lord for the Baptism.' A great joy came into my soul and I began to say, 'I praise Thee,' and great floods of laughter came into my heart. Psalm 126:2. I tried to praise the Lord in English but could not. So I just let the praise come as it would in a new language that was given. The floodgates of glory were wide open. The Holy Spirit had come to me, even to me, to speak not of Himself but to magnify Christ. And oh, what a wonderful, wonderful Christ He revealed. All around me I heard great rejoicing while others spoke in tongues and magnified God. One sister had a wonderful language. She spoke in tongues and immediately following came the interpretation, a beautiful poem about Christ, the worship of Christ, bringing the words of the Saviour, 'When the Comforter is come ... He shall testify of Me.'

"With a simultaneous movement, we began to sing together, each one singing in his new language but all in perfect harmony. As we sang 'All Hail the Power of Jesus' Name' and other familiar hymns, it would be impossible to describe the glory of His presence in our midst. The cloven tongues of fire had been seen by some when the evidence was received.

"As we went into meetings it seemed impossible that any one could resist the messages given. Some, understanding the languages spoken, were convinced. But with others the prophecy was fulfilled, 'With men of other tongues and other lips will I speak unto this people; and *yet for all that will they not hear Me, saith the Lord.'* 1 Cor. 14:21; Isa. 28:11, 12.

"On one occasion a Hebrew rabbi was present when one of the students read the lesson from the Bible. After the service this rabbi asked for the Bible from which the lesson was read. The Bible was handed him and he said, 'No, not that one; I want to see the Hebrew Bible. That man read in the Hebrew tongue.' On another occasion, during the sermon there was a message in tongues. At the close of the meeting a man arose and said, 'I am healed of my infidelity; I have heard in my own tongue a Psalm I learned at my mother's knee'."

It was soon noised abroad that Pentecost was being repeated and an article appeared in the Topeka paper ridiculing the speaking in tongues. Other newspapers began to hear of it and sent reporters. Articles appeared in Kansas City and St. Louis papers. These advertised the work, and some came to see what the Lord was doing.

Mrs. LaBerge writes: "After some weeks of blessing in the school our hearts were burdened for other cities. The Lord made it clear to a company of twenty of us to go to Lawrence, Kansas. An old theater was rented for the meetings. We made house-to-house visitations throughout the city, going two by two, praying for the sick in homes wherever we could get admittance. Large numbers came to the meeting, and many were saved, the sick were healed, and a goodly number of believers received the Baptism just as we had, speaking in tongues and glorifying God. Francene Dobson, of Joplin, Missouri, was one who received the Baptism in this meeting. A company of us visited Kansas City and had a good meeting there. Some were saved and healed and a number received the Holy Spirit, speaking in tongues as the Spirit gave utterance.

"From the beginning we proclaimed the importance of a clean, holy life of victory and power for every believer. We honored the Father, Son, and Holy

Ghost. We believed and taught all the words and commands of the Lord Jesus Christ, repentance, forgiveness of sins, a sanctified life, separation unto the Lord, and power over sin through the indwelling Christ.

"After a while the work of the school seemed to have been finished and those connected with it went into evangelistic and missionary work. Some went south, bringing the light of Pentecost into Missouri, Texas, and other fields."

CHAPTER III

The Outpouring Throughout the South

IN THE year 1903 a most gracious Pentecostal revival came to the city of Galena, Kansas. In this city was a good sister, Mrs. Mary A. Arthur, who was a great sufferer. She says, "I was afflicted with dyspepsia for fourteen years, also with prolapsus, hemorrhoids, and paralysis of the bowels, but my greatest distress was in my eyes. My right eye was virtually blind from birth. I sought the help of many prominent oculists, and tried allopathy, homeopathy, osteopathy, and Christian Science. In the summer of 1898 a Kansas City doctor operated for the second time on my eyes after which they grew much worse. I spent two summers in a dark room and could neither read, write nor sew for the pain. Five years passed in which I knew no moment apart from pain. Everything I tried for relief only ended in a new disappointment."

In August 1903, at the insistence of her husband, Mrs. Arthur went to Elorado Springs. It was there that she heard the gospel message that Jesus Christ is the same yesterday, and today, and forever, and that He heals the sick in our day as surely as He did in the days of His flesh. She was prayed for and anointed according to James 5:14, 15 and was perfectly healed.

She testifies: "I was healed on August 17, 1903, and joy and gladness filled my soul continually. With this came a deeper thirst for God than I had ever known before. As I sought the Lord He gave me

many promises concerning the Holy Spirit. One
morning while I was praising, the Lord told me that
the Comforter would come to me that day. It was a
busy day in the home, and it was not until in the
evening that I got alone to pray, and I said, 'Now He
will come to me according to His word.' And as I
praised the Lord for His faithfulness and asked Him
to take the throne of my heart, the blessed Comforter
came in and my joy overflowed in utterance in other
tongues. Then He gave me the words in English and
later many languages, often interpreted by friends who
spoke the different languages. He also gave me the
most beautiful songs in the Spirit, indescribably glorious and so different from our ordinary singing.

"In October 1903 a meeting was started in our
home for two days, but so many came we did not have
room. On October 20 we opened up a meeting on a
large lot adjoining our home. The meeting continued
until Thanksgiving, and after that we secured the Grand
Leader building on Main Street. This building was 50
feet by 110 feet, but the doors to it stood wide open
as the crowds overflowed into the street. Two meetings
were held each day until January 15, and all the city
was moved. Large numbers from surrounding towns
came, for God stretched forth His hand to heal the
sick by the hundreds. Many signs and wonders were
wrought, and hundreds were saved and filled with the
Holy Ghost.

"One night when we were in a tent meeting the
Holy Spirit was manifested in heavenly song. An
interpretation came in English. The tent was filled
with angels and these were seen even by sinners. Those
who stood outside saw a white cloud come down and
rest on the tent. Two nuns from St. Louis, who were
visiting friends, came to the meeting and heard the
anthem that the Spirit gave. They said it was sung in
the most perfect Latin and that it was translated into
perfect English. They said their cathedral church choir

had tried to learn that anthem for a month but had finally given it up as too difficult.

"A three-year-old child fell from a second-story window of a large store building on Main Street. She fell about eighteen feet to the sidewalk. Three doctors were called and they said, 'Nothing can be done for the child, she will die from internal bleeding; or if she becomes conscious she will have convulsions until she dies.' They advised the mother to call for prayers, agreeing among themselves it would be a test case, as they knew the child's condition. In response to prayer God healed the child."

The revival soon extended to the near-by cities of Baxter Springs, Columbus, and Joplin. A short while later a company left Galena for Orchard, Texas, to carry the fire there. Mrs. John C. Calhoun, of Houston, Texas, writes: "In the early spring of 1904, a report reached the writer in the city of Houston, that the Latter Rain was falling in a prairie village named Orchard, forty-five miles west." She searched the Word diligently to see if what was reported was Scriptural, and decided to visit the scene. Attending the community church one Sunday morning, she realized a supernatural power in the songs, prayers, and testimonies, the like of which she had never seen before, and her heart was strangely warmed within her. A matronly lady, whom she afterwards learned was Mrs. Anna Hall, gave a soul-stirring message. The Spirit of the Lord was present in marked power, speaking for Himself from time to time in a strange language through the lips of His handmaiden. In the evening meeting Mrs. Hall again preached. It was a never-to-be-forgotten occasion. In that hour Mrs. Calhoun heard the call and received the promise of the Father.

Returning to Houston, she testified to the congregation and to Pastor W. F. Carothers, who was a leader of the Holiness Church in Brunner, a suburb of Houston. The testimony was received kindly and a great searching of the Word began among these noble

Bereans, with the result that when two months late,
an evangelistic party came from Kansas to hold a
campaign in Bryan Hall, this church was ready for the
message. Almost immediately God set His seal upon
the work by baptizing in the Spirit a sixteen-year-old
member of the congregation. Others were soon filled
with the Spirit and many healings followed.

There were many saved in this meeting in Bryan
Hall and there were some notable cases of healing.
Mrs. Delaney, who was well known in the city, had
been seriously injured in a street-car wreck about two
years previous to this first meeting. She was paralyzed
and had to go about in a wheel chair. One day she
was being wheeled around the street and came to a
street meeting. Previously she had been given a vision
of one of the workers and the Lord had shown her
that he would pray the prayer of faith for her. In the
street meeting she saw the man the Lord had shown her
in the vision. She stopped to listen to the preaching
and inquired where the meetings were being held. A
few days later she was brought to the meeting and was
carried, chair and all, up the stairs. She was prayed
for and instantly healed. This caused quite a stir.

A special conference was held in Houston in 1905
and at the close several bands of workers went forth
to near-by towns. Oscar Jones, a former Baptist
preacher, and some other workers went to Alvin,
Texas, and took the opera house. God visited this
place with a very gracious revival. About 200 were
converted and 134 received the Baptism in the Spirit.
Hugh M. Cadwalder, who at the time of writing is
laboring in Egypt as a missionary, is one of the fruits
of this meeting. The revival soon began to spread
throughout the State of Texas and many hundreds
were saved and filled with the Spirit.

In the fall of 1905 a Bible school was held in
Houston, and from this school about fifty preachers
and workers went out into new fields and were soon
having gracious revivals.

A convention was held in Orchard, Texas, in April 1906. At the close of the convention a number who had attended were unsatisfied, as they had not received the Baptism in the Spirit as they expected. However, as they went to the railroad station to take a certain train they were full of expectation. The train was late and so while they waited the time was spent in singing, testifying, and preaching. When the train arrived the seekers were full of the joy of the Lord and in one hour twelve were filled with the Spirit. Three of these who received later became ministers of the gospel.

It was just at this time that the power began to fall in Los Angeles, but previous to this it is estimated that at least 1,000 had received the Baptism in the Spirit and spoken in other tongues as the Spirit of God gave utterance, and there were some 60 preachers and workers in the State of Texas alone.

CHAPTER IV

Pentecost in Los Angeles

AMONG those who attended the Bible school held at Houston, Texas, was a colored Holiness preacher named W. J. Seymour. He was convinced in his heart as he listened to the Word explained at this Bible school that the Lord meant His saints in these days to receive the Baptism in the Spirit in identically the same manner as they received on the day of Pentecost with the initial evidence of speaking in other tongues as the Spirit of God gives utterance. He was convinced that "this is that" which was promised through the prophet Joel, and that nothing else is "that."

It happened that a sister from Los Angeles, who was associated with a small colored Nazarene church, visited Houston, Texas, and on her return to Los Angeles she told about a "very godly man" she had met in Houston. These colored saints in Los Angeles were moved to send an invitation to Brother Seymour to hold a meeting in their church. In due time he came to Los Angeles, and he took for his text on the first Sunday morning that he stood in that Nazarene pulpit, Acts 2:4. He said that when any one receives the Baptism in the Spirit according to the original pattern, he will have a similar experience to that which the disciples had on the day of Pentecost, and speak in tongues just as they did on that occasion.

That afternoon, when he returned to this mission, he found the door was locked against him because these

colored saints thought he was preaching a false doctrine, and they would not allow him in the mission
any longer. He was invited to a home where he gave
himself to prayer.

Some Baptists, who lived at 214 North Bonnie
Brae Street, invited Brother Seymour to hold a meeting in their home. In a short while a number of
hungry souls were meeting nightly to pray in this
Bonnie Brae Street home.

It was on April 9, 1906, that the power of God fell
upon those praying saints, and seven received the
Baptism in the Spirit and began to speak in tongues.
The shouts of praise were so tremendous that it was
soon noised abroad that there was a gracious visitation
from on high. Sister Emma Cotton writes: "People
came from everywhere. By the next morning there
was no getting near the house. As the people came they
would fall under the power, and the whole city was
stirred. The sick were healed and sinners were saved
just as they came in.

"Then they went out to find another meeting place
and they found an old discarded building on Azusa
Street that had been used for a Methodist church but
had been vacant for years. It seemed to have been
waiting for the Lord, and there began the great world-
wide revival. People came from all over the country
by the hundreds and thousands. That meeting lasted
for three years, day and night, without a break.

"The noise of this great outpouring of the Spirit
drew me. I had been nothing but a walking drug
store all my life, with weak lungs and cancer. As they
looked on me (and Sister Cotton had a terrible cancer
on her nose) the saints said, 'Child, God will heal you.'
In those days of that great outpouring, when they said
God would heal, *you were healed.* For thirty-three
years I have not gone back to the doctors, thank God,
nor to medicine. The Lord saved me, baptized me in
the Holy Ghost, healed me and sent me on my way
rejoicing."

The one who gave this testimony became a preacher of the gospel and is still preaching that our glorious Christ will save, heal, and fill thirsty souls with His blessed Holy Spirit.

The premises at 312 Azusa Street which had formerly been a Methodist church had been converted in part into a tenement house, leaving a large, unplastered barn-like room on the ground floor. It was in the vicinity of a tombstone shop, some stables and a lumber yard, where no one would complain of all-night meetings.

A witness wrote of those early days: "The news spread far and wide that Los Angeles was being visited with a 'rushing mighty wind, from heaven.' The how and why of it is to be found in the very opposite of those conditions that are usually thought necessary for a big revival. No instruments of music are used. None are needed. No choir. Bands of angels have been heard by some in the Spirit and there is heavenly singing that is inspired by the Holy Ghost. No collections are taken. No bills have been posted to advertise the meetings. No church organization is back of it. All who are in touch with God realize as soon as they enter the meeting that the Holy Ghost is the leader. One brother states that even before his train entered the city he felt the power of the revival. Travelers from afar wend their way to the headquarters at Azusa Street. There they find a two-story whitewashed store building. You would hardly expect heavenly visitations there unless you remember the stable at Bethlehem. But here they find a mighty Pentecostal revival going on from ten o'clock in the morning until about twelve o'clock at night. Pentecost has come to hundreds of hearts. We remember years ago, when a bright young missionary was dying in Bombay, India. In his last hours, unconscious from the fever, he kept crying, 'Pentecost is coming! Pentecost is coming!'

"As soon as it is announced that the altar is open

for seekers for pardon, sanctification, the Baptism in the Holy Ghost, and healing for the body, people rise and flock to the altar. There is no urging. What kind of preaching is it that brings that? The simple declaring of the Word of God. There is such power in the preaching of the Word in the Spirit that people are shaken on the benches. Coming to the altar many fall prostrate under the power of God and often come out speaking in tongues. Sometimes the power falls on people and they are wrought upon by the Spirit during the giving of testimonies, or the preaching, and they receive the Holy Spirit. It is noticeably free from all nationalistic feeling. If a Mexican or a German cannot speak English he gets up and speaks in his own tongue and feels quite at home, for the Spirit interprets through the face and the people say 'Amen.' No instrument that God can use is rejected on account of color or dress or lack of education. That is why God has so built up the work.

"Seekers for healing are usually taken upstairs and prayed for in the prayer room. Many have been healed there. There is a large room upstairs that is used for Bible study. A brother fittingly describes it this way: 'Upstairs there is a long room furnished with chairs and three California redwood planks laid end to end on backless chairs. This is the Pentecostal upper room where sanctified souls seek the Pentecostal fullness and go out speaking in tongues'."

A leading Methodist layman said: "The scenes transpiring here are what Los Angeles churches have been praying for for years. I have been a Methodist for twenty-five years. I was leader of a prayer band for the First Methodist Church. We prayed that Pentecost might come to the city of Los Angeles. We wanted it to start in the First Methodist Church but God did not start it there. I bless God that it did not start in any church in this city, but in a barn, so that we might all come and take part in it.

If it had been started in a fine church, poor colored people and Spanish people would not have got it."

The following is an extract from the *Apostolic Faith,* a four-page, free paper that was published from the Azusa Street headquarters: "The waves of Pentecostal salvation are still rolling in Azusa Street Mission. From morning till late at night, meetings continue with about three altar services a day. We have made no record of souls saved, sanctified, and baptized in the Holy Ghost, but a brother said last week he counted about fifty in all who had been baptized with the Holy Ghost during the week. Four Holiness preachers have received the Baptism in the Holy Ghost. One of these, Brother William Pendleton, and his congregation have been turned out of their church and are holding meetings at Eighth and Maple. There is a heavenly atmosphere there. The altar is filled with seekers, people are slain under the power of God and are filled with the Holy Ghost.

"Different nationalities are now hearing the gospel in their own tongue wherein they were born. A sister, Anna Hall, spoke to the Russians in their church in Los Angeles in their own language as the Spirit gave utterance. They were so glad to hear the truth that they wept and even kissed her hands. They are very poor and simple, but hungry for the full gospel. The other night, as a company of Russians were present in the meeting, Brother Lee, a converted Catholic, was permitted to speak their language. As he spoke and sang, one of the Russians came up and embraced him. It was a holy sight and the Spirit fell upon the Russians as well as the others, and they glorified God."

In December 1906 the *Apostolic Faith* was able to report: "Hundreds of souls have received salvation and healing. The Lord God is in Los Angeles in different missions and churches in mighty power, in spite of opposition. This revival has spread through the towns round about Los Angeles, through the States, over the United States in different places, and across the ocean. The blood of Jesus Christ prevails against every force and power of the enemy. Glory to God!"

Writing of what they believed, they said: "We stand for Bible truth without compromise. We recognize every man that honors the blood of Jesus Christ to be our brother, regardless of denomination."

Writing of those early days in Azusa, Frank Bartleman stated: "Brother Seymour generally sat behind two empty shoe boxes, one on top of the other. He usually kept his head inside the top one during the meeting, in prayer. There was no pride there. The service ran almost continuously. Seeking souls could be found under the power almost any hour, day or night. People came to meet God. He was always there, hence the continuous meeting. God's presence became more and more wonderful. In that old building, with its low rafters and bare floor, God took strong men and women to pieces, and put them together again for His glory. It was a tremendous overhauling process. Pride, self-assertion, self-importance, and self-esteem could not survive there.

"No subjects or sermons were announced ahead of time and no special speakers for such an hour. No one knew what might be coming, what God would do. All was spontaneous, all of the Spirit. We wanted to hear from God through whomsoever He might speak. We had no respect of persons. The rich and educated were the same as the poor and ignorant, and found a much harder death to die. We recognized God only. All were equal. No flesh might glory in His presence. He could not use the self-opinionated. Those were Holy Ghost meetings, led of the Lord. It had to start in poor surroundings to keep out the selfish human element. All came down in humility together at His feet."

A. H. Post, a Baptist minister of Pasadena, California, wrote: "About the middle of June, I was led into the meetings in Azusa Street. I was convinced that God was indeed working. In the altar service I quietly presented myself before the Lord. On the second day, while at the altar, as distinctly to my inner consciousness as a clear voice to my ear, the Lord said, 'Receive ye the Holy Spirit.' As a hungry person would readily take food, I eagerly accepted the gift of my Lord. This was Saturday afternoon. On the Monday following I returned to Los Angeles and was in meetings all day. The meeting at night seemed very remarkable. As Brother Seymour preached, God's power seemed to be increasing in him. Near the close of the sermon, as suddenly as on the day of Pentecost, while I was sitting in front of the preacher, the Holy Spirit fell upon me and literally filled me. I shouted and praised the Lord and incidentally I began to speak in another language. Two of the saints quite a distance apart saw the Spirit fall upon me. Oh, how God did fill my whole being in a way indescribable! I had not been seeking the gift of tongues, or any gift; but oh, how I did long for God Himself to completely fill me, and in His great love He surely did! In an experience of over thirty-five years God has kept me, and I am sure that in no time in my life was I more fully surrendered to God and free from all desire aside from just His will alone. I know that God has come into my life in a fuller and more profound sense than ever before. His love completely permeates my whole being."

The writer of the above testimony later went to Egypt as a missionary. God gave to him a mighty ministry of intercession. As a result of his constant life of prayer there came gracious visitations in Egypt, especially in the great orphanage at Assiout in charge of Miss Lillian Trasher. (See Chapter XIV.)

A. W. Orwig wrote of those early days at Azusa Street: "One thing that somewhat surprised me was the presence of so many people from different churches. Some were pastors, evangelists, or foreign missionaries. Persons of many nationalities were present. Sometimes these, many of them unsaved, would be seized with deep conviction of sin under the burning testimony of one of their own nationality, and at once heartily turn to the Lord. Occasionally some foreigner would hear a testimony or earnest exhortation in his native tongue from a person not at all acquainted with that language, and thereby be pungently convicted that it was a call from God to repent of sin.

"In the first year of the work in Los Angeles I heard W. J. Seymour say, 'Now, do not go from this meeting and talk about tongues, but try to get people saved.' I heard him counsel against all unbecoming or fleshly demonstrations and everything not truly of the Holy Spirit. Brother Seymour constantly exalted the atoning work of Christ and the Word of God and very earnestly insisted on thorough conversion, holiness of heart and life, and the fullness of the Holy Spirit, yet some uninformed persons uncharitably declared that the whole thing consisted of talking in tongues and was of the devil.

"A reporter from one of the daily papers was assigned to write up an account of the meetings held by those supposedly ignorant, fanatical, demented people, but it was to be from the standpoint of the comic or the ridiculous—the more highly sensational the better. The reporter went to the meetings with feelings in harmony with his employers. He was going to a circus. But he witnessed some very touching, solemn scenes, and heard the gospel truth so admirably presented in the Holy Ghost by different persons, that his frivolous feelings gave way to devout ones.

"After a while a Spirit-filled woman gave a mighty exhortation, an appeal to the sinner to turn to God. Suddenly she broke out in a language with which she was utterly unfamiliar. It was the native tongue of the foreign-born reporter. Directing her earnest gaze upon him, she poured forth such a holy torrent of truth, exposing his sinful licentious life, that he was dumbfounded. No one seemingly understood the language but himself.

"When the services were over he at once forced his way to the woman, asking her if she knew what she had said concerning him while speaking in that particular foreign language. 'Not a word,' was the prompt reply. At first he could not believe her, but her evident sincerity convinced him that she knew absolutely nothing of the language. Then he told her she had given an entirely correct statement of his wicked life and that now he fully believed her utterances were from God in order to lead him to true repentance and acceptance of Jesus Christ as his personal Saviour. He at once faithfully promised to follow such a course. Going from the meeting he informed his employer that he could not give them such a report as they expected him to present. He added, however, that if they wanted a true and impartial account of the meetings he would gladly give it. But they did not want that.

"A woman who knew only English, addressed a man in French. He was a grocer, a Frenchman. While both of them were crossing the street, in opposite directions, she suddenly spoke to him in his native tongue. It was in the form of a gospel message with a view to his salvation. Utterly surprised he asked, 'Since when have you been able to speak French?' To this she replied, 'I did not know that I spoke French, for I do not understand a word of that language.' The man answered, 'You certainly spoke in very excellent French, warning me to repent of my sins and to give my heart and life to God'."

S. J. Mead, a missionary who had labored for over twenty years in Liberia, attended the Azusa Street meetings. He heard many African dialects spoken with which he was familiar. A colored woman spoke at length in tongues as the Spirit was pleased to use her. Immediately after she had spoken, Brother Mead arose and interpreted the message and gave the name of the tribe in Africa that spoke this language.

It was soon noised abroad that God was giving a gracious visitation in Los Angeles and many workers came from different parts of the country, received the Pentecostal enduement and, returning to their home towns, witnessed to what they had seen and heard, with the result that hungry souls began to tarry and wait before the Lord and they too received a like Pentecostal enduement. Before the year 1906 closed, the Pentecostal power had fallen in scores of cities on the West Coast.

We take the following testimonies from the *Apostolic Faith* of December 1906.

"Pueblo, Colorado, is a city of many nationalities. In the steel works where they employ five hundred men, seventeen languages are spoken. There are Greeks, Chinese, Japanese, and many others. The Lord opened up a mission there when the Pentecostal gospel came. The woman in charge of the mission went right to seeking the Baptism, and before she got off her knees she was speaking in Chinese. One day when she was speaking, the Spirit began to speak another language through her. Nobody seemed to understand until they saw some uneasiness manifested in the back of the room where some Japanese were seated. They began to wring their hands and cry and bury their faces in their hands. Someone went to them and one of them said, 'She talked my tongue. Told me all about my God and how He died for the Japanese.' They had never heard anything like that before.

"In Denver, Colorado, in Brother Fink's home, a woman who had been hurt in falling from a wagon, was brought in. She had been a cripple for thirty-two years, unable to walk. Her toes were drawn up under her feet and could not be straightened. She was unsaved. The next morning as she was sitting in the front room alone, a six-year-old girl who had received the Baptism and speaks with tongues, walked in and put her hands on the woman and said, 'Jesus wants to heal you. The Spirit has sent me to put my hands on you.' Instantly those toes on the woman's feet straightened and she arose and walked."

CHAPTER V

The Revival Spreads

ONE OF those who received the Baptism in the Spirit in the early days at Azusa Street was Elder G. B. Cashwell, a Holiness minister of Dunn, North Carolina. He returned to Dunn and rented a large warehouse. People of all denominations came from all over the South to attend the meetings. A large number of the ministers of what was known as "The Holiness Church" and many of the lay members came to this meeting to seek God. It continued for about one month. G. F. Taylor, one of the ministers of this church, wrote: "What did our preachers and people do about this? They went to Dunn by the thousands, went down for the Baptism with all the earnestness they could command, and were soon happy in the experience, speaking in tongues, singing in tongues, shouting, weeping, dancing, praising, and magnifying God. They returned to their respective homes to scatter the fire. A great Pentecostal revival broke out in practically all the churches. A revival had come, and nobody was able to stop it."

This Pentecostal visitation became so universal in "The Holiness Church" that it had to be renamed. It is now known as "The Pentecostal Holiness Church."

One of those who received in a meeting held by Elder G. B. Cashwell was Evangelist F. M. Britton. He held a meeting at the Pleasant Grove Camp Ground, Durant, Florida, during June and July, 1907, during which many were saved, reclaimed, and revived, and

41

about seventy were filled with the Holy Ghost, speaking in other tongues as the Holy Ghost gave them utterance. Among those who were filled with the Spirit were many ministers and Christian workers who went everywhere scattering the fire.

Elder G. B. Cashwell was used of God in a remarkable way in establishing the truth of Pentecost in many sections of the Southeastern States. Many ministers and workers were baptized in the Holy Ghost at Atlanta and went from there in many directions to spread the truth of Pentecost. The standard held up was: Full salvation from sin through the blood of the Lord Jesus Christ, the Baptism in the Holy Ghost accompanied with the speaking in other tongues, the healing of the sick through the merits of Jesus by prayer and faith and laying on of hands and the anointing with oil in the name of Jesus.

There was a gracious revival in London, Kentucky. A Methodist minister named Blackburn received the Baptism there and was much used in preaching the gospel in the eastern counties of Kentucky. A Jew who lived in the city went one night to the meeting, and heard a minister speak in other tongues. He stated the following day, "I did not believe in Jesus, but your preacher spoke in Hebrew last night and talked about Jesus." The preacher was not an educated man at all. When he heard this he said, "I do not know any language but English, and but little of that, but this is about the eighth time I have been understood when speaking in some other language."

In the city of Dallas, Texas, in 1912, the Lord gave a gracious visitation and His hands were stretched forth in a very special manner to heal the sick. Many came from different parts of the country and were not only healed of the Lord but filled with His Spirit. Throughout the States of Oklahoma and Arkansas there were many gracious revivals. Because the South has kept wonderfully true, on the whole, to the fundamentals of the Faith, God has given many wonderful outpourings of the Holy Ghost throughout the Southern States.

A very large number of colored people have received the Pentecostal enduement. In 1895 a number of colored ministers organized a movement known as "The Church of God in Christ." The overseer of this church is Elder Charles H. Mason. He and his coworkers heard of the revival in Azusa Street, and Elder Mason made his way to Los Angeles. He received the Baptism in the Spirit in March 1907, and returned to his headquarters in Memphis, Tennessee. Before he reached Memphis the power had fallen and many in his church were being filled with the Holy Ghost as at Pentecost. He came in the fullness of the Spirit and a remarkable revival resulted in the churches of this organization. The growth of this fellowship has been phenomenal. Today they have more than 1,200 churches and a membership of over 200,000.

In 1906 a party from Azusa Street Mission visited Chicago. In the fall of this year Miss Mabel Smith preached nightly to overflowing crowds and wonderful scenes were witnessed. During her messages she would almost invariably break out in other tongues and give a lengthy message followed by a clear and inspiring interpretation, which seldom failed to bring pungent conviction to the hearts of the hearers. Her speaking in tongues was often understood by foreigners. On one occasion she met a German who addressed her in the German language, and without knowing a word of German she replied in that language and they carried on a conversation in German. The man could not believe that Sister Smith was not acquainted with the German language. Two of the first to receive the Baptism in Chicago were J. C. Sinclair and W. E. Moody, both of whom became active workers in the new movement. Pastor W. H. Durham, who was in charge of the North Avenue Mission in Chicago, received the Baptism on March 2, 1907, in Azusa Street Mission in Los Angeles. Previous to that time about fifty had received the Baptism in Chicago, but on his return the work received a new impetus. Meetings were held nightly at the North Avenue Mission, where the power of God was mightily manifested.

Writing of those early days of the North Avenue Mission, Pastor Durham stated: "People began to come in considerable numbers. Soon our little place would not hold them. Best of all, God met those who came. We had meetings every night and they generally ran more than half the night—sometimes all night. The teaching was simple—to repent of every known sin, yield fully to God, resting on the finished work of Christ, fully trusting in His precious blood, and that God would pour the Spirit upon us. One after another, God met the seekers. It was nothing unusual to hear people at almost all hours of the night receiving the Spirit, speaking in tongues and singing in the Spirit."

Among those who received the Baptism in the Spirit at this North Avenue Mission was a Baptist minister of Fort Worth, Texas, E. N. Bell, who became the first chairman of the fellowship of Pentecostal ministers known as General Council of the Assemblies of God in 1914, and held this position at the time of his going to be with the Lord in 1923.

Another minister who received the Baptism at North Avenue Mission was Pastor A. H. Argue of Winnipeg, Canada, who has been greatly used of God in Pentecostal ranks since the early days.

A large number of Italians came to this North Avenue Mission and received the Baptism in the Spirit. They were encouraged to start a work of their own and God marvelously visited this Italian Pentecostal Mission, and many remarkable miracles took place among them. One day a mother brought her dead baby to the church. The prayer of faith was uttered, and God gave life back to that child whose spirit had departed. From this Italian work many missionaries went forth to South America to labor among the Italians there.

A number of Persian young men also came to that North Avenue Mission and received the Baptism. They too started their own work in Chicago and God greatly blessed. Some of these Persians went back to their own land to preach the gospel.

One of those who received the Baptism in the Spirit in 1907 was F. A. Sandgren who was connected with a Scandinavian weekly religious paper published in Chicago. He was able to spread the news of this Pentecostal revival through the columns of this paper. This was the means of opening hearts and doors in the Northwest, in the Dakotas, Minnesota, Wisconsin, and Northern Michigan. The pastor of the Swedish Baptist church in Menominee, Michigan, received the Baptism in the Spirit in Chicago in 1909. Later with Brother Daniel Berg he sailed to Brazil. Since that time a number of Swedish Pentecostal brethren have gone to Brazil, and as a result thousands of Latin-Americans have been saved and filled with the Spirit.

Miss Iva Campbell, who was among the early recipients of the Baptism in Azusa Street, returned to her home city, Akron, Ohio, and gave her testimony to the members of the Christian and Missionary Alliance church, of which C. A. McKinney was pastor. The pastor and a great many of the congregation received the Baptism in the Spirit, and ever since Akron has been a center of Pentecostal activity.

A Methodist presiding elder from the South visited Akron, was baptized in the Spirit in Brother McKinney's meetings, and early in January 1907 was called to Homestead, Pennsylvania, to hold Pentecostal meetings in a branch of the Christian and Missionary Alliance where God began to pour out His Spirit in great measure. Among those who received the Baptism at the Homestead meeting was Elder J. T. Boddy, who in 1919 became the editor of the Pentecostal Evangel. Another one to receive a mighty Baptism in this meeting was the late George Bowie, who later became a missionary to Africa. Mrs. George Murray, a missionary belonging to the Christian and Missionary Alliance, received the Baptism early in 1907 and was greatly used of God in the Pentecostal testimony in and around Pittsburgh, Pennsylvania. Scores of young and old were saved and baptized in the Spirit at the Christian and Missionary Alliance Headquarters and numerous other places.

God also sent a gracious visitation to the Christian and Missionary Alliance Tabernacle at Newcastle, Pennsylvania. One day Elder John Coxe was endeavoring to deliver a message there, but through the pressure of the Spirit he was unable to proceed, as the people kept coming to the altar. Suddenly he fell prostrate to the platform and was immediately baptized in the Spirit, speaking in tongues. The meetings continued unabated for months and many were saved and baptized in the Spirit. Brother John Coxe later went to Wilmington, Delaware, and founded the Pentecostal work there.

In August 1907 there was a gracious visitation of the Spirit at the Christian and Missionary Alliance camp at Beulah Park, Cleveland, Ohio. The minister in charge, William Cramer, had some time before received the Baptism.

J. T. Boddy who was present at this camp states: "Here God marvelously worked unhindered, practically all the leaders being earnest seekers for the Baptism in the Spirit. Here Elder D. W. Kerr and wife on the same night were blessedly baptized in the Spirit. Brother Kerr had been announced to speak in the morning, and although deprived of sleep all night, under the new anointing of the Spirit, he delivered a most powerful message. The late Pastor John Salmon of Toronto, Canada, vice-president of the Christian and Missionary Alliance, also received the Baptism in the Spirit. Among scores of others thus baptized was the wife of

Dr. Wm. A. McArthur of the Christian and Missionary Alliance.

"Conventions and camp meetings, in the interest of Pentecostal truth, were held everywhere, and the fire fell in a remarkable way on these occasions. At one camp meeting in Ohio in 1908, I saw what could not be less than from fifty to seventy-five people prostrated at one time under the power of God, numbers of whom received the Baptism in the Spirit."

David H. McDowell, who was a student at the Christian and Missionary Alliance training school at Nyack, New York, tells of a gracious visitation that came to that school in those early days: "In May, when the Christian and Missionary Alliance Council opened, preachers and workers poured in from every point of the compass. Many of these workers were already filled with the Spirit, and spoke in tongues as the Spirit gave utterance. Several nights of prayer were entered into. At one of these nights of prayer at midnight, we had the presence of Brother Cramer, Brother John Coxe, and Brother Cullen, all of whom had already received the Pentecostal Baptism. The power of God came mightily among us until the chapel was one volume of prayer, tears and crying to God. In the gray of the morning one of the lady students who had been confessing and pouring out her heart, as she lay prostrate on the rostrum, began to speak in tongues. Miss Lucy Villars, a returned missionary from the Congo, who was sitting by her, declared that she was speaking in a tongue of the Congo which she understood and translated for us."

Many of these Nyack students later received the Pentecostal enduement and are now giving their whole time to the ministry. Among these are W. I. Evans, principal of Central Bible Institute, Springfield, Missouri, D. H. McDowell who has labored unremittingly as pastor and evangelist during the past thirty-three years, G. F. Bender, who has spent 27 years in Venezuela.

When Pentecost came to Zion, Illinois, one who was filled with the Spirit, Miss Marie Burgess, stepped out of her employment and went to work for the Lord. For some months she preached the Pentecostal truth in Chicago, Toledo, and Detroit, but later on invitation went to New York City. Together with her co-worker, she held a two-weeks' meeting in a Holiness mission. Here God met many hungry hearts and baptized three in the Holy Ghost.

After this, different homes were opened and tarrying meetings commenced. In May, 1907, they opened Glad Tidings Hall on Forty-Second Street, and God began pouring out His Spirit in a blessed way. One night in June, 1908, Robert A. Brown, then a minister in the Methodist Episcopal church, with another Christian worker, Alfred Monroe, who was superintendent of a mission in the Bronx, New York, and G. Anderson, for many years treasurer of the Glad Tidings Tabernacle, all received the Baptism in the Holy Ghost.

In October, 1909, Miss Burgess was married to Robert A. Brown, and together they have labored in the Pentecostal work in New York ever since. Today the Glad Tidings Tabernacle is situated on Thirty-third Street, just opposite the post office, in a large church adapted in every way for the Pentecostal work. Right from the beginning there has been a wonderful spirit of prayer in this New York mission. Large numbers have been saved there and many have been filled with the Spirit. There is also a remarkable missionary spirit.

In June, 1907, a Pentecostal convention was held in Rochester, New York. During this convention a number were prostrated under the hand of God and were speaking in tongues, singing in the Spirit, and prophesying. Speaking of the remarkable singing, Miss Susie A. Duncan wrote: "We had heard of the 'heavenly choir,' but never imagined its power and sweetness until we actually heard its notes sounding out like a great oratorio of angelic voices. One of our workers who had no knowledge of music and no natural voice for song was given a gift so that she sang clear as a bird and sweet as an angel with a range and compass past belief. At times several were singing together, yet in perfect harmony. A dozen voices would be swelling into a grand oratorio, then sinking into the softest whispers, with all the trills and variations of a practiced choir, not one of them knowing a word nor the melody until it burst forth from their lips."

Miss Duncan further wrote: "Many times the tongues have been understood by missionaries and linguists who have heard the Spirit-filled speak Greek, Hebrew, German, Italian, French, Hindi, Chinese, and other languages. A most convincing incident occurred in our midst one Sunday evening. After the opening hymns were ended, John Follette, then one of the students in our Bible school, arose and began to speak with great feeling in the new tongue. After this he burst forth in rapturous song and then all was quiet. At the close of the service a lady and a gentleman, who were strangers, came to us and asked, 'Who is that young Jew who spoke and sang?' They were surprised to learn that he was not a Hebrew but only a young American. The gentleman then stated that he had lived in Paris and understood several languages and said that the young man sang and spoke in perfect Hebrew, rendering a Psalm which he had heard in the synagogues of Paris. He said the rendition was impossible to an American, the intonation and variety of expression was unique and could not be reproduced by a foreigner except in this supernatural manner.

"At the time of the outpouring, probably twenty-five or thirty received the Baptism. We kept a record until the number had reached something like two hundred, when we felt a check in our spirit as to 'numbering the people,' and from that time desisted.

"Many have received healing as well as the Baptism, and at our conventions testimonies have been given of the healing of all manner of diseases."

We regret that we have not space to tell of blessed visitations of God's Spirit in many other parts of the United States. We desire, however, to mention two outstanding characteristics of this revival. It has been evangelistic from the beginning. The pioneers of the early days were willing to endure hardship as good soldiers of Christ. Many of them knew what it was to go hungry, sometimes for several days together, as they went into new territory to open up new works. They knew what it was to sleep on a hard board or schoolhouse floor for many nights in succession. But God rewarded them by letting them see glorious outpourings of His Spirit. They saw many under deep conviction of sin and crying to God for forgiveness, coming through to a clear experience of the new birth, and into the mighty Baptism in the Spirit as received at the beginning. They saw the sick healed as they laid hands upon them in the name of Jesus Christ. The signs which Christ indicated would "follow them that believe" as recorded in Mark 16: 17, 18, have been everywhere seen. It can be said of these pioneers, "They went forth, and preached everywhere, the Lord working with them, and confirming the word with signs following." Mark 16:20.

This Pentecostal revival has also been decidedly missionary from the beginning. The Spirit-filled have heard the word of the Master, "Go ye into all the world, and preach the gospel to every creature," and have responded to this call. They went forth in simple faith trusting God for all their support, and as a result there have been gracious revivals in every part of the world. There have been mistakes made, and some undoubtedly went to the field before they were sent, just as John Mark did in the early church. But despite this, the gracious stories of the outpouring of the Spirit in different lands read as someone has said, "like a twenty-ninth chapter of the Acts of the Apostles."

In the year 1914 a number of Pentecostal ministers assembled at Hot Springs, Arkansas. They realized the movement was growing and that some form of organization was essential. The missionary problem alone had become a great one. A simple constitution was drawn up to which they all agreed, and two years later a statement of fundamentals was prepared with the purpose of encouraging all to speak the same thing. From the beginning the statement was made, "The Bible is the inspired Word of God, a revelation from God to man, the infallible rule of faith and conduct."

The Assemblies of God is not the only organized Pentecostal work in this country. There are several others that are doing a splendid work and standing for the same fundamental truths of the Word.

From the early days of the outpouring of the Spirit young men and young women have been attracted to the revival because of the marked touch of reality and life. Thousands of these young people have consecrated their lives for ministry in the service of the Lord.*

---

* Current statistics and facts on the Assemblies of God are available by writing Public Relations Department, Assemblies of God, 1445 Boonville, Springfield, Mo. 65802.

CHAPTER VI

The Pentecostal Flame in Canada

ONE remarkable feature of the Latter-Rain outpouring in the early days was the way the Spirit of God fell upon one and another in different parts of the world who had never come in contact with anyone who had received the Pentecostal experience.

In 1906 Mr. and Mrs. Hebden were conducting an independent mission at 651 Queen Street East, Toronto, Ontario, in a small store about 20 by 35 feet. On November 17, 1906, the Lord graciously baptized Mrs. Hebden with the Holy Ghost and gave her a most wonderful experience. Mrs. Hebden had been praying for more power to heal the sick and cast out demons. The Lord spoke to her concerning the speaking in tongues, but she answered, "No, Lord; not tongues, but power, power." She realized that the Spirit of God was grieved and then cried, "Anything, Lord, tongues or anything." The power of God came upon her and she began to speak in an unknown language.

Pastor G. A. Chambers, who at that time was a Mennonite preacher in Toronto, states: "When the Holy Spirit fell, the mission hall on Queen Street became too small. They began to remove partitions until finally it was extended to a length of about 90 feet. This hall was filled to capacity each night and people came from near and far to seek for the Baptism in the Holy Ghost. Mr. and Mrs. Hebden belonged to the common class of people rather than to the

53

educated class, yet their services were attended by doctors, lawyers, professors, schoolteachers, and people from every rank." New assemblies soon began to open in the city. As a result of the outpouring of the Spirit in Toronto, missions were soon opened in various other parts of Ontario and Canada. Before long missionaries began to leave for foreign fields. C. W. Chawner, who went to South Africa, was the first to go.

Possibly the first from Canada to receive the Baptism in the Holy Ghost with the initial evidence of speaking in other tongues was Pastor R. E. McAlister, who received the experience in Los Angeles, Calif. Brother McAlister opened a mission at Ottawa and the Lord gave a very gracious revival. The truth spread all over the Ottawa valley. A number of ministers and workers received the Baptism as a result of this work. Two of those who received were Mr. and Mrs. C. E. Baker, who went to Montreal and opened a work there. Mrs. Baker was marvelously healed of cancer. God has graciously visited Montreal and many hundreds have been saved in that mission and filled with the Spirit. Many of the French-speaking saints of Montreal are filled with the Spirit and today they have their own French Assembly.

In Eastern Canada, there was an organization of Mennonites. Its founder, Solomon Eby, was formerly a Mennonite minister whom God greatly used in evangelistic work. One of their ministers states that sixty years ago the whole Mennonite Church in Canada was dead and formal and there was no sympathy with evangelism. This resulted in the withdrawal of those in the church who had an evangelistic spirit. This new movement was called "Mennonite Brethren in Christ." Solomon Eby was elected as its head.

Pastor A. G. Ward, who had been conducting a work in Winnipeg, was invited as guest-speaker by the local pastor of the Mennonite Church at Berlin (now Kitchener), Ontario. Brother G. A. Chambers writes:

"He was to conduct a New Year's convention which was attended by many of the workers. This convention ran through January and February and into March without a break. Many of those dear people were filled with the Holy Ghost and were speaking in other tongues as the Spirit gave utterance. One of them was the founder of the work, Elder Solomon Eby, who passed away in 1934 at the age of ninety-six.

"A great separation came at the following conference of the above mentioned church. Some of the leaders who had sought the experience and had not received, now became fearful and doubtful. At this convention the writer with a number of others took their stand for God with regard to this outpouring of the Holy Spirit. One day they were sitting in the church in Kitchener. While singing the opening hymn two doves flew in through the open window and circled overhead, lighting on the balcony, and then after circling over their heads again the doves departed through the same window. At this point Solomon Eby arose and said, 'Brethren, see these doves. Cannot we be at peace?' "

Those who objected to the Pentecostal teaching were in the majority and a split was the result. Solomon Eby was turned out of the church that he had served for forty years and of which he had been the founder. However, a Pentecostal mission was opened in the city and this assembly prospers today. It has sent a number of missionaries to the field.

"From that convention there came a separation which led us step by step into what later became known as the Pentecostal Assemblies of Canada." At the present writing there are 574 associated Assemblies throughout the Dominion, and 1,097 affiliated workers. In the 1941 Census in Canada there were 57,646 persons listed as Pentecostal.

Writing concerning the early days of the work in Winnipeg, Manitoba, A. H. Argue states: "After returning from Chicago, where the Lord so wonderfully baptized me in the Holy Ghost with the accompanying sign of speaking in other tongues as the Spirit gave utterance, in the spring of 1907 a number of hungry saints began tarrying in my home. One afternoon the Holy Ghost mightily fell on three and they began to speak with other tongues as the Spirit gave them utterance. This intensified the hunger of many and soon a real Pentecostal meeting was started at 501 Alexander Avenue, Winnipeg, where the power fell and a mighty revival began.

"One night while I was preaching I quoted from Acts 10:44-46. Suddenly the Holy Ghost fell on two sisters sitting side by side. One of them was Mrs. James Chafe of Winnipeg, who instantly burst out speaking in other tongues, in a wonderful way magnifying God. The other was Evangelist Ella M. Goff, now wife of Pastor G. S. Paul of Vancouver.

"Almost like a prairie fire the news spread that God was fulfilling His Word as recorded in the book of Acts, and soon the hall was packed to overflowing. Often many were unable to get in. People came from surrounding districts to seek the Lord, and many received the Baptism, and as they would return filled with the Spirit, the revival would spread.

"A company of Indians from Fisher River and other Indian reservations, about two hundred miles north of Winnipeg, hearing of this gracious outpouring, came to see for themselves. Soon they were down on their faces before God and a number of them received this wonderful Baptism. On the return of these Indians to their reservation a remarkable revival broke out in their midst, and God's Word truly was confirmed with signs and wonders and divers miracles and gifts of the Holy Ghost."

One of the first to receive the Baptism in those early days was Pastor A. G. Ward, who went out to preach among the Indians of the Fisher River reservation. He had to speak through an interpreter. One day when he was preaching under the power of the Spirit, he began to speak in other tongues and his interpreter suddenly exclaimed, "Why, you are now speaking to us in our own language." It was a call for these Indians to advance. This remarkable manifestation had a marked effect on the hearers.

During 1907 hundreds in the city of Winnipeg received the Baptism in the Holy Ghost, including a number of ministers and Christian workers. Among those who received the Baptism was Archdeacon Phair, an Episcopal minister who had labored for about fifty years among the Indians of Northwest Canada. In his testimony he wrote: "God led me to the foot of the Cross and humbled me in the dust before the One who loved me and gave Himself for me. I saw Him as I never had seen Him before. For some time I lay prostrate at His blessed feet, gazing on Him, and so enraptured with His unspeakable glory I felt lost to every being and everything but Himself alone. He touched the temple He wanted to occupy and moved it in His own way. Being the Lord's doing, 'it was marvelous in our eyes.' He came in and spoke in an unknown tongue, and I had no words with which to praise Him for ever deigning to do so. He shed abroad His love in my heart by the Holy Ghost, and there was great joy. It may appear strange when I assure my brethren that I am just beginning to understand my Bible, to see light in its light. If this great boon alone were all, I would most heartily urge upon all saints to wait upon the Lord patiently until they received the promise of the Father."

Brother A. H. Argue tells the following incident: "I was in prayer in the home of Brother and Sister Murray in Toronto, returned missionaries from Palestine, when I suddenly burst out speaking in other tongues. This was understood by both of them, and they declared I spoke in the Arabic tongue, a language which was utterly unknown to me."

CHAPTER VII

The Pentecostal Outpouring in the British Isles

THE Welsh revival made a deep impress on the life of the British Isles in the early days of the century. In different places prayer groups gathered and constant prayer was made for revival.

Mrs. Catherine S. Price, of London, was a member of one of these prayer groups. We shall let her give her own testimony: "At twelve o'clock one night in my room I knelt in quiet worship and adoration. I seemed to go to Calvary in spirit. I saw the Lord Jesus suffering for a poor, lost world, and He called me to enter into His sufferings, His longings and His love for those for whom He died. Then, in spirit, I was taken beyond things of time and sense. I saw Him exalted in glory, far above all, surrounded by heavenly hosts, and He brought me also into the train of His triumphs over death and hell. I opened by mouth to adore and worship the Lamb who had been slain, and who now was raised in glorious victory. Strange sounds fell upon my ear. It was another language than my own—soft, flowing, beautiful sounds."

Attending a convention the following night, Mrs. Price says: "While sitting there, to my great surprise, the Spirit of the Lamb overshadowed me. I seemed to see the Lamb of God enthroned, but pleading with His people to humble themselves before

59

Him, yield wholly unto Him, and cease from their own works. He gave me a great burden to say this to those present, but I found I was speaking by the Spirit in another language. I was asked by a minister sitting near me if I knew the language, and that if it was by the Holy Ghost would I ask for an interpretation. The Lord at once gave it to me in English. The result was conviction, confession and whole-hearted yieldedness to the Lord Jesus all over the hall, and some were anointed with the Holy Ghost. One dear young woman who had always lacked assurance of salvation, had a revelation of Calvary that night and entered into a joyous triumphant life in the Holy Ghost, and stands firm to this day. She was a great stammerer but has since been completely delivered from this infirmity. The following night at the convention the Spirit continued to fall and several of God's children came under such an anointing of the Holy Ghost as they sat in their seats that they were brought into a life of revelation and knowledge of Jesus Christ as never before."

Prayer meetings were held in Mrs. Price's home and many received the Baptism in the Holy Ghost there. She writes: "A few of us who met for prayer at the beginning will never forget the awe of God's holy presence in the room when everything in it gently rocked. This occurred on two occasions. The second time it happened I opened my eyes to look around and felt I had grieved my Lord for He does not want us to be occupied with the *manifestations* of His presence but with *Himself alone.*" Many were filled with the Spirit in this home.

Mr. J. Nelson Parr writes of the early days of the Pentecostal outpouring in Great Britain: "In 1906 a company of Christians commenced to hold prayer meetings in Sunderland for revival and enduement with power, and about the same time revival prayer meetings were being held in various parts of the country.

"Pastor A. A. Boddy, who was vicar of an Episcopal church in Sunderland, after a visit to Norway was convinced that the Lord was visiting His people in Pentecostal power. In September, 1907, during a visit of Pastor Barratt of Norway, the Holy Spirit commenced to fall in Sunderland. In 1908 the small showers of Latter Rain blessedly became a cloudburst, and by 1910 the land was being flooded by a deluge of Pentecostal power. In Sunderland the streams became a mighty river reaching Lytham, Preston, Bradford, and various towns in Wales, Scotland, and Ireland. Thousands were baptized in the Holy Ghost and spoke with new tongues, magnifying the Lord, who had put no difference between them and those mentioned in the tarrying company in Acts 2, having given them the same gift."

The following account from the pen of Mr. Thos. Myerscough describes the commencement of the Pentecostal work in Preston: "In the year 1908 a small company of Christians who met privately for seeking the deeper things of God, heard the report that a company of Christians had received the Baptism in the Holy Spirit with the same manifestations as the apostles in the Upper Room. A deputation of four went to see and hear. There was great power and glory in the meeting, with speaking in tongues. On leaving the meeting we stood together in the road, each of us confessing we had never before heard such glorifying of the Lord Jesus nor such fervency in prayer. Subsequently our own company were informed of what we saw and heard. It was determined that we begin to search the Scriptures to find if these things ought to be so. This went on for nine months, with the result that we were convinced the gifts of the Holy Spirit had been lost to the church through unbelief and not because God had withdrawn them. We also expressed the belief that simple faith would bring about a restoration of the gifts. The writer received the Baptism in the Holy Ghost at

Sunderland convention in 1909. Work started in Preston and has continued to this time. Other assemblies have sprung up at Blackpool, Blackburn, Burnley, Bury, Chorley, Manchester and Liverpool.

"Scores have had like experience. Multitudes have been saved, and hundreds baptized in water. Glory be to God for everything, including the growth in grace and truth, and for the unspeakable blessing of worship and songs in the Spirit! And still there is more to follow.

"There has also sprung up from Preston the very much blessed mission known as the 'Congo Evangelistic Mission' through our dear brethren, Wm. F. P. Burton and James Salter. In the Congo thousands have been saved and filled with the Holy Spirit. Signs and wonders and healings have moved the heathen crowds to seek the Lord. For all of which we praise our great God and Saviour."

Mr. Parr continues: "Many marvelous healings were seen, but in those days, more abundant than all other divine manifestations, was the speaking with tongues, and yet this was only the outward evidence of the presence of the Spirit who had filled them as at the beginning. The outstanding features of this great outpouring were: the worship, adoration and praise given to our exalted Lord and Saviour. It was a glorious foretaste of heaven to be in those early meetings when the glory of the Lord came down and hundreds of believers joined in the heavenly anthem, and baptized saints were singing spiritual songs of praise to the Lord in other tongues.

"Other features of this Pentecostal revival were the prominence given to the atoning blood of Christ, in song, prayer, and preaching, and an amazing love for the Word of God.

"As in the days of the apostles, these people were villified, slandered, ridiculed, and denounced by pulpit and by the religious press. Men predicted that it would soon fade away and become a thing of the past. But notwithstanding all the persecution, the revival is burning with intensified flame today.

"From the commencement of this great Pentecostal outpouring in 1907 till 1914 there was a steadily rising tide of marvelous revival. After the commencement of the great World War there appeared to be a lull, and the work passed through internal and external storms. Many were put into prisons for refusing to take arms, and the fires of trials, testings, and tribulations burned for approximately another seven years, refining and purifying the various meetings which had been started all over the country.

"Since about the year 1922 the tide has again risen in revival blessing. Thousands have been saved and baptized with the Holy Spirit, and they all speak with tongues as the Spirit gives utterance.

"Marvelous miracles of healing have been witnessed. We can give the names and addresses of many who have been healed of malignant cancer. The glorious deluge of Pentecostal revival sweeping this country is greater now than it has been in any previous period.

"While the Lord is still filling numbers with the Holy Spirit there are far more miracles and healings being witnessed than in the early days of the outpouring of the Spirit, and sinners by the thousands are accepting Christ as Saviour. We are finding, as Philip found in Samaria (see Acts 8), that the people are giving heed to the full gospel message, seeing and hearing the miracles that are done in the name of the Lord Jesus. Scores of people are being healed each week. The lame walk, people brought in ambulances and wheel chairs are delivered. Empty chapels and churches are being occupied."

In 1907 the Pentecostal revival swept Scotland. From Kilsythe, where the fire first fell, it spread all over the country. Scotch fires were again rekindled during two great campaigns held in 1927 by Pastor

George Jeffreys in Glasgow and Paisley. One report of the former campaign stated: "Revival fires burning in Glasgow. Crowds flocking to the services. Hundreds converted. Remarkable healing testimonies. Blind eyes opened. Running wounds dried up. Paralysis, rupture, tumor, growths, disappear under the power of God."

Another report stated: "Seven hundred and fifty publicly accepted Christ as their Saviour, and we heard of a number who were converted in their seats. The place was charged with the Spirit of revival, and people came from all districts of the city and country to share the blessing."

Wales was mightily visited by this Pentecostal revival. During the great Welsh revival at the beginning of this century, large numbers were truly born of God. When the revival fires ceased to glow, these "Children of the revival" as they called themselves, did not feel at home in the churches where things had grown cold. How these dear Welsh people welcomed this new revival, and thousands of Welsh miners were filled with the Spirit as on the Day of Pentecost. Pastor Techner was invited to hold a meeting at Cross Keys, an important mining center in South Wales with a population of seven thousand. Numbers speedily came into the experience of Acts 2:4, including Mr. Sydney Mercy whom God raised up as a leader. In a few years 36 assemblies have directly or indirectly been formed as branches of the mother assembly in Cross Keys. During eleven years the Cross Keys assembly, composed of working class people, all of them receiving a small salary, probably averaging not more than $12 to $15 per week, contributed for foreign mission work more than $16,000. In addition to this, considerable amounts were contributed for home work.

From Wales God raised up two brothers who have been wonderfully used of God in the Pentecostal work in the British Isles. George Jeffreys, the younger of the two while yet in his teens, began preaching the full gospel. God gave him some very gracious revivals in Ireland. The old people in Ireland, who remembered the revival in 1859, when God's power was so mightily manifested, were delighted to see revival of like nature. The first meeting hall was established in Belfast, Ireland, with a seating capacity of 300. Today in the same city there are two large tabernacles with a seating capacity of 2,000.

Reared in an earnest Christian home, George Jeffreys never knew a time when he did not love Jesus, but he can definitely fix the date of his new birth. Not many years after he started a business career as a lad, he abandoned it for the more serious business of proclaiming the gospel to perishing souls. Before he left business one side of his face was struck with paralysis, and for a time he partially lost the power of speech. Ever since 1911, when he was completely healed, he has publicly preached Divine Healing in the atonement, and has been markedly used of the Lord in healing of the sick. The campaigns held by George Jeffreys have packed some of the largest halls in the British Isles, including the historic hall of St. Andrews, Glasgow, with its seating capacity of 4,500; the Guild Hall of Plymouth, which accommodates nearly 4,000; the Military Riding School of Carlisle, which holds 4,000; and the Royal Albert Hall of London, which accommodates 10,000. Each Easter three meetings have been held in this great hall and at each meeting the building has been filled to capacity. One Easter 1,000 were baptized in water. At a testimony service given at Albert Hall at Easter, 1933, to quote the account given in the *Daily Express:* "Of those who testified there were 72 guaranteed cures of cancer and malignant growths; 20 had been crippled; 17 had been blind; 70 had been afflicted with stiff muscles or useless limbs; and 18 had been deaf."

Over 1,200 were swept into the kingdom in one campaign held in Brighton, and 300 gave testimony to the Lord's healing power. One who attended this meeting writes: "Hundreds of people have testified in the meeting to having been healed. People who only a few weeks ago were bedridden, or wheeled about in chairs, are today walking and praising God for His kindness in healing them. Lame ones, who moved only by the aid of crutches, are able to dispense with these. Deaf ones have been made to hear, blind ones to see, fourteen testified to having been cured of cancer, tuberculosis, or tumor."

Mr. Percy G. Parker wrote of a revival campaign held by George Jeffreys at Portsmouth: "Hundreds testified to healing, two at least had been wheeled into the meetings a few days before. One for fifteen years and the other for twenty years had been wheeled about helpless, but lo! they walked before us healed! The useless leg of one had faded to a skeleton. Not only was she instantly healed but her flesh returned as fresh and full as the other. A little girlie of about three years of age had been healed of paralysis of both arms. She held them up before us. Another had been blind in her right eye for many years. Now she sees! Growths, dislocations, deafness, rupture, even sugar diabetes have all disappeared before the touch of the Master.

"We are living in the days of the acts of the Holy Ghost—thank God for it! Our eyes are seeing what hundreds of thousands of the redeemed ones have been groaning for. At this last meeting no less than 130 people signified their acceptance of Christ."

The following is a newspaper clipping from the *Bournemouth Times and Directory,* by a special reporter, Marion Holmes: "If I had gone to the big tent—where Principal George Jeffreys has been holding revival and healing meetings—to scoff, I should certainly have remained to pray. But I did not go to scoff, I went to see if the wonderful cures of which I had heard were really taking place, and to decide—if I could—whether they were due, as some said, to hysterical excitement, or to something much greater and more permanent in its effects. I went, I saw, and I was conquered.... The gift of sight to a boy, who—so I was told—was born blind, was conferred at the same meeting; and I was given the particulars of the healing of a severe and long-standing case of spinal trouble by the grateful patient himself. Cases of cancer, goiter, rheumatism, nerve trouble, curvature of the spine, hereditary deafness, asthma, and numerous others have been cured at other meetings."

The following incident is one of the after-effects of the revival meeting held at Bournemouth. It is taken from the *Daily Chronicle,* a London newspaper: "After being crippled from early childhood, owing to a diseased hip, Lindley Lodge, aged 26, of Highfield Road, Salisbury, has been cured by prayer. She has cast aside a surgical shoe, a splint, and surgical irons, and now wears ordinary shoes. Miss Lodge has been a patient in Salisbury infirmary about 20 times since she was five years old, and has had a number of operations, yet for the most part she has had to be wheeled in a chair. When last discharged from the infirmary a few months ago she was told that, failing relief of her pain, it would be necessary to amputate the leg. She agreed to this course, but decided to wait until after Christmas. In the meantime, however, a friend communicated with Pastor Fergus Trevor, of Bournemouth, who sent a message that at 3:20 p. m. on a certain day, special prayer would be offered for her. 'I had heard of a person at Bournemouth being cured of curvature of the spine by prayer,' she told a *Chronicle* reporter, 'and just before three o'clock that day I went into my room, took off my splint and irons, and feeling sure that I should not wear them again, I began to pray. Then something happened—I do not know what—but when I came to myself I could walk around the room. That was at 3:25. I flew downstairs to tell my parents. They were dumbfounded.' Within a week Miss Lodge had discarded her shoe, which had a sole 3½ inches thick, and has worn shoes one of which had merely an extra layer of leather on the sole. The leg which was previously four inches short is now practically normal."

God has graciously honored the ministry of Pastor Stephen Jeffreys, brother of George Jeffreys, in the salvation of souls, and has continually confirmed the Word with signs following. J. W. Adams, an Episcopal minister of Wall, Litchfield, Staffs., writes: "While in London I went to Surrey Tabernacle, Walworth, and though at first somewhat prejudiced, I was profoundly impressed that Pastor Jeffreys and his helpers were instruments of the Lord Jesus in healing all manner of sickness. After being given up by doctors and turned away from hospitals, the blind received their sight, the deaf heard, the dumb spoke, cancer was cured, and the lame leaped for joy. Above all, the gospel was preached to rich and poor alike."

One who attended Stephen Jeffreys' campaign at Bishop Auckland wrote as follows: "There have been as many as 1,500 turned away disappointed after waiting in line two hours before the commencement of the service, who have complained, 'When we have a bit of gospel we cannot get in to hear it.' There have been some wonderful divine healing cases—the lame walking, the deaf hearing, and all manner of diseases healed in the name of Jesus. A born-blind girl, twelve years of age, from Newcastle on Tyne, received her sight, and the first face she saw in the world was the pastor's. A dear man who had been in an invalid's carriage and on crutches for seven years, came to the meeting on Friday night and could hardly move on his crutches, an object of pity. The pastor laid hands on him as he sat helpless in the chair. Immediately he came to his feet, and putting his crutches on his shoulder, walked home. This man walked into the meeting on Sunday night, and as soon as he was noticed the whole congregation of 1,000 began clapping their hands as they saw him mount the platform. This man has come every night since, dancing and leaping

for joy. Another woman, Monday night, never able
to walk from birth, of about forty-five years, was
prayed for. As the evangelist laid hands on her she
stood and walked, and then in sheer joy sobbed."

Mr. T. D. Dorling writes: "During the month here
at Bishop Auckland, over 2,000 souls confessed the
Lord as their Saviour, a church being formed which
now fills the Eden theater holding 1,200 people on a
Sunday evening."

"On September 3, 1927, a campaign commenced
at Victoria Hall, Sunderland. The Lord came down
in mighty power and testified to His presence in a
manner that set the county heaving. Crowds gathered
from distant towns, creating a situation which had to
be taken in hand by the police. Twice a day thousands
of people were divided into queues by mounted and
foot police, and when 3,000 had been admitted to the
hall, often a larger number remained outside to be dis-
persed by the police or reformed into queues to wait
for the next meeting. Probably never before in England have such services been witnessed in the outpouring of the Holy Spirit. So mightily was the
Spirit outpoured that at ten p. m. queues were formed,
standing or sitting, throughout the whole night till
three p. m. the next day, sympathetic hearts ministering to the crowds—some with their sick—throughout
the night, supplying hot tea and eatables.

"An inspection in the early hours of the morning
revealed some stirring examples and deep pathos of
human love and sympathy. An aged mother reclining
on the flagstone was holding the place for a crippled son,
who could not spend the night in the open. A young
woman resting on the pavement was ministering
throughout the night to her sick husband. Each story
told a need and a sacrifice through love. Ambulances,
cabs and a variety of vehicles brought the sick and
suffering and numbers were immediately raised from
stretchers and testified in a practical manner of their
healing. Such mighty demonstrations of the power

and virtue of Calvary increased the interest, and the crowds, from which the Lord drew an abundant harvest —3,300 souls passed through the enquiry rooms or confessed the Lord as their Saviour; forming a church so numerous as to create a difficulty to find a place to accommodate them. This work has since spread to Seaham Harbour, where a second church has been formed in a hall holding 1,000."

One who attended the revival meeting held by Stephen Jeffreys in Bury, wrote: "We have daily seen wonderful miracles of healing and salvation. Seven blind eyes have been opened, deaf have regained their hearing, the lame have discarded crutches, and the dead in trespasses and sins have been raised to newness of life. One Thursday afternoon two cases of cancer were prayed for and both were healed. One of these two was Mrs. Wall, The Homestead, Woodland Ave., Gorton, Manchester. Mrs. Wall preached in the United Methodist Church the Sunday morning after her healing."

Pages could be filled with remarkable stories of similar meetings.

The Assemblies of God in Great Britain and Ireland is a co-operative fellowship organized on similar lines to the Assemblies of God in America.

CHAPTER VIII

Revival in Norway and Denmark

IN THE year 1906, Pastor T. B. Barratt, a minister of the Methodist Episcopal church, paid a visit to the United States in order to raise funds for a building for a large city mission in Christiania (now known as Oslo), Norway. There was a very poor response to his appeal for funds, but the Lord gave him something infinitely better. He heard of the Pentecostal outpouring in Los Angeles and gave himself to prayer, sometimes praying for twelve hours a day. On October 7, 1906, he was filled with the Spirit, and spoke and sang in a number of different languages as the Spirit gave him utterance.

He returned to Norway and it was not long before there was a gracious outpouring of the Spirit there. On January 29, 1907, he wrote, "God is wonderfully demonstrating His power here in the Norwegian capital. It is about ten days since I held the first meeting in the large gymnasium that will take, when crowded, from 1,500 to 2,000 people. Folk from all denominations are rushing to the meetings. A number have received their Pentecost and are speaking in tongues. Some have seen Jesus at our meetings, and tongues of fire have been seen over my head by an infidel, convincing him of the power of God. Many are seeking salvation and souls are being gloriously saved. Hundreds are seeking a clean heart, and the fire is falling on the purified sacrifice. People who have attended the meetings are taking the fire with them to the towns round about.

"Some of the languages spoken are European. One man, a preacher, was thrown on his back last Sunday, and when he arose he spoke in four languages; one of these was English. He could speak none of them before. After that, he prophesied and invited sinners to come to Christ. Numbers cried for salvation, cleansing, and the fiery Baptism in the Spirit."

Ministers came from various countries to see what was going on in Norway. Alexander A. Boddy, an Episcopalian minister, came from Sunderland, England, and wrote: "My four days in Christiania cannot be forgotten. I have stood with Evan Roberts at the Tonypandy meetings but never have I witnessed such scenes as in Norway." Pastor Paul of Berlin, a great Holiness teacher and evangelist, also visited Christiania to see the movement, and shortly afterwards received his personal Pentecost, and began to spread the Pentecostal message.

The work grew in Oslo, and in 1938 the Filadelfia Assembly, of which Brother Barratt was pastor, erected a large modern building to hold 2,100. This main assembly has a membership of 2,100. There are three other affiliated assemblies in Oslo that have a joint membership of 1,350.

Writing about the opening of this Filadelfia Temple, William S. Johnson states: "There is a name which is the center of our divine service, and that name, seen in large letters on the front of the platform, is—'JESUS.' Everything centers around this one point—this holy name of JESUS. Our preaching is centered around this name. Many are of the opinion that we Pentecostal people are always in a state of ecstasy, because we, like the first Christians, speak in tongues and believe in miracles. But the main points of our doctrine, *our speaking in tongues and interpretation, our prophesying, our song and music, our meetings, all are centered around Jesus.*"

In June, 1907, Pastor Barratt paid a visit to Copenhagen in Denmark. Meetings were held in several churches and halls. Within about twelve days of his arrival a very gracious revival commenced in this city. One of the results of this revival was the salvation of a well-known Danish actress, Anna Larssen. She was one of Denmark's favorite stars. She began her work on the stage at the age of six years. Her father was an actor and her mother was also on the stage in her early days. Special opportunity was given to Pastor Barratt to preach to actors and actresses.

Her conversion created a great stir in Copenhagen and was discussed in the papers. Some thought she would soon get out of this "hypnotic spell" and go back to the stage. Pastor Barratt was much persecuted. A number of doctors apprehended Anna Larssen for observation. They thought there was something wrong with her mind, but after six weeks she was allowed her liberty. Not long after this she was married to Mr. Sigurd Bjorner, who was secretary of the Y. M. C. A. in Copenhagen. Mr. Bjorner received the Pentecostal experience, and they have been ministering together ever since. In 1922 they built a large hall in Copenhagen at a cost of $27,500.

A few years later Ernest Gordon wrote in the *Sunday School Times*: "A dozen years ago Anna Larssen was the most brilliant figure on the Danish stage, and a worldling of the purest type. Then she was converted to Christ and became an evangelist. On the occasion of her fiftieth birthday an interview appeared in *Kopenhavn*. She speaks of herself as the happiest person in Copenhagen. 'We believe in God's Word—the whole of it—and have been baptized with the Holy Spirit. You ask wherein we differ from the State church? We are more old-fashioned and orthodox. We have the principles and teaching of the Early Church. We build more upon what Paul says than what the church does. We are not against the church. The church is against us. We feel it a

great injustice that the church should call us sectarian.
A sect is a party that takes a single evangelical truth
and builds a system on it. We believe in the whole
truth, and that God's Word can be practiced as in the
early Christian community. When it says that the
sick of the church should send for the elders to anoint
them with oil and pray for them in Jesus' name, we
practice the admonition. My husband and I hold
meetings all over'."

Another Danish actress, Anna Lewini, also was
saved and filled with the Spirit. Today she is a missionary in Ceylon. This sister writes enthusiastically
about meetings held by Smith Wigglesworth in Copenhagen: "For three weeks, thousands daily attended the
meetings. Each morning 200 or 300 were ministered
to for healing. Each evening the platform was surrounded. Again and again, as each throng retired,
another company came forward seeking salvation.
Many were baptized in the Holy Ghost. One brother
was lost in intercession for the hundreds of sick waiting to be ministered to for healing, and was given a
vision."

In 1921, Smith Wigglesworth visited Norway and
Sweden as well as Denmark. Vast crowds attended the
meetings. At times it was necessary to move into the
open air, where stands were erected for the occasion,
because the buildings were too small. A great number
were saved and blessed. Pastor Barratt wrote at that
time that all Norway was stirred. He said, "A man
and his son came in a taxi to the meeting. Both had
crutches. The father had been in bed two years and
was unable to put his leg to the ground. He was
ministered to. He dropped both crutches, walking and
praising God. When the son saw this, he cried out,
'Help me, too.' And after a little while, father and
son, without crutches and without taxi, walked away
from the hall together. The wonder-working Jesus
is just the same today."

Niels Thomsen, who visited Norway a few years

ago, reports: "Two evangelists, who were blessedly used in the ministry, felt led to visit Bergen. In a short time they were turned out of the hall, because of the teaching on Pentecost. Having no other opening, they started to preach on the street. Souls were saved and baptized in the Spirit on the streets of that city. The street meetings continued for nine or ten months with blessed results. When they had water baptism, there were 60 or 70 baptized at one time; and at the end of the year about 200 people had been saved. In two years' time they had a congregation of nearly 1,000 people.

"This wonderful meeting was not without its distressing sorrow. One of these young men, who was so gifted and so greatly used of God, became puffed up and took the glory for what God had done as if he were some great one. In this condition he opened the door of his heart to the enemy, and one evening, while sitting by the fireplace, an evil spirit in visible form, came to him and asked for admittance. Being out of touch with God he said, 'Yes.' From that moment he became a raving maniac. How like Nebuchadnezzar who said, 'Is not this great Babylon, that I have built . . . by the might of my power, and for the honor of my majesty?' For six or seven months he was possessed and had to be confined. Much prayer went up for him. One day God called him by name. At that time something snapped within him, the enemy's power was broken, and he was absolutely delivered. He is today perfectly normal and today preaching the gospel, humbled in spirit, and being blessedly used. Some might say we ought not to tell what the enemy does, but there are some lessons in these experiences. We give it as a warning to those that may be tempted to take the credit for what God does through His Holy Spirit."

CHAPTER IX

Continuous Revival in Sweden

IN THE years of 1905 and 1906 many Christians all over Sweden were moved to gather in groups to pray for a revival. God answered their prayers. There was a special moving of the Spirit of God among the Baptists. Pastor Lewi Pethrus, who was formerly a Baptist minister, told the following story at the Central Assembly of God, Springfield, Missouri: "I had a wonderful experience in 1905. The Lord cleansed my heart and then I had a great desire to be filled with God. I was holding revival meetings and a few souls, from ten to twenty, were coming to the Cross in the meetings. But when I saw them coming, weeping, I also saw the emptiness of my own soul and heart. I got away from the revival meetings, threw myself on the floor in my room, and cried to God that He might fill me. There were thousands of others with the same experience, crying to God to give us a revival and fill us with the Holy Spirit.

"In January, 1907, I picked up a Stockholm paper and saw the picture of a man I knew very well, Pastor Barratt of Norway. The heading of this article was, 'A Remarkable Revival Has Broken Out in Christiania. People are talking in tongues, just as on the day of Pentecost.' I said to my helper, 'I am going to Christiania tomorrow.' When I was leaving the church, they told me I was welcome back again, but I answered, 'I will never come back again unless the Lord baptizes me with the Holy Spirit.' I will not describe how it happened, but praise God, it did happen, and a little later there were thousands and thousands baptized in the Spirit in Sweden.

"In 1910, a Baptist church was organized in Stockholm which stood for Pentecost, and I was called to be their pastor. All the members were baptized in the Spirit and they said, 'This assembly shall remain Pentecostal.' The church began with 29 members but in 1913 it had grown to 500 members. Then something happened. The Baptist church excommunicated us from their denomination. But when the church was put outside of the camp, then it got freedom. Today there are 300 Pentecostal assemblies that stand completely free; many of them being great, powerful churches." (The number of assemblies has since increased to 800, and the number of the members to approximately 100,000.) "When we started our church it was one of the smallest in the country. Now for several years it has been the largest one." (The Filadelfia church in Stockholm has a membership of over 6,000 today.)

"None of the papers would announce our services. I wrote an article about our work but no paper would print it. We prayed much and decided to get out a paper of our own. We had not a cent to start with, but we borrowed 1,000 crowns (approximately $300) out of the building fund we had. At the end of the year we paid back the thousand crowns and since that time the paper has paid for itself. (This paper has now a circulation of 45,000, and has been used of God to spread the Pentecostal message all over Sweden.)

"When we started our paper, we prayed for an editor. We had to wait several years for the answer to our prayers. Then God gave us Sven Lidman. He was one of the best known authors in Sweden, had published many books and poems, and was very prominent in society. God saved him in his own home while alone. Someone asked him to subscribe for our paper.

He did, and in that way the movement became known to him. He could not write novels any more. He wrote a book telling how he was converted and in it he said a good deal about Pentecost. He was such a popular author, that all his old readers bought his book. The newspapers began to talk about him, saying that he had turned Pentecostal already. He was baptized in the Spirit, and has become the editor of our paper. He is one of the most humble men you can meet. He sent a book to the publishing house that printed all his novels. They printed it and asked to be allowed to print his sermons. They have sent them out in book form by the thousands all over the country. This man preaches the whole truth without compromise."

Sven Lidman wrote a book entitled *Bryggan Haller* (The Bridge Holds). This book takes its name from the dying words of a good woman who had carried on a little orphanage on faith lines. She lay in a coma, and all those around her bed thought she had actually passed over. Suddenly she opened her eyes and looking on her relatives smiled and said, "Greet the friends, and tell them that the bridge holds." Then she shut her eyes and crossed over the chasm which separates us from the next world. For He who is the Way of life is also the Bridge of death.

Pastor Pethrus continued: "Up in the northern part of Sweden, the people were living very careless lives. A young evangelist was baptized in the Spirit and went up to these parts preaching the gospel. A revival broke out wherever he went. This young evangelist soon broke down, contracted consumption and died in a few years. But a wonderful work was started. Nearly all that country is now Pentecostal. It is just wonderful to have meetings there. I have seen young mothers come seventy miles with their babies tied to their bodies. It is not hard to preach to those folk. You have to start in the morning and keep it up all day.

"Since this revival began in Stockholm, it has continued summer and winter, all these years. We have a campaign the year around; souls are being saved, filled and healed. It is wonderful to know that God can start a fire that will keep on burning, just as it was on the altar of burnt offering. God commanded that this fire should always be burning on the altar; it was not to be put out. That is the way God wants it to be among us. There is a question that arises with all Pentecostal people in the world today, and that is, 'Is this Pentecostal revival going to continue?' I have prayed night and day regarding this question. I feel that life is not worth living if God cannot continue this revival."

In 1921 Smith Wigglesworth held some special meetings in Sweden. Anna Lewini, a former actress of Denmark, who attended these meetings, wrote, "Hundreds of people received Jesus as their Saviour. Thousands of believers awoke to new life. Many received the Baptism in the Holy Ghost as on the day of Pentecost. For all this we give God the glory. Here are a few examples of miracles our eyes have seen. The first meeting I attended was at Orebro. I came to seek help myself, being worn out with long, unbroken service in the Lord's work. There was a meeting for healing. After the preaching service, I went forward into the other hall and was surprised to find a crowd following. As hands were laid upon me the power of God went through me in a mighty way. I was immediately well.

"It was wonderful to notice, as the ministry continued, the effect upon the people as the power of the Lord came upon them. Some lifted their hands, crying, 'I am healed! I am healed!' Some fell on the platform overcome by the power of the Spirit. A young blind girl, as she was ministered to, cried out, 'Oh, how many windows there are in this hall!' During the three weeks the meetings continued, the great chapel was crowded daily, multitudes being healed and many saved. The testimony meetings were wonderful. One said, 'I was deaf, they prayed, and Jesus healed me.' Another, 'I had consumption, and I am free.' And so on.

"At Stockholm crowds waited for hours to get in. At nearly every meeting, crowds were unable to enter the building, but they waited on, often hour after hour, for the chance, if any left the building, to step into the place. Here a man with two crutches, his whole body shaking with palsy, is lifted onto the platform. This man is anointed and hands laid on him in the name of Jesus. He is still shaking. Then he drops one crutch, and after a short time, the other one. His body is still shaking, but he takes the first step out in faith! He lifts one foot and then the other, and walks around the platform. The onlookers rejoice with him. Now he walks around the auditorium. Hallelujah!

"During this meeting a woman began to shout. The preacher told her to be quiet, but instead she jumped upon a chair, flourishing her arms, and crying, 'I am healed! I am healed! I had cancer in my mouth, and I was unsaved; but during the meeting as I listened to the Word of God, the Lord saved me and healed me of cancer in my mouth! I am saved! I am saved! I am healed of cancer!' The people laughed and cried together.

"Here was another woman unable to walk, sitting on a chair as she was ministered to. Her experience was the same as hundreds of others. She rose up, looking around, wondering if after all it was a dream. Suddenly she laughed and said, 'My leg is healed!' Afterwards she said, 'I am not saved,' and streams of tears ran down her face. They prayed for her, and later she left the meeting healed and saved and full of joy. We have a wonderful Saviour!"

The Stockholm church also does a very splendid rescue mission work. It has a night refuge for homeless men and gives meals to many unemployed during the winter, distributes provisions and clothes to many poor people outside the assembly, as well as taking care of the poor who are members of the assembly. There is a splendid Sunday School work in connection with this church.

A large number of members and ministers in the Baptist church in Sweden have received the Pentecostal experience. Dr. C. B. Miller, a Baptist minister of Springfield, Mo., who visited Stockholm in 1923, wrote a letter which was published in the *Springfield Leader,* giving an interesting account of a visit he made to a Baptist church. This is part of the letter:

"The service this morning was unique. I spoke a few sentences and the pastor spoke by interpretation. The service began with a voluntary prayer service, several taking part. The singing was spirited. The people seemed deeply spiritual. There were many Amens, etc.; you would think you were in the midst of a big revival.

"At the close, a man of humble appearance, spoke voluntarily. The pastor interpreted. He spoke in an 'unknown tongue.' The pastor did not know the language he used—neither did the man. The pastor says he was given the power of interpreting the unknown tongues about a year ago. Several of his people both speak and interpret. He is a very sensible fellow and not given to foolishness. He says the tongues movement is general in the Baptist churches in Sweden and Divine Healing is generally practiced. He tells of hundreds, who have been healed. One man taken from a tubercular sanitarium was healed and passed a satisfactory examination before the Board of Health —is working regularly now. I do not understand it all, but he is so intelligent and so sensible one cannot doubt his testimony."

Marvelous Miracles in France

FOR MANY years there had been a Pentecostal revival in Le Havre, France, in charge of a godly woman, Mlle. Biolley. She was a woman of faith and believed that the key to the heart of the Catholics... France would be the truth of the ... of its teaching. In the year 19.. Douglas Barr went from England to Le Havre, and at the beginning of his ministry there he proved to many present in the ... God healed him right on the spot. This healing completely advanced one who had attended a ... meeting of the seventh-day Adventists. This man worked on the railway and ... easy opportunity to testify ... what he had seen and heard. He brought one whole family to be healed. The mother was incurable. She could not move her arms or legs on account of rheumatic arthritis. The Lord healed her and several others in the same family. There they saw the mind of ... prayer. After they were baptized ... Holy Spirit had the joy of baptizing all the members of this family in water.

A continued drunkard and gambler, being in the meetings in Le Havre declaring that Jesus was not the Son of God. The Spirit of God kept him under conviction night after night, him through the fire and pointing out all his sins one after the other... He was glad to find Jesus as his Saviour and a mighty healer of ... He was saved ... This man was converted and ... the salvation of many others, led many who knew ...

CHAPTER X

Marvelous Miracles in France

FOR MANY years there had been a Pentecostal center in Le Havre, France, in charge of a godly woman, Mlle. Biolley. She was a woman of faith and believed that the key to the heart of the Catholics in France would be the truth of the Lord's healing. In the year 1930, Douglas Scott went from England to Le Havre, and at the beginning of his ministry there he prayed for a man gassed in the war. God healed him right on the spot. This healing completely convinced one who had been attending the meetings of the Seventh-day Adventists. This man worked on the railway and took every opportunity to testify to what he had seen and heard. He brought one whole family to be healed. The mother was incurable. She could not move her arms or legs on account of chronic arthritis. The Lord healed her and several others in the same family. They saw their need of conversion. After they were converted Douglas Scott had the joy of baptizing fifteen members of this family in water.

A confirmed drunkard and gambler came to the meetings in Le Havre declaring that Jesus was not the Son of God. The Spirit of God kept him awake for three nights, taking him through his life and pointing out all his sins one after the other. He was glad to find Jesus as the Saviour from sin, and acknowledged Him as the Son of God. This man was instrumental in the salvation of many others, for many who knew him were struck by the change in his life. One night he came at midnight and asked the Scotts to go and pray for his nephew who was dying with double pneumonia. God healed the little one while they prayed. The father went to the meetings. His life was transformed, and today he is secretary of the Assemblies of God in France and pastor of two assemblies. This brother while away on a vacation one year prayed for a number of sick people and so many were healed that he gave up his holiday. As a result a new assembly was formed where from 200 to 300 meet together to hear the Word of God.

Writing of the work that he has witnessed in France, Douglas Scott says: "The Lord moved in His own inimitable way in bringing to nought the work of a spiritist healer who attracted a great number of persons after him in much the same way as Simon the magician of the eighth chapter of Acts. Among his many clients was a little girl who fell with about 25 epileptic fits a day. She could no longer take her food, and was not responsible for her actions. This child was brought to our meetings, and the demon rebuked in the name of Jesus. When he was cast out, the little girl became normal. Within a short time she was no longer a skeleton, but a fine, healthy child. This came to the notice of many people who had seen her at the 'magician's house' and they inquired where she had been healed. In simple childlike faith she told them and one night we had the joy of seeing about 50 strangers, all people who had been to the spiritist to be healed but who had forsaken him to be healed by the power of God. Many of these were converted, healed, baptized in water and in the Holy Ghost, and the name of the Lord was glorified.

"Just at this time, the Lord sent back to France Brother Domoustchieff, who had been converted some years before in the mission of Mlle. Biolley. He immediately opened another work in another part of the town and the revival spread abroad. Let me give

you the testimony of a clown who gave his heart to the
Lord Jesus. He used to make others laugh when on
the stage but went behind the scenes to cry because of
his misery and sickness. One day on coming back from
a tour he was surprised to meet a little girl who formerly was a cripple, walking with crutches, but who met
him trotting gaily downstairs. This completely stag-
gered him and that very night he was at our meeting,
where the Lord saved him and healed him. He immediately gave up his job on the stage and the Lord
found him other work. After his receiving the Baptism in the Holy Ghost he placed his gifts on the altar
for the Lord and today in the assembly it is the ex-
clown who conducts the singing. Hallelujah!

"Today we can number in the town of Le Havre
over 1,000 baptized in water and nearly 500 baptized in
the Holy Ghost. In two strong assemblies souls were
saved unceasingly and people from far and near come
to find healing from sorrow and sickness in Jesus'
name.

"Now a few words about the revival at Rouen, the
town of the hundred steeples, perhaps the most clerical
in France. This work was started with the small number of ten people at the first meetings, and nearly all
of them sick, but God stretched forth His hand to heal
and their testimonies brought others along to hear the
message, so that soon nearly a hundred met several
times a week. Among the converts there was one whom
God has specially blessed and used. He was the banner carrier in the Communist association, but was
brought to the meeting by his niece who was healed in
a remarkable way. Lying ill in a sanatorium, she received a handkerchief upon which hands had been laid
in Jesus' name and the Lord healed her. This convinced her uncle and he also came along to be healed.
This God did at the first meeting, delivering him of a
sort of paralysis in the side, and saving his soul. He
also was a drunkard, a quarreler, and a gambler, but
God took away all his vices, gave him victory, trans-

formed his life, gave to his wife a new husband, saved
her as well, and gave them a ringing testimony to His
grace.   Today he takes his stand under the banner of
the Cross and has been instrumental in bringing many to
the Saviour's feet, and also in opening up new works.
In this town there was also a man deaf and dumb from
birth who received his speech and hearing after the
laying on of hands.   There was also another brother,
suffering from a grave illness the result of his sinful
life, but God proved to him the words of Psalm 103,
verses 3, 4, in pardoning his sin and taking away also
the consequences.   This man was night watchman in a
garage and amongst his other duties was that of ex-
tracting petrol from the autos and replacing it in the
pump.   After his conversion he told the owner he
could no longer continue that work, and so leaving his
job, he threw himself on the goodness of the Lord,
who has supplied and met his every need.

"Our greatest difficulty in this town was the question of halls.   We had a good one facing the cathedral,
but the Catholics succeeded in getting us out at a
moment's notice.   However if the Episcopal clergyman
had not loaned us his church for three months, the
work would have been to the ground.   God blessed
this brother and servant of His although his action
cost him his place and the disapproval of the English
Consul, and once again the assembly was without a
home.   God however provided a hall just the size to
house our rapidly increasing assembly.   One day we
found that the whole house had been taken over our
heads.   Just at that time there was a disused factory
available, but the size seemed too large to Mr. Nicolle.
the pastor.   He however took it in faith, and praise
God, he has now seen the whole floor filled at the
evangelical meetings with 800 people.   Pastor Nicolle
testified in 1938: 'In six years we have seen 400 baptized, and our church has already opened eight outstations.'

"Just a word here of how God called Pastor Nicolle,

who is now the president of the Assemblies of God in
France, into the Pentecostal movement. He was col-
porteur-evangelist in a little town near the old battle
front, when the pastor arranged for us to hold a mission in this church. Our Brother Nicolle who was
a fundamentalist to the last degree, was surprised to see
the power of God in healing the sick and casting out the
demons. Without saying anything to us, he began to
search again the Scriptures to see whether these things
were so, and when the written Word gave testimony
to what he was seeing around him, he asked for prayer
for the Baptism in the Holy Spirit. After 51 days of
waiting upon God for several hours a day, the Lord met
our brother and gave him a powerful Baptism in the
Holy Ghost, and at the same time to us a message in
tongues and interpretation to the effect that he would
have an abundant ministry, and that the years of dry-
ness would be more than made up for, in the blessing
that would come. This has literally been fulfilled in
our brother's ministry at Rouen and the neighboring
towns, where healings of all kinds of diseases are the
everyday happening, with striking conversions.

"After the establishment of the second assembly
at Le Havre, the Lord led our Brother Domoustchieff
to Paris. He was able to found an assembly at Argen-
teuil, which is today standing strong, with a congregation of 350. After that he entered Paris where a real
fight against all the forces of Satan, Spiritists, Anton-
ists, Catholics and Communists awaited him, but nevertheless God gave him grace to stand. Souls were saved
and many brands plucked from the burning, so that
today there is a church of 250 supporters.

"We ourselves had the pleasure of taking one or
two meetings in the Communist suburb, known as the
Moscow of Paris, in July last, and had the joy of
seeing at least 250 gather to hear the Word of God in
a theater. This was the result of a real miracle which
the Lord wrought before at least 130 people. A woman
really at death's door, with several internal illnesses,

each one sufficient to cause her death, was brought into
the meeting, stretched out on a deck chair. Immediately upon the laying on of hands, the power of God
penetrated and touched the whole of her body, so that
instantly she was able to get up and stand to give
the testimony of her healing, and it was this miracle
that brought the people even in the height of summer,
and which enabled us to sell over 150 New Testaments
in one meeting. Without the ministry of healing, it
would have been impossible to reach all these people
and bring them into the knowledge of the Son of God.

"God who knows the need and who possesses the
key to their hearts, has shown forth His glory with
the result that on every hand assemblies are springing
up. The Holy Spirit gives the gifts severally and as
He wills, and we praise Him; for up to the present
He has given to each of our pastors and evangelists
the gift of healing, so that the balm of the Spirit can
be poured out upon broken hearts and suffering
bodies."

In October, 1934, a new work was commenced in
Marseille. After seven weeks people began to have
confidence. One elderly lady, who had a broken ankle,
came to the altar and was prayed for. She was perfectly healed and walked home. Another had arthritis in
the jawbone, could not open her mouth properly. She
was instantly healed and was not afraid to give her
testimony. Another woman was in a terrible condition
through rheumatism. She was healed. People began
to come, and soon they had four halls in different sections of the city at the same time with an average of
200 people in each. After this they began to pray for
a large hall and the Lord gave them a disused factory.
It was converted into a large central hall for Pentecostal services. In 3½ years this assembly had 350
baptized members and 13 outstations. Douglas Scott
writes: "I will give you a little account of what I saw
at Lisieux. This is a place of pilgrimage to the latest
Catholic saint, St. Therese, and it might even rival

Lourdes. There have been supposed Catholic miracles
and a shrine has been built costing 140 million francs.
Our evangelist opened up in a transformed granary on
the first floor, and God has given him some remarkable
healings. I listened to the following testimonies: A
little girl who was blind from birth had her eyes opened
by the Lord. Another little girl who was deaf and
dumb can now both hear and speak. Cases of cancer
have been healed. A woman who had a short leg,
after being prayed for, found that her leg had grown
two inches in one night, and the next day she had to
change her shoes. There were also many who had
been brought back from the edge of the grave through
the prayer of faith and the laying on of hands in
Jesus' name. The number of people attending the
meetings varied from about 400 to 650 and most of
them were from Lisieux and the surrounding country.
Some had come on pilgrimage to the shrine, and had
been directed by the hotel keepers into our meetings.
It is Ephesus over again, God working special miracles
by the hand of His servant, Mr. Le Maire. There are
30 people at least who are asking for water baptism,
and I fully believe that God will make this place a
center of revival which will touch thousands and
thousands of hearts."

Brother Scott wrote us at the beginning of 1939:
"At this time, nine years after the foundation of the
Pentecostal work in France, we can look back and say,
'The Lord has done wondrous things for us, for which
we are glad.' We have now 51 established assemblies
and gospel meetings, some of which are very strong
in numbers, and the others just commencing. Each
one of these assemblies sees a continual stream of
conversions, baptisms in water, baptisms in the Spirit,
and miracles of healing. In fact, the revival goes on
steadily and gradually, without any special evangelistic
effort. Every new work is opened on the ministry of
Divine Healing, for without the supernatural it would
be impossible to get any interest created in the gospel

message in this half-Catholic, half-atheistic country; but praise the name of the Lord, He is there to meet the need.

"An ex-Communist brother, in his spare time, has been instrumental in the opening of at least three assemblies, God bearing witness to His Word with numerous miracles of healing in his ministry.

"In nearly all the coast towns there is a testimony to Pentecost, on the north, west and south coasts. In nearly every assembly God has been pleased to give spiritual gifts, and the work is thus alive with the power of God.

"Since last year the Lord has led us to the Riviera, and we have had the joy of seeing 6 assemblies opened, some of which are really established, with a wide range of testimony, for people come from all parts to these centers and go back to the towns in France, and to many foreign countries with the blessings of the Lord as we know them in Pentecost.

"This year the assemblies have decided, by His grace, to send out their first missionary, Brother Vernaud, who had a real Pentecostal revival in the Gabon, French Equatorial Africa. He was turned out of the Reformed Church in consequence of his stand. He feels the Lord would have him go back to feed these sheep and to encourage the native evangelists who have received the 'like gift.'

"In Belgium there are 13 Pentecostal assemblies in the French-speaking part, in all the large centers. The work has gone steadily forward after a shaky beginning; and now every month, there are baptisms in water, and every week those who come through into the fulness of the Spirit, with a continuous stream of healings and miracles.

"There have been so many Bibles and New Testaments sold during these last nine years in France that the British and Foreign Bible Society has sent a delegate to tour our assemblies to find out what is doing."

CHAPTER XI

Pentecost in Various European Lands

A T THE time the Lord began so graciously to pour out His Spirit in Los Angeles and other parts of the United States, two evangelists came to the city of Mulheim in Germany and pitched a large tent in the city. In a few weeks there were 2,000 converts. There was a great awakening throughout this district. Following this there came a most gracious visitation in the form of a Pentecostal revival. The first Pentecostal Conference in Germany was held in Mulheim in 1908. This conference was so blessed of God that it was agreed to hold a second conference in 1909. Many attended and according to Pastor Emil Humburg of Mulheim, "During the days of the conference hundreds were anointed with oil according to James 5, with the laying on of hands. The pains vanished immediately with few exceptions. The following cases have been certified by doctors in writing: Heart disease of long standing, brain disease, gall stones, rheumatism, consumption, internal cramp, violent chronic neuralgia, internal diseases in many forms. nervous diseases, throat disease, ear disease, etc. One woman testified, 'I have suffered for twelve years with internal cancer, and have been fully healed through the prayer of faith'."

Pastor Humburg said, "We were greatly rejoiced as we heard a sister speaking in tongues in English, of which she did not know a word. I heard suddenly the words, 'Blessing, Blood.' My wife, who sat near the sister, heard it more clearly, 'The Blessing of the Blood of the Lord Jesus Christ.' It was a challenge to honor the Blood of the Lord Jesus Christ."

Fifty-five were filled with the Holy Spirit in this meeting, and each one spoke in other tongues as the Spirit of God gave utterance.

In September, 1909, a number of German pastors met in Berlin and sent out a declaration concerning the Pentecostal Movement. Among other things they said: "We thank the Lord for this present spiritual movement. We consider it the beginning of God's answer to the prayer of faith for years concerning a world-wide revival. We recognize therefore in it a gift from *above* and not from below.

"What is the fundamental feature and the con-straining power in this movement? It is the love for Jesus and the desire that He in all respects may fulfill His purpose in and through us. We wish nothing else but that He may be glorified. The purpose of this movement is that the full atonement of the Blood of Jesus may be manifested in power and that the Holy Spirit may have way and dominion to prepare us for the coming again of the Lord."

Pastor Emil Humburg stated in 1911: "During the last two years in Germany, we have experienced what is written in the answer of Jesus to John's disciples: 'Go and show John again those things which ye do hear and see: The blind receive their sight, and the lame walk, the lepers are cleansed, and the deaf hear, the dead are raised up, and the poor have the gospel preached to them.'

"First of all, we have seen the *blind receive their sight*. A blind young man seventeen years old, blind from his childhood, came to the house of a sister, and she was led of God to preach to him a full salvation. The young man said: 'I should like to see the same as other people.' She read to him from James 5, and asked if she should anoint him and pray for him according to the Scripture. 'Yes,' he said. So she anointed his eyes with oil and laid her hands upon him. What happened? He could see, but very indistinctly. You remember the blind man in the gospel who, when healed, at first saw men as trees walking. She prayed the whole day, and about the middle of the next day he could see quite clearly. He saw the pigeons flying, green grass, and other delightful objects, and did not know what to do owing to his great joy. One result of this was that members of his family were converted. With the opening of the outward eyes the inward eyes were also opened. It was through the outward that Jesus reached the inward.

"Secondly, *The lame walk*. Last year we were in Stutgart. Brother and Sister Polman were also there. We were often together in that place. There was a woman there who could not walk without a stick or other help, and she had been prayed for very much. We said we must pray for her once again, but the sister who led that morning, said: 'No, we shall not pray for her again. We must now believe and she will be healed,' and she took hold of her by the hand and said: 'In the name of Jesus, stand up and walk,' and she stood up and went a few steps, and a stream of blood came from her nose. The sister said to her: 'That's from the devil, don't let it affect you.' Four months afterwards, when I went to Stutgart again, I saw that she was completely healed.

"*The lepers are cleansed*. Pastor Meyer of Hamburg tells how a leper was healed. He was permitted to go into the hospital and pray over a leper. The leper was healed. However the doctors would not let the man go out, although they could not find any trace of leprosy upon him. The man managed to escape from the hospital, and now he is free. The authorities are not troubling to go after him.

"Then, *The deaf hear*. A shoemaker came into our meeting. He was absolutely deaf. He said: 'I will make no boots today. I am going to Mulheim, and God will heal me.' He came to us and asked us to pray with him. We anointed him with oil. He went home and for the first time heard the voices of his children. That was a great joy.

"And, *The dead are raised.* In June, 1909, our Sister Wex was wonderfully healed of tubercular consumption of the lungs, and received the Baptism in the Holy Ghost with the Scriptural sign of tongues. The great power of voice with which she sang in tongues showed that the Lord had done a complete work in her body as well as in her spirit. However on Good Friday, a hitherto unknown power fell suddenly upon her. She felt it to be the power of death which was seeking to obtain the mastery of her body, and noticed how it commenced at the feet and how the lifelessness proceeded upwards. Darkness and great fear overcame her. The Lord showed her that this was a case of wrestling against the powers of darkness described in Ephesians 6. She distinctly felt as if a cold hand had touched her heart and sought to grasp it and make it stand still. Some brethren and sisters hastened to her help in prayer. Suddenly, before their fervent, persevering supplications, the powers of darkness gave way, and the Lord Jesus became visible to one sister in a wonderful light, and said to her, 'My child, trust Me, I have given thee strength.' All of us who were present with her realized the blessed presence of the Lord, and soon there rose up to the Lord much praise and thanksgiving in German, also 'in other tongues,' with psalms and hymns and spiritual songs. Then we all went home, powerfully quickened by the Lord.

"The two Easter days were spent by our sister in stillness, and in the power of the Lord, but with an ever-increasing longing to be soon at home with Him, and behold Him face to face. On Tuesday, the third Easter day, came the removal of the family to another house. In the evening she went early to bed in her new home. She had hardly lain down when she noticed that something wonderful was taking place within her. She describes it thus: 'Lying quite still, looking up to the Lord, all the events of my life began to pass rapidly, as in a dream, before my inward view, and I realized how blessed and holy it was to know that all my sins had been forgiven and that He had loosed me from everything of earth. After a "Hallelujah," I received the distinct consciousness that now my spirit would depart from the body. I felt some throbbings of the heart, then convulsive movements in the neighborhood of the heart, and then it stood still. I distinctly noticed how the last breath left my life, and how my spirit left my body to ascend to its Lord. Blessedly happy and ravished was my soul before Him, my beloved Lord, and it was now as if I lived on by the breath of His mouth. Ever fresh streams of life and power went out from Him, and I was permitted to receive them into myself.'

"While Sister Wex was thus with the Lord, a brother and four sisters remained in fervent prayer before the Lord. Before eleven o'clock at night two sisters came to fetch me. Before they left to come, my mother-in-law (who lives in the same house), who had seen all the signs of death upon Sister Wex, said to them: 'Children, it is useless, you can see it is all over,' for she thought that now that death had stepped in, there was nothing more to be done. Notwithstanding this, the others cried all the more to the Lord. When I arrived with the sisters at the bedside of the deceased, I took her left hand from the chest where it lay, and it fell down lifelessly at the side. I felt for the pulse; there was none. There was also no breath, the lower jaw hung down, and the body was cold.

"Then we prayed on fervently, each independently, but the heavens seemed as brass and shut up. We said to the Lord: 'Thou hast conquered even death!' and realized we might count upon His power. Suddenly the heavens opened above us, and there was given to us great joy in believing. While we continued thus, each for himself or herself, praying fervently and praising God for this joy in believing, I received the inward summons to command death to give way. I did so, though tremblingly, but hardly had I spoken when there fell upon me a power of doubt such as I had never before experienced. However, the Lord showed me at once that this came from the enemy. Then I uttered a second time the command: 'In the name of Jesus, Death, let go!' and behold, at the same instant Sister Wex breathed deeply, and said with this first returning breath, 'Jesus, Hallelujah!'

"Overcome by the power and presence of God, we all sank down and praised Him long into the night. After the 'Hallelujah,' Sister Wex commenced to worship God in new tongues. The first words of prophecy which came from her lips were these: 'Rejoice and exult, for I have done great things; go and proclaim what you have seen and experienced; I have taken away the power of death.'

"Never have I felt the power of the presence of the Lord in so humbling and yet at the same time so uplifting and overpowering a degree, as at this time. Sister Wex had remained two and one half hours with the Lord, in this 'fallen asleep' condition. It is also very characteristic that thus 'present with the Lord' and at rest, she suddenly noticed that the Lord breathed upon her powerfully and in a special way, and thus gave her a new life, caused her spirit to be reunited with her body for further life on earth for Him. This return to life could take place only when the Lord had given us all full faith in its possibility, and we had acted in accordance therewith. Sister Wex said, 'May this which the Lord in His great grace has done to me, serve this purpose—that He shall be honored and glorified, and may He be able to give all the confidence of faith, that He can do everything, and that all things are possible to them that believe.'

"A month before this wonderful experience, the Lord prepared us for it, having suddenly in a prayer meeting where about one thousand were present, given this message through a sanctified sister: 'My servants will, before long, raise the dead.' As this message came, there fell upon me a sort of holy horror, whereupon I foolishly groaned within myself, 'Then, O Lord, permit that I may not be present.' Yet now our hearts are filled with praise and thanksgiving, and with a much greater assurance of faith in our blessed Lord.

" 'And the poor have the gospel preached to them.' About last New Year's night the Lord gave us a glorious song in tongues, and during the singing of this song between thirty and forty people were converted and thoroughly saved. I could relate many wonderful cases of healing, but I believe this will be sufficient."

There have been very gracious revivals in Switzerland through the ministry of Smith Wigglesworth of England. After visiting Switzerland in the early part of 1921, he wrote: "At Berne hundreds have been saved by the power of God. At Neuchatel, God worked marvelously. At my second visit to Neuchatel, the largest theater was hired and it was packed. God moved upon the people and scores of souls were saved each night. Many were healed through God's touch. I preached one night on Ephesians three, for three and a half hours, and so powerful was the word that the people did not seem inclined to move. I preached and prayed with the sick until eleven-thirty p. m. Four people brought a man who was paralyzed and blind; the power of God fell upon him and us and he now walks and sees and is praising God. I have not been to one meeting where the power of God has not been upon us. I say this to His glory.

"In French Switzerland, where Pentecost was not known, seven different meeting places have been opened, and the work is prospering. At Berne there was a band of praying people; there we have seen wonderful things. A girl was brought to me sitting in a chair. I did not minister to her at first, but told

her she must wait and hear the Word of God. Her
mother, who had come with her, was greatly moved
as she heard God's Word expounded. I then laid
hands on the girl, who had never walked. The power
of God was manifested and she now walks. A man
had had a cancer taken out of his neck, after which
he could no longer eat, not being able to swallow. He
told me he could not even swallow the juice of a cherry.
He had a pipe inserted in his neck so that food could
be poured through it into his stomach. I said to him,
'You will eat tonight.' I prayed with him. He came
the next day. I saw that the color had come back into
his face, and he told me he had been eating and could
swallow comfortably. He had looked for the hole
where the pipe had been inserted but could not find
it. God had completely healed him. He was well
known. He was a tea grower. People said that he had
come to life again.

"Every afternoon people were baptized in the Holy
Ghost or brought down into the dust, for the power of
God always lays a man low. In Lausanne the power
was mighty. Also at Vevey and Geneva. God has
raised up Spirit-filled leaders in these towns.

"A man came to me suffering from diabetes. The
power of God was upon me and I realized that God
was working upon him. I said: 'God has healed you.'
His address was taken and the case followed up. He
went to the doctor to be examined because he knew
he was healed. The doctor examined him and stated
he was unable to find any trace of the disease. He
asked the doctor to give him a certificate, which he
did, and which I saw. A young woman was dying of
consumption, and a doctor had given her up. I laid
hands upon her in the name of Jesus and she knew that
the disease had passed away. This girl went to the
doctor, who examined her and he said: 'Whatever has
taken place, you have no consumption now.' She replied: 'Doctor, I have been prayed over. Can I tell
the people I am healed?' 'Yes, and that I could not

heal you.' 'Will you put it in black and white?' she asked the doctor. He gave her a certificate which I saw. God had healed her.

"A man was brought into one of the meetings in a wheel chair. He could not walk except by the aid of two sticks, and even then his locomotion was very slow. I saw him in that helpless condition and told him about Jesus. Oh, that wonderful name! I placed my hands on his head and said: 'In the name of Jesus thou art made whole.' This helpless man cried out: 'It is done, it is done, glory to God, it is done!' He walked out of the building perfectly healed. Many suffering with cancer, tumors, tuberculosis, rupture, rheumatism and many other diseases were miraculously healed through the prayer of faith. One man, who was suffering with tuberculosis of the stomach, was brought to the meeting in a dying condition on a stretcher in a wagon. By his side was a basket of food, and a friend, knowing his condition, asked the reason for its presence. 'I shall eat it going back,' was his simple answer, and he did. Four 'spies' sent by doubting 'believers' to detect the counterfeit, were all convinced of God's work and are today working in the Pentecostal movement, one of them filling the place as leader in one of the twelve assemblies that have sprung up in the wake of the revival."

Mr. Wigglesworth tells of a remarkable miracle which took place in a town just on the Swiss border of Germany. He had been holding an afternoon meeting in the Pentecostal mission there. Some time later, as he and the pastor were walking through the streets, some one came to them and said, "There is a blind man in the mission and he says he is not going to leave there until he gets new eyes." Brother Wigglesworth turned to the pastor and said: "Brother Ruff, this is the opportunity of our lives." They hastened back to the mission. Brother Wigglesworth laid his hands on the empty sockets in the name of Christ and immediately God wrought a miracle. Instantly this brother could see, and he wanted to see his father and mother. He was familiar with the streets of the city for he had walked through them so often, feeling his way with a stick, and so he rushed to his home to tell the wonderful news that now he could see. That night when Pastor Ruff and Brother Wigglesworth arrived at the meeting, the blind man had taken charge. Brother Wigglesworth said: "I did not preach that night, for the blind man completely took the meeting out of my hands. We surely had a wonderful time, for God gave us a great visitation."

In the early part of 1926, Smith Wigglesworth wrote: "I had a call into Italy to visit some sick. I had the joy of my life preaching in Rome. I prayed much about this, that God would provide me with an interpreter, and the first man I met in Rome was a man that was in my meetings in San Jose, California, an Italian, and he really did good work for me. We had a great meeting that reminded me of a red-hot Welsh revival. There was a great crowd of Italians crying to God for mercy, many fine men among them, and after this, many seeking the Baptism. Quite a number received and others were under the power. A number were healed. I understand there are thirty Pentecostal assemblies in Italy."

There was a flourishing Pentecostal work throughout Italy, but the work has been subjected to great persecution. The saints, like the early church, met in catacombs but they were betrayed by a spy who pretended to be one of them and the the result was the leaders were cast into prison. Many of the Italian Pentecostal saints have known what a prison in Rome is like, just as the Apostle Paul did in the first century. In that century Nero covered the saints with tar and set them on fire, and used them as torches. The spirit of modern Rome is no more favorable to true saintship than it was in the days of Nero.

The Lord has done a very great work in Poland. In the years prior to 1939 there were gracious Pentecostal visitations in many parts of Poland. As a result there arose 700 meeting places where the full gospel message was given. A number of the Pentecostal saints emigrated to Canada, to Argentina and other South American countries, but it was estimated that before the war there were at least 24,000 Pentecostal people in Poland.

God has given a spiritual awakening to Greece also and there are assemblies in Athens, Salonika, and other places.

There has been much opposition to the Pentecostal work in Rumania. Brother Peterson writes: "We have been told that the total number of assemblies exceeds 300, but since all meetings must be held in secret the groups are not large. The number of believers is probably between 5,000 and 6,000.

It is difficult to write concerning the work in Soviet Russia. In 1909 there were about 500 assemblies with a membership of approximately 25,000. But the Russians have done their very best to destroy this work.

Pastor Barratt of Norway visited Finland in the early days of the revival and wrote: "A great revival broke out there, especially after Pastor Smidt began to work there. I have visited Finland several times since and crowds have attended, and remarkable revival scenes have taken place. Several of the ministers of the State church accepted the Pentecostal message and left the church, her mansions and luxuries, and are preaching the gospel of Christ with Pentecostal power. Wm. Pylkkanen, who was working in China as a missionary under the Lutheran board, received the Pentecostal Baptism and as a result had to drop his board. He returned to Finland and has since been working in the Pentecostal movement and the Lord has blessedly used him. One movie director, who owned fifty movie shows, was wonderfully saved. Two lawyers have also been saved and are a great testimony to the saving power of a living Christ."

Donald Gee writes concerning the work in Finland

in 1939: "There are about 25,000 Pentecostal believers in Finland, and a vigorous Publishing House in Helsinki. There are some large assemblies. Their missionaries have gone to the ends of the earth."

Writing from Estonia at the same time, Donald Gee says: "We had good meetings. Some 700 or 800 persons were crowded into their main church in Tallinn, the capital. That church now has 1,300 members, including the outstations. There are now between 3,500 and 4,000 Pentecostal saints in Estonia. They are grouped into membership in about 10 main assemblies."

You will find Pentecostal assemblies in all European lands. In Holland there is a good work, and even in Catholic Portugal there are eleven flourishing assemblies.

Brother Gee writes in 1946: "When war again burst upon Europe in 1939, we wondered how the Pentecostal assemblies all over the Continent would survive. They have survived. More than that, they are manifesting a remarkable tenacity of life by the Spirit of God. They are going forward, filled with an aggressive vision. The fiery trial has convinced them of the reality of the spiritual experience with which God has blessed them: and they feel assured that they have a message which the war-stricken peoples need."

CHAPTER XII

Latter Rain Falling in India and Ceylon

THE PENTECOSTAL revival of the twentieth century has had no outstanding leader such as Luther or Wesley, but in different countries where the saints have definitely prayed for an enduement of power from on high, God has answered by giving them a Pentecostal outpouring. During the latter part of the nineteenth century God graciously saved a well-educated Indian widow named Ramabai. In a season of famine in India, God put it upon Ramabai's heart to gather together a large number of destitute children, all of them widows. She looked to the Lord alone for support just as George Muller, of Bristol, England, had looked to the Lord for the support of his ten thousand orphans. The Lord gave to Ramabai some very splendid co-workers to assist her in training her young widows in the ways of the Lord. One of these, Miss Minnie F. Abrams, tells the story of how the Spirit fell in 1905:

"In January, 1905, Pandita Ramabai spoke to the girls of Mukti concerning the need of a revival, and called for volunteers to meet with her daily to pray for it. Seventy volunteered, and from time to time others joined, until at the beginning of the revival there were 550 meeting twice daily. In June, Ramabai asked for volunteers to give up their secular studies and to go out into the villages round about to preach the gospel. Thirty young women volunteered. We met daily to pray for an enduement of power.'

105

"On June 29, at 3:30 a. m., the Spirit was poured out upon one of these volunteers. The young woman sleeping next to her awoke when this occurred and seeing the fire enveloping her, ran across the dormitory, brought a pail of water and was about to dash it upon her, when she discovered that this girl was not on fire. In less than an hour nearly all of the young women in the compound gathered around, weeping, praying, and confessing their sins to God. The newly Spirit-baptized girl sat in the midst of them, telling what God had done for her and exhorting them to repentance.

"The next evening while Pandita Ramabai was expounding John 8, the Holy Spirit descended and all the girls began to pray aloud. All in the room were weeping and praying, some kneeling, some sitting, and some standing, many with hands outstretched to God. God was dealing with them and they could listen to no one else.

"From that time the two daily meetings of the praying band became great assemblies and the Bible School was turned into an inquiry room. Girls were stricken down under the power of conviction of sin. Regular Bible lessons were suspended, and the Holy Spirit Himself gave to the leaders such messages as were needed by the seeking ones. After strong repentance, confession, and assurance of salvation, many came back in a day or two saying, 'We are saved, our sins are forgiven. Now we want the Baptim of fire.'

"One Sunday the text spoken from was, 'He shall baptize you with the Holy Ghost, and with fire.' Matt. 3:11. The Holy Spirit evidently taught the girls through this passage and the one in Acts 2:1-4, as well as through the experience of the first baptized girl, to expect an actual experience of fire; and God met them in their expectation. They cried out at the burning that came into and upon them. Some fell as they saw a great light. While the fire of God burned, the members of the body of sin, pride, love of the world, selfishness, uncleanness, etc., passed before them. There was much suffering for sin under view of the self-life. This would have been too much for flesh and blood to bear, save that all these sufferings were intermingled with joy, wooing the stricken soul on, until the battle was won. Finally complete assurance and joy took the place of repentance. Some who had been shaking violently under the power of conviction, now sang, praised, and danced with joy. Some had visions, others had dreams. The Word of God confirmed all this. The Holy Ghost had been poured out according to the Scriptures. Such seeking could not have been endured save as it had been done in the power of the Spirit. They neither ate nor slept until victory was won. Then the joy was so great that for two or three days after receiving the Baptism in the Holy Ghost they did not care for food."

A goodly number of foreign missionaries and workers in Mukti and other stations round about sought and received the same enduement with power from on high that the girls had received. Writing of this revival at a later date, Albert Norton, venerable missionary of Dhond, wrote: "About six months ago we began to hear of Christian believers in different places and countries receiving the gift of speaking in a new tongue which they had never known before. One week ago today, I visited the Mukti Mission. Miss Abrams asked me if I should like to go into a room where about twenty girls were praying. After entering, I knelt with closed eyes by a table on one side. Presently I heard someone praying near me very distinctly in English. Among the petitions were 'O Lord, open the mouth; O Lord, open the mouth; O Lord, open the heart; O Lord, open the heart; O Lord, open the eyes! O Lord, open the eyes! Oh, the blood of Jesus! the blood of Jesus! Oh, give complete victory! Oh, such a blessing! Oh, such glory!' I was struck with astonishment, as I knew that there was no one in the room who could speak English, beside Miss Abrams.

I opened my eyes, and within three feet of me, on her
knees, with closed eyes and raised hands was a woman,
whom I had baptized at Kedgaon in 1899, and whom
my wife and I had known intimately since, as a devoted Christian worker. Her mother-tongue was Marathi, and she could speak a little Hindustani. But she
was unable to speak or understand English, such as
she was using. But when I heard her speak English
idiomatically, distinctly and fluently, I was impressed
as I should have been had I seen one, whom I knew to
be dead, raised to life. A few other illiterate Marathi
women and girls were speaking in English, and some
were speaking in other languages which none at Kedgaon understood. This was not gibberish, but it
closely resembled the speaking of foreign languages
to which I had listened but did not understand.

"Again I was at Mukti last Saturday and the Lord's
Day, when some twenty-four persons had received the
gift of tongues. Quite a number had received the
ability to speak in English, a language before unknown
to them. Just why God enabled these women and
girls to speak in English, instead of Tamil, Bengali,
Tugulu, or some other language of India, unknown to
them, I cannot say. But I have an idea that it is in
mercy to us poor missionaries from Europe and America, who, as a class, seem to be Doubting Thomases, in
regard to the gifts and workings of the Spirit, and are
not receiving the power of the Holy Ghost as we ought.

"On Saturday I was much impressed with the
speaking of a Hindu woman who was rescued in the
famine of 1897. She was praying in English. Among
other things, she was saying: 'Oh, the love! the love!
the love! Oh, the love of Jesus! Oh, my precious Lord!
My precious Lord! My precious child!' One not
knowing her history, would not see the force of the
last sentence. This was an only child, whom she had
been separated from for ten years, and with whom she
is not allowed to have communication. I was struck
with the English which she used, as being idiomatic,

and the words being a class she would not have used had she been learning by study. I have no doubt from what I know of her, that she, by her own powers, could no more have spoken in English than she could have taken wings and flown."

The revival soon spread throughout Alfred Norton's school for boys in Dhond, and in a short while sixty-five were baptized in the Spirit and a number received the gift of interpretation.

It is very evident that the enemy has no love for the Pentecostal outpouring. Alfred Norton wrote of an incident that took place in a Pentecostal conference at Fyzabad, in North India. There were two clear cases of demon possession in the meeting. He wrote: "The evil spirit in one of the possessed persons, after much prayer that it might be cast out, said many times with a hissing voice: 'I *hate* the Pentecostal people.' I think we all felt that this attack of demons was a testimony to the divine character of the work done in the meetings, and a testimony that the work was done by the Holy Spirit."

Miss Minnie Abrams tells of a meeting held by one of the Mukti bands in Anrangabad in 1906. It was in the Church Missionary Society schoolroom. A little girl of nine was wonderfully anointed with prayer. Before going back to the Church Missionary Society boarding school in Bombay, from which she had come for a vacation, she asked her father if any one might receive the Holy Spirit. He told her that God would give the Holy Spirit to all who asked Him. On returning to the school she succeeded in getting four girls to join her in prayer, daily, for the Holy Spirit. Upon one of these, a girl of sixteen, the Holy Spirit was poured out with the speaking in tongues. She asked daily to retire to a room for prayer. She would become oblivious to her surroundings and time, wholly occupied in communion with God, praying always aloud. When it was discovered that she was speaking in a language not understood, Canon Haywood was brought in. He decided this might be the speaking in tongues, and took measures to find out what she was saying. In the cosmopolitan city of Bombay where many languages were spoken, he found one who could understand much of what she said. She was pleading with God for Libya, in North Africa. She did not always speak the same language.

Miss Abrams also tells the following incident that took place in Mukti early in 1907: "At midnight, from a room where three head matrons were sleeping, an English hymn rang out in a clear voice, followed by prayer. Manoramabai (Ramabai's daughter) sent word to me that Gulabbai was praying in good English. That night no one went near her to disturb her. At the close of the Sunday morning service, Gulabbai asked to be excused from teaching her Sunday School class, she felt she must pray. She asked Miss Carrie Couch to join her in prayer. It was only a few minutes before Gulabbai was lost to her surroundings and was praying in English. Miss Couch sent for Pandita Ramabai, her daughter, myself, and one by one for all the English-speaking workers on the place. All had known Gulabbai since the time she had been driven over the mountains, a sad and oppressed Brahman widow, unable to read a word of any language, unable to speak anything but Marathi. We know she did not understand English.

"That day tongues became a sign, not to them that believed, but to the Mukti workers that believed not. For four hours she prayed continually. She seemed to want fellowship in prayer, and in our ignorance we prayed in English thinking she would understand. At last someone prayed in Marathi. Immediately there was a response, and after a season of prayer in Marathi the burden was lifted, and the prayer service closed. Gulabbai prayed in Sanskrit the following Sunday morning in the church. Ramabai and Mr. D. G. B. Godre, both testified that she used perfect classical Sanskrit while under the power of the Spirit. She has since spoken

Guzerathi and Canarese, all of which languages are unknown to her.

"The power of the Holy Spirit which rested upon Gulabbai was marked. Others began to speak in unknown tongues. The effect was wonderful. Unsaved ones, hitherto unreached, began to seek the Lord. The discouraged ones were encouraged, and the ones that felt they could not lead a victorious life repented of their sins. Daily the number of those who spoke in tongues increased."

The well-known journalist, William T. Ellis, was visiting India in 1907 and wrote a lengthy article in the *Chicago Daily News* concerning what he saw at Mukti. He was amazed at what he saw in this revival. He spoke to Ramabai concerning this and he states that she said to him: "We do not make a special point of the gift of tongues, but our emphasis is always put upon the lives. Undoubtedly the lives of our girls have been changed. About 700 of them have come into the place. We do not exalt the girls that have been gifted with other tongues, nor do we in anywise call special attention to them. I move among the girls listening to them in awe and wonder. I have heard girls who knew no English at all utter prayers in your tongue. I have heard others pray in Greek and Hebrew and Sanskrit, and others pray in languages that none of us understood. One of my girls was praying in this very room a few nights ago, and although in her study she has not gone through the second book, she prayed so clearly and beautifully in English that the other teachers marveled who could be praying since they did not detect the voice."

Miss Sarah Coxe tells how the Spirit of God was outpoured in the station of the Christian and Missionary Alliance at Gujarat: "We were a most needy lot of missionaries and our Indian people also needed a new touch from God. We had heard that God was working in America and other parts of the world, and so we began to wait upon Him. From the very first our waiting times were seasons of blessing. God kept searching our hearts and cleansing us, and getting us ready for the great gift He was about to give us, even the Baptism in the Spirit. One of our Indian evangelists received a mighty Baptism. One day he came to our station at Kaira, where we were all on our faces seeking God. I shall never forget the shine on his face. To look at him just made one desperately hungry for God. He spent most of his time in prayer and when he gave a message, it was in the power of the Spirit.

"One day he came into the bungalow and said he had been walking and talking with God all around our compound, and that God had told him He was soon going to pour out His Spirit upon Kaira. And it was so, for soon after, the Spirit of God fell upon our missionaries and school (we had then about 400 Indian girls), carrying everything before Him in a mighty Pentecostal revival. Our Indian Christian girls would gather in groups to pray, some in the schoolroom, some on the veranda, others under a tree, and the missionaries in the bungalow, until a mighty wave of prayer ascended to God like an incense. It reached His throne, touched His heart, and He came down and met us. Sometimes these prayer meetings lasted all night.

"One after another we missionaries and our Indian Christians were baptized according to Acts 2:4. One little Indian girl was so happy that she had been baptized, that she laughed and laughed, and then finally went up to Mrs. Schoonmaker, who lived with us then, and said, 'God loves me as well as He does you. I am black, you are white, but He has given me the Baptism too.'

"Many of our small girls, many of our middle-sized Indian Christian girls, a number of young men and missionaries received this precious Baptism at that time. The tiny girls had a saying that was very precious to me. As soon as anyone was baptized in the Spirit, they would say, 'She is in the boat too!' They were so happy when anyone received Him they would often clap their hands for joy. I had fifteen of these little Indian girls in my Sunday School class. They were baptized before I was, and so also was Mrs. Schoonmaker, who was rooming with me at that time. They and she were concerned because I did not yet have my Baptism, and one day Mrs. Schoonmaker prayed with me about it. She was so concerned for me that she cried, and that broke my heart and made me desperate after God. The word came to me, 'A broken and a contrite heart . . . Thou wilt not despise.'

"Later in that same morning, I went out where those fifteen girls were waiting for me. They said, 'Why have you not received the Baptism when God is pouring down the rain? Shall we pray now?' I said, 'yes,' and they began to pray. In a few minutes all fifteen were pleading with God for me and soon I began to sway under the power of the Spirit, then fell back on the floor. It was very hot on the cement floor in India. One child ran and got a fan and kept fanning me, praying all the time. The rest made a circle around me and prayed hard. The enemy had tried hard to counterfeit Pentecost in India, so one of our best Indian evangelists had taught the girls that if anyone who was seeking the Baptism could not say 'The blood of Jesus!' they were not right in spirit. So three of these little girls drew near me and said, *'Ban* (sister), *Esau nu Iohi bolo,'* (say 'the blood of Jesus'). This they did three times and then they all praised God and said: 'She says, "The blood of Jesus!" She is quite ready for the Baptism.' That very day, I was really, truly baptized in the Spirit, according to Acts 2:4. I received the Baptism in the Holy Spirit and spoke in tongues as an evidence of the Baptism. The little girl ran to tell Mrs. Schoonmaker. They said, 'Did you know that Miss Coxe is in the Pentecostal boat, too?' "

In January, 1907, the Lord sent A. J. Garr and his wife from Los Angeles to Calcutta where a number of missionaries were assembled in a convention. A large number of missionaries sought and received the Pentecostal enduement and took the blessing back to their various stations.

Because of the excessive heat in the plains in the middle of summer, many missionaries have of necessity to go to the hills where it is cooler. At Landour a Pentecostal sister, Miss Barber, has opened a rest home, and a large number of missionaries of various denominations have received the Baptism in the Spirit in this home.

A missionary, Frank B. Rhenstrom, writes of the revival that came to his station after his return from a period of blessing in this rest home:

"When we left for our station we were convinced that the time had come when God would pour out of His Spirit upon Christians. On August 1, when our Bible School was reopened, the presence of God was so real. We had been praying that no one might leave this institution and go out to preach the Word of God without being baptized with the Holy Ghost and fire. We could not go on with our studies. No one could pray without breaking down.

"We were convinced that all hindrances in the church were due to sin. When the Holy Spirit brings all kinds of sin to light, people are convinced. The most piercing cries that I have ever heard came from Indian Christians, when the Holy Spirit's convicting power came over them. Never have we seen anything more moving than during those wonderful days of prayer, when one after another broke down and confessed sin. All manner of sin was confessed and put away, and all kinds of quarrels were made up and wrongs righted. In this way the hindering stone was removed, and the Holy Spirit broke through in all the fullness of His convicting power.

"Two meetings were conducted every day during ten weeks. At the beginning of this revival meetings were held only for our preachers, Bible women, and the students in the Bible School, but when they *all* were baptized in the Spirit, we closed our carpenter shop and all the young men joined us in prayer. Those who were not on right terms with God were saved and some of them received the Baptism. Also many of our Christians here were baptized. When the news about the outpouring of the Holy Ghost reached other mission stations, preachers and Bible women were sent here to receive the Promise of the Father. During these meetings more than forty people were baptized with the Holy Ghost and with fire here in our station. People from other stations who had been baptized here went back to kindle the fire. In this way the revival spread to all our stations and about one hundred persons received the Baptism in the Holy Spirit.

"The spiritual atmosphere was so electrified by the Holy Spirit that outsiders who came into our compound were brought under conviction, and believers who were hungry for God, were often baptized with the Holy Spirit in the very first meeting they attended. Many times during these meetings I was prevented from giving an address due to the great brokenness among the people. Although the meeting lasted more than four hours, many would go back to the church, others would go to their rooms and continue in prayer. Even throughout the night we could find groups here and there engaged in prayer. The spirit of prayer was poured out in such a way that someone was always praying."

Walter H. Clifford, a missionary who was laboring in North India, paid a visit to Ceylon and held meetings in a number of churches in Colombo and other cities. The Lord confirmed His Word with signs following. People were healed of tuberculosis, blindness, deafness. The dumb spoke and the lame walked. Hundreds sought the Lord for salvation.

Brother Clifford writes: "In the spring of 1924, while on our way home on furlough, we stopped off in Ceylon and held meetings. Again the Lord blessed.

Many sought the Lord for salvation, and He graciously healed all sorts of diseases.

"A Roman Catholic woman who had been in labor pains for four days, suffering great agony and could get no deliverance, sent word to me and asked for prayer. Prayer was offered and the baby was born about an hour later. As soon as she was able to get out of bed she came to the meeting and gave her heart to the Lord. A paralyzed man was brought into the meetings, unable to walk. When the altar call was given he was brought to the front, and dealt with about his sins. He confessed, accepted Christ as His Saviour, was anointed and prayed for in the name of the Lord, and was instantly healed. He walked home."

Brother Clifford held a four days' meeting at a Methodist church in Galle, where seventy souls were dealt with for salvation, and many were healed.

In 1925 Brother Clifford settled permanently in Ceylon. In the first three years he reports there were records of over 2,000 coming to the altar for salvation.

He writes: "A prominent lawyer was at death's door. He had been a church member for twenty years, and had represented his church at the Synod, but on his deathbed he found that he was unsaved. Pentecostal people showed him the way of salvation and he was saved. They prayed for him and God healed him. He and his wife and twelve of his fourteen children have been saved and baptized in the Holy Spirit. Only the youngest have yet to be saved and filled. I saw six of that family receive the Baptism in the Holy Spirit in one service, all speaking in other tongues as the Spirit gave utterance. Acts 2:4.

"In these years we have had the joy of seeing scores of Hindus saved, dozens of Buddhists, and hundreds of nominal Christians. Hundreds in the islands have been filled with the blessed Holy Spirit. Ruined homes have been restored, broken hearts and lives have been mended, barren women have become joyful mothers of children, and the sick have been healed."

Recently a Ceylon Council has been organized, known as "The Assemblies of God of Ceylon." The Executive Committee of this Council consists of three missionaries and four Ceylonese brethren. The work is becoming a self-supporting, self-governing and self-propagating part of the body of Christ. Also a Ceylon Bible Institute has been established, giving a complete course of Bible training for ministers and Christian workers. At the time of writing, there are more Ceylonese young people applying for admission to the Institute than can be accommodated.

Brother Maynard Ketcham, in an address given in 1938, said: "It is a joy to report that at the present time the Pentecostal message is making remarkable advance in denominational circles. Several missionaries, some of them holding key positions in their respective missions, have recently received the Baptism in the Holy Spirit. Others are earnestly seeking.

"I have personally had the privilege of being associated with a work that is being maintained by Abdul Munshie, a dear Indian brother, who is working as a faith missionary in East India. This brother was saved as a boy. His open confession of Christ so enraged his Mohammedan parents that more than once they attempted to take his life.

"Shortly before Mrs. Ketcham and I returned to America on our first furlough we had a very precious outpouring of the Holy Spirit, and at that time Brother Munshie received the Baptism. After some time the Lord called this brother to take up his abode in his ancestral home in East Bengal—cut off entirely from all visible means of support—to live in the midst of a hotbed of fiery opposition. Many were the days when his next meal was provided by God in answer to prayer. Many were the times when only the hand of God protected him and his family from the physical violence of the Mohammedans. God supplied needs protected from dangers, and established this work.

"The remarkable ministry of healing given to our brother has been largely instrumental in breaking down prejudice and winning him favor. One man possessed of a violent evil spirit was delivered in answer to Brother Munshie's prayer. A child with epileptic fits, being treated then by the seventh doctor, was instantly healed, resulting in the conversion of this doctor. A demon-possessed woman who had a power of divination and was also near death's door with cholera, was healed of cholera and freed from the demons. She became a radiant witness for Christ, all in an instant. Other instances too numerous to mention have transpired. Thus many have been drawn toward the gospel, and become the nucleus of a Pentecostal church in this part of India.

"Brother Munshie has also had many calls to work among small independent groups of Indian Christians scattered here and there throughout Eastern Bengal. A hunger for the Pentecostal experience has attended his ministry everywhere, and now he has approximately twenty churches, representing perhaps 600 Christian people, who look to him for spiritual leadership. Brother Munshie also had about 400 inquirers in different villages whom he is training for water baptism. The Lord has remarkably provided two Spirit-filled Indian helpers to carry on the existing work and to answer new calls, but many more are needed."

Today there are large numbers of mission stations of the Asemblies of God in both North and South India. Close to the Nepal border in North India there are sixteen mission stations. J. H. Boyce writes: "While our work is largely evangelism, we have a large girls' school at Bettiah, a men's Bible school at Laheria Sarai, a small girl's orphanage at Purulia, a large boys' school at Nawabganj, a home for lepers at Uska Bazar, a girls' industrial school at Siswa Bazar, a babyfold at Rupaidiha, a women's Bible School at Hardoi, and recently a Bible School has been opened at Calcutta. Some of our missionaries are ever pressing forward to open other stations.

"Hundreds of orphans, boys and girls, and widows have been taken into these school and homes during recent years, and have been brought to a saving knowledge of the truth as it is in Christ Jesus, and also have received the Baptism in the Holy Spirit according to Acts 2:4. Many adults have been won to the Lord from time to time from these thickly populated districts in which we work, in which there are about 20,-000,000 people.

"We are not the only Pentecostal missionaries who are working in these areas, as there is a Swedish Baptist Pentecostal work which has over 20 missionaries. There are possibly another 20 missionaries of a 'like faith' from Sweden, Norway, and Denmark."

CHAPTER XIII

The Outpouring in China

MISS Blanche Appleby writes: "In the year 1807 Robert Morrison, the first Protestant missionary, arrived in China. In the city of Macao he and William Milne began their missionary labors for China. Here the first Protestant Christian convert was baptized and the first Protestant Christian church organized. It was here in October, 1907, just one hundred years later, the first Pentecostal missionary landed. Missionaries were gathered for a summer conference. The Lord had prepared them for the message, and missionaries connected with many societies and many Chinese workers were graciously baptized in the Holy Spirit according to Acts 2:4. It is estimated that some 200 Chinese and missionaries were baptized in the Spirit in Macao, Hong Kong, and Canton in five or six months."

Miss Nettie Moomau, a missionary in China, heard of the outpouring in Los Angeles. Leaving China in October, 1906, she made her way to Los Angeles, sought and received the Baptism with signs following. Of the revival that followed on her return to China she writes: "A Chinese woman, who was very ill, was taken to the mission hospital, and returned home in despair, unhealed. A testimony of healing was given to this woman's husband, who had been a member of a denominational church from which he had been expelled because of gross sin which he refused to confess. The wife, who was suffering from typhoid fever.

was in a critical condition. We dealt with them faithfully on the lines of repentance and obedience. God answered prayer, and in a few days this woman was able to walk a distance of about four miles to the mission.

"This healing was the beginning of a wonderful work of grace in this dear woman, in her family and relations. The Holy Ghost wrought mightily in her in convicting power. Repentance followed, and the cleansing of back tracks and a thorough work of sanctifying grace, followed by the baptism in the Holy Ghost with signs following. For many years this woman, under trying circumstances, has in her daily walk adorned the gospel of our Lord and Saviour. Her husband was soon gloriously saved, confessing his sins and making restitution. This man had a relative who was an idolater, who upon hearing his kinsman's testimony, was saved. *This* man had a sick child who seemed to be at death's door. This child was anointed with oil and then received the laying on of our hands in Jesus' name. This child began quickly to mend, and the little one's healing resulted in the conversion of the relatives.

"Numbers of demon-possessed people have been gloriously delivered through the power of Jesus' blood, including some insane persons. One of these lunatics had been insane for nine years. So violent was he that he would, at times, break the chains that bound him. Neither Chinese doctors, nor those of the denominational mission hospital could bring this man any relief. With the consent of the mother of this man, the images were smashed and burned. A message on salvation was given to the crowds of people present. Then the crazy man was prayed for. That night he rested better than usual. In a few days' time he could help his mother to cook. In a few weeks' time he was instantly and completely delivered and returned to the government position he had left. The day he was prayed for, his mother, who had been an opium smoker and gambler, was completely delivered from both vices.

In less than a month she was wonderfully saved and received the anointing of the Spirit.

"In the same house as the lunatic, lived a sister who was afflicted with epilepsy. One day, resting on the couch, she had a seizure. With eyes closed, teeth clenched, pale of countenance, and body rigid, in response to an inquiry, she slightly moved her head, indicating that she desired to be prayed for. Besides the workers, a number of Christian neighbors gathered to join in prayer. Outside in the courtyard was a large crowd of people who could plainly see through the windows this afflicted young woman and the praying band. The uncle in the courtyard was raging, and he threatened to hang us if the girl died. Inside the house the spirit of prevailing prayer continued for almost an hour. Suddenly the epileptic began to sing in her native tongue, 'Jesus breaks every fetter,' and in a few moments she sat up, and with arms uplifted, continued to sing: 'I will shout hallelujah, for He sets me free.' From this time she has never had another attack. The crowd of neighbors were amazed at the power of the living Christ.

"Another healing resulted in the awakening of a professor of science in the Methodist Episcopal University, who received full salvation and the baptism in the Holy Ghost according to Acts 2:4. This university professor is now one of our native preachers.

"The circumstances of this healing to which I referred were as follows: This man had one leg two and one-half inches shorter than the other. Until invited by one of our native Christians, he had never before been in a Pentecostal mission. He was anointed and prayed for the first night he came, but received no manifestation of healing until the fifth night, when he sat well up toward the front. The Lord put a spirit of prayer upon us workers and for half an hour we battled with the powers of darkness, praying that the Lord would break through and glorify the name of Jesus. During this season of prayer, the young man affirmed that it seemed as if someone took hold of his arms and wrists and lifted him up with a jump, and when he came down he was completely healed.

"The only daughter of an American doctor in a Methodist hospital was in a critical condition with rapid consumption. I received an express letter inviting me to come immediately and pray for the afflicted young woman. An opportunity was thus afforded to witness to the full gospel in this missionary doctor's home. God heard prayer and raised up the consumptive, putting flesh on her bones and restoring her to health so completely that she was scarcely recognizable as the person who had been ill.

"Two blind persons received sight, one of whom had not seen light for seven years. Two persons who had stooped backs were straightened. Persons suffering from cholera, diphtheria, scarlet fever, consumption, asthma, and various kinds of fever have been healed completely through faith in Jesus' name."

Writing of a convention held in 1914 Miss Blanche Apppleby states: "Conviction and confession of sin were evident. A little Bible woman, who had no knowledge of English, with face radiant, began singing in clear English. 'The angels are surrounding me.' There is no sound in the Chinese language equal to the 'R' sound, but this Chinese woman was able to say the 'R' sound."

Writing of some special meetings at Lo Pau, Miss Appleby states: "On the third night an altar call was given and many responded, among them Yeung Tai Koo, a blind Bible woman. After praying a short time she was filled with the Spirit. She knew nothing of the English language but the Holy Spirit soon began to speak through her in English and the first word was 'Worship!' While prostrate on the floor the Spirit of God spoke this word through her perhaps a score of times. Other words followed in English, among them the word 'His.' Then the word 'Rest!' and the very expression suggested rest. Then the words 'Father' and 'daughter' and 'Jesus.' Close by her at the altar was another blind sister. She turned to her and began to say these two words in English, *'Fill her.'* Then after that she repeated the word *'Love.'* She also spoke in French giving the French word for *'Rejoice.''* Miss Schultz, one of the missionaries present, understood French.

"A few days later, at a tarrying meeting in our home, this blind sister was mightily prostrated under the power of the Spirit again and the Holy Spirit began to speak through her in English—this time giving sentences instead of words. She started by saying, 'The Bible! *The Bible!'* Then she sang through the song, 'Jesus loves me, this I know,' in perfect English She said again and again, 'I go this way with Thee!' and then with great expression, 'Be strong, be strong— it will not be long.' At this time she spoke also in Mandarin, a language with which she was also unfamiliar. She spoke at some length and much of what she said was understood by three evangelists and one Chinese woman present. It was a prophetic message concerning the Antichrist. This manifestation made a great impression on some of the other workers and caused them to seek the fullness of the Spirit in earnest."

The following is a letter written by Miss Ethel Abercrombie, from The Door of Hope in Shanghai in 1910: "You will rejoice with us before the Lord that over a month ago He poured out Pentecost on us. In less than a week, five of our native helpers and about ten of the girls had received their Pentecost as at the beginning with the sign of tongues. (There must be more than twenty now.) Others of the girls who were hard characters have yielded to the Lord."

W. W. Simpson wrote of this Door of Hope work in 1923: "This place provides a Christian home, giving industrial training to young slave girls who are rescued from a destined life of sin. It is in charge of Miss E. G. Dieterle, who has received the Spirit and spoken in tongues. Some of the Chinese have also received. There are about 160 girls, 20 helpers, and a few people from the United States in the meetings, nearly 200 in constant attendance. From the first the Spirit gave me such a yearning, loving compassion for these dear girls who had been destined, so far as it is in the power of man and devil, to eternal slavery to sin and Satan. The Lord gave me the unutterable joy of beholding the travail of His soul in the mightiest flood of broken-hearted repentance I have ever seen. I one time counted more than one hundred crying, weeping, wailing, screaming in the agony of conviction as they confessed their sins and called on God for mercy.

"Some went through to the Baptism, we know, for we heard them speaking in tongues as the Spirit gave utterance. On Monday they began at ten a.m. and continued without intermission until ten p.m. On Tuesday they began at eight a.m. and continued right on until ten p.m. Almost uninterruptedly there were nearly two hundred girls and young women who poured forth a solid stream of confessed sins for three days.

"I gave a short message on the third parable in Luke 15, showing how the Father, Son, and Spirit were longing, seeking, searching for the salvation of the lost; and the confessions began again. All night long they continued, one girl after another rising with streaming eyse and broken voice to praise the Lord for dying on the cross for such a sinner as she; then recounting the sins she had formerly cherished hidden deep down in an impenitent heart, but now flung from her bosom in pitiless abhorrence. If angels rejoice over one sinner that repents, what must have been their joy over the one hundred that repented that night. And after the burden of sin was gone, these girls would kneel in adoration of the Prince and Saviour who had given repentance and remission of sins to such sinners.

"Then I hurriedly ate breakfast, for I had to leave for Shanghai at 9:30, and I had not packed my suitcase and bedding. But they pressed into the dining room with their gifts and offerings—poor slave girls, some rescued only a month ago—laying before me all they had, handkerchiefs, towels, pennies, dimes, and dollars—sacred, holy things, for they are sacrifices unto God. The value of it all is more than $50, but what must it mean to God?"

In the latter part of 1926, Brother Simpson wrote from Michow: "Your prayers and offerings, and our toils and labors have resulted in a mighty revival, and the sending forth of twenty-seven additional laborers into this big harvest field. On June 8 a man came to the meeting from Taochow, asking Mr. Chow, who has charge of the work there, to come and pray for his niece who had been sick about three months and was now dying, but wanted to be saved ere she passed away. He hurried to her bedside while we prayed for him and her. His uncle joined him and they prayed for the young woman who was indeed dying. She confessed her sins, and the Lord saved her. The two men then asked the Lord to heal her also and had the assurance that He would do so. Then they went home for the night. But the next morning they were called again as she was plainly dying. According to the Chinese custom she was already dressed in her burial clothes. Her limbs had lost all feeling and were growing cold and stiff. Her father, the doctor, and all her family knew she was dying, but the two men held on in faith. Gradually she sank into unconsciousness, her entire body growing cold and stiff as death claimed her. Finally she ceased breathing, and her tongue dropped back into her throat. But the two men still kept their hands on the lifeless body, praising the Lord for victory over death.

"After a few minutes they heard one word from the dead throat, 'Faith!' Reassured, they redoubled their praises, and soon the mighty Spirit of Life from Christ Jesus filled that lifeless clay and all heard clearly the dead lips speaking in tongues as He gave utterance! And the same Spirit who gave utterance in tongues raised the dead woman to life! Calling to her father she said, 'Except you believe in Jesus, your daughter cannot live.' He dropped to his knees and accepted the Lord he had rejected for thirty years. She then told her husband he too would have to accept Jesus as his Lord. When he said, 'Yes, I will believe,' she said, 'It must be with all your heart.' And he confessed his sins and accepted the Lord. She said there were three who were mocking, and her uncle looked outside and found three members of an idolatrous society making fun of the work of God. She challenged them to prove their religion and the Spirit of God declared through her, 'To show you that Jesus is true and your religion false, I will cause this woman to stand on her feet today, sit up tomorrow, and walk on the third day.'

"Immediately. with no assistance, and to the consternation of all, the woman who was dead but a few moments before stood up in their midst and *preached the gospel for two and a half hours.* She who had never heard the Bible read, and who could not read a word herself, proclaimed the terrible judgments now impending, going over much the same ground as the Revelation! The next day she sat up, and the third day she walked in the presence of many. As a result of this mighty miracle her entire family have been saved and deep conviction has come to many others. Her father came sixty miles to the Minchow convention to tell everybody about it and to be baptized."

In 1927 a blessed outpouring of the Spirit came to the Baptists in a Chinese church in Canton. "In one week twenty have received the baptism in the Holy Spirit, and about a hundred girls from the school are now seeking. Those in charge of the school of 600 students were alarmed and sent for one of the head teachers from Shanghai to come down and stop this movement. But she was taken sick and was prayed for and healed in the Pentecostal mission in Canton, and received the baptism in the Holy Ghost. Also another one of her companion teachers received. As many as five have received in the Presbyterian compound, in the school for the blind. A Chinese lady doctor has recently been filled with the Spirit. She has left her hospital work and gone out to preach the gospel. Another remarkable report is regarding an old lady who was miraculously healed, and whom God has used to bring hundreds into the kingdom. She is over eighty years of age. Lately God has given her a wonderful faith in praying for the sick. Hundreds are now coming to her for prayer, and a revival has broken out. Some twenty-five received the Baptism under her ministry in two weeks' time."

David Leigh who labored in Yunnan, wrote of a gracious revival that God sent to Siimao: "Brother Fullerton belonged to the China Inland Mission: One day he went to a Pentecostal meeting, received the baptism in the Holy Ghost, and began to speak in tongues. He severed his connection with the mission he loved, and came out to trust God alone for his support. The Lord directed him down to the south. At the end of twelve months Brother Fullerton saw absolutely nothing for his labor. All through the second year he labored faithfully, but at the end of the second year there was still no result. He had toiled night and day and had taken nothing. One night there were just four Chinese seated in the chapel. None of them were converted. They were just a little interested. He went to the vestry and wept bitterly. He said, 'My Lord, another year of labor and not a single soul!' He went back to the chapel and began to preach. Another man came in, a man who belonged to the tribes people. The moment this man entered Brother Fullerton felt God had sent that man. He forgot all about the four Chinamen and directed everything to that man. After the meeting he came forward and said, 'This is wonderful. I have not heard anything like this before. Have you any books so that I can understand better. Brother Fullerton gave him books and he went away. The following Sunday he returned, bringing ten others with him. And these eleven sat and listened most attentively. After the service he invited the eleven to a meal, and at the table he explained more simply the gospel. After prayer they left his home. The following Sunday forty came. And in a remarkably short space of time Brother Fullerton had the joy of seeing 9,000 of this same tribe gathered to the Lord. He wrote to me one day and said, 'You must come down here. This is spreading far beyond my control'."

Miss E. M. Cook wrote from Yunnan in 1927: "There is a continuous revival in the district where Brother and Sister Hector McLean are laboring. Over a hundred have received the baptism in the Holy Spirit, and as in all God-given revivals, deep confiction of sin and genuine repentance have been the outstanding features."

In 1934 W. W. Simpson wrote of a convention of native workers in Kansu: "Just recently a convention of over 300 Christians, nearly all from the China Inland Mission, was held. Toward the close of the ten days the Spirit was poured on them, shaking the place where they were assembled. Many heard beautiful music in the sky above the building. Sixteen came through in tongues, several had visions and danced in the Spirit. Altogether 43 were under the power. The rest are very hungry and some of the leaders have written asking me to come and help them."

Brother Leonard G. Bolton, who labors among the tribal people in Southwest China, writes "I think we can safely say that since the work was opened in 1921, over 1,000 souls have been saved and there have been remarkable healings through simple faith in Christ. Four other Lisu districts have been opened from this center in the last ten years, where they also report thousands of converts. Our Lisu native workes are not employed by us but are on an indigenous basis. We have fifteen such workers who are teaching and spreading the gospel among their own people."

H. A. Baker was a missionary of the Christian Church. While on furlough he received the baptism in the Spirit and returned to China as a Pentecostal missionary, trusting the Lord fully for his support.

Brother Baker and his wife gathered together in the city of Yunnan a number of children. Brother Baker writes: "There was a very remarkable outpouring of the Holy Spirit on the Chinese children of the Adullam Mission in Yunnanfu, China. The children, mostly boys, the majority below the teen age, had nearly all been rescued out of a beggar life on the streets of the city.

"Meetings were held with these children twice a day. Suddenly in one of these services the heavens opened, and the veil was so drawn aside that the children were allowed to see the things of the unseen world as face-to-face. This continued for a period of eight weeks.

"The first two weeks the glory of God so rested on the place that all ordinary activities were suspended, while the things of the Lord were sought earnestly day and night. Sleeping and eating appeared but mere incidents. After going to bed, children would often get up again, return to the prayer room to seek the Holy Spirit, and be lost in heaven-sent blessings until morning. Almost all that time, day and night, there were those who lay prostrate under the power of the Lord, lost in the things beyond the veil, while at times the glory of the new Jerusalem seemed to descend upon the group who in vision were in the heavenly city dancing with the angels, though in reality they were dancing in the prayer room, sometimes describing in prophecy what they were seeing in vision.

"Walking through the golden streets of the New Jerusalem in the third heaven, visiting mansions of indescribable glory, playing by the streams with the animal pets in the heavenly Eden, enjoying the delicious fruits, flowers, birds, and other glorious wonders of Paradise more than restored, and ten thousand wonders that cannot be told, were such constant and general experiences of these children that for those weeks they seemed to be translated from earth to heaven. They thought they actually left their bodies and ascended through the first heaven where they could feel the heavenly air as a breeze on their faces, then on through the starry realm and on and on though the third heaven into the golden city.

"Hell and the realms of the kingdom of darkness were sometimes visited. Events of the Old Testament were seen as actual realities. Likewise New Testament events were seen as eye witnesses. Events as related in the Gospels in the life of Christ, His capture, His crucifixion, His burial, His resurrection, His appearance to His disciples, and His ascension to heaven were clearly seen. The children saw and lived through these events.

"Nearly all the things of the Book of Revelation were seen by the children and given through them in prophecy. Things seen in vision were acted out by the children, and what they were experiencing in the unseen worlds was described aloud, while, so far as the children knew, they were in another world altogether.

"Some of the most profound revelations and wonderful visions were given to small and ignorant children, revelations and visions of things in the Bible they had never heard of.

"The greatest emphasis was on coming events. The great dragon cast out of heaven to earth, the Antichrist, the persecutions of believers, the plagues and other events of the great tribulation were constantly witnessed. These children repeatedly saw the believers supernaturally anointed with power from God to miraculously preach the gospel in these days of distress and persecution, to a degree that even the Early Church did not know. In their vision they saw men preaching to the tribes of the earth in prophecy through tongues and interpretations and with a testimony attended by signs and wonders. Villages that rejected the testimony were sometimes destroyed by fire from heaven. Persecutors were sometimes smitten by plagues. Believers were sometimes miraculously fed with food from heaven and like Philip miraculously transported to the place of testimony or carried away from the hands of persecutors. An outstanding impression of all this was the miraculous and prophetic preaching of the gospel to the tribes of the earth in the midst of great persecution, attended by constant miracles and supernatural works of God.

"Even children eight or ten years old could preach freely under the unction of the Holy Spirit in the streets of the city or out in the villages, there being some instances of preaching through tongues and interpretation and some instances where the Holy Spirit came upon the boy preacher, lifting him into the realm of the Holy Spirit so that he preached in pure prophecy like an Old Testament prophet.

"By anointing children as well as older ones and sending them out to preach in the power of God, the Lord seemed to be showing what He wants the final church to be in the last days of its testimony upon the earth.

"We expected that after those days of preparation the Lord would send the older of the Adullam boys into the surrounding mountains to preach the gospel to the many primitive tribes who occupy these unevangelized regions. But God opened other doors among other mountain tribes twelve days' journey away.

"This new door was miraculously opened by God. A young married man of the Ka Do tribe who had never heard the gospel, but who knew a little about the claims of Christianity to present a way of getting through the present life without the heavy demands of constant sacrifices to appease devils, for material motives more than any other, decided to become a Christian. Accordingly he discussed this with the other fifteen families of his village

"This village was soon followed by other villages turning to Christianity in a mass movement until there were soon six hundred families. At this time I was invited to be the first missionary to visit this movement. Everywhere God-prepared hearts were found who heard the gopel for the first time. The mass movement soon spread to 2,500 families of perhaps 10,000 people.

"The young man who had first decided to become a Christian returned with us to the Adullam Mission on that first trip into Ka Do Land. He was converted, received the Holy Spirit and after a few weeks returned to his home in the mountains. He was uneducated and knew only the fundamental things of the Lord. But upon his return to his village and upon his telling the people about the working of the Holy Spirit among the Chinese children at our home, where he had received the Holy Spirit, the people in the village wanted to seek the Holy Spirit.

"This they did, and He fell among them mightily. This fire of God rapidly spread to other villages. Other young men now came with the former one to the Adullam Mission in Yunnanfu to learn more of the Lord, study the Bible, and seek the Holy Spirit. Their stay was short, but as soon as they arrived the Holy Spirit began to fall among them in power, until nearly all who came received anointings, some speaking with other tongues, some speaking in prophecy. The importance of leading men and women to Christ was always emphasized to them in the meetings.

"Upon their return to their mountain tribes they went everywhere among the villages preaching repentance, and the soon coming of the Lord, and the need to receive the power of the Holy Spirit, and to give a real testimony in the midst of a wicked generation. Everywhere these men went the Lord poured out the Holy Spirit. Within a few months the fire spread all over Ka Do Land and into the other tribes, until the villages where no one received miraculous anointings of the Holy Spirit were very few.

"These outpourings of the Holy Spirit, with very few exceptions, were attended by much prophetic utterance. Women and children especially, who could not have said anything in public, when under the anointing of the Holy Spirit had often, when in a trance, spoke, of the mighty works of God, the Maker of heaven and earth. They spoke of the glories of heaven, the wonders of the life to come, the certainty of the Lord's return, and of coming judgment, the Cross of Christ, the love of God, and the necessity to turn from all sin to the Saviour of sinning men. This prophetic speaking under the unction of the Holy Spirit was so evidently miraculous that those present could not doubt that God was speaking to them from heaven. There were some who like those in Bible days mocked and received no good. There were a host whose hearts the Lord opened who turned to God.

"This prophetic speaking under the unction of the Holy Spirit was so usual, that I doubt if there was any place where the Holy Spirit fell in power without one or two or many of those present speaking in this miraculous way. In this way the Lord spoke to these tribespeople and led them to repentance. These new, untried, untaught workers preached what they could. But the Lord attended their preaching with mighty outpourings.

"In one place where an uneducated and untalented young man was preaching, there was a night when fifty-six people were prostrated in the open court where the meeting was being held, while thirty more were dancing or shaking under the power of the Holy Spirit. Many of those prostrated lay in a state of heavenly ecstasy singing the praises of God until late into the night. Such scenes were not unusual wherever the Holy Spirit was outpoured. Heaven came down, angels were seen, and God talked to people almost as He did to Moses face-to-face.

"This outpouring of the Holy Spirit was so clearly a call of the Lord that few of those who slighted or refused that call have subsequently turned to the Lord.

☉"Men gathered twice a year for periods of two or three weeks' training in Bible teaching. At these times the Lord poured out the Holy Spirit and in a remarkable way opened the minds and hearts of these men to understand the Word. The greater part of those who came began to study the Chinese Bible as their first lesson in reading. After these short periods of study the men would return to their native Bibles, or rather a Gospel or New Testament they had been studying, and with the anointing of the Holy Spirit, began to preach.

"The Lord developed leaders, taught them to understand the Bible, and helped many to learn to read who could otherwise never have learned to read. No workers were paid salaries. No one was promised food or clothing. They labored in home duties, or at times of opportunity for more extensive work they made itineraries, traveling from section to section, trusting the Lord to meet their needs. He did.

"At this time, six years after the initial outpourins of the Holy Spirit, buildings ranging from grass-covered sheds to very usable thatched native churches have been built in over thirty centers, and the work is being cared for by those whom the Lord has called out of paganism and made shepherds of His sheep. As the Lord began this work supernaturally, He continues it supernaturally. Miraculous manifestations still continue in the work."

The Holy Spirit continues to be poured out in China. B. T. Bard wrote from Peking in the early summer of 1940: "Never before have I witnessed such a mighty manifestation of the power of God. His glorious presence fills the school through day and night as many are baptized in the Spirit, and God moves in ways that are more marvelous than we had ever even imagined. There are confessions of sins and short-comings, messages in tongue and interpretation, pro-phetic utterances, spiritual dreams, heavenly visions of Christ and the glory land, divine healings, and, above all, a spirit of prayer and supplication and wor-ship.

"God began in our midst with prayer in the chapel. Only a few students were present; then God filled one with His Spirit and began to call others from their beds. Soon they were gathered in prayer and, as a great and roaring wind, the Spirit swept over them, slaying them under the mighty power of the living God.

"For more than a month now this wonderful visita-tion of the Spirit has continued and the end is not yet, praise the name of the Lord! About one hundred have been filled with the Spirit since that first night, and we know that God has accomplished and is accom-plishing great things in the lives of our students, pu-rifying, strengthening, and instilling in their hearts holy zeal for the things of God.

"After the opening of the school term we found that a number of our students were opposed to the work of the Spirit, the Baptism, and particularly the evidence of speaking in tongues. During the great outpouring a marvelous change has taken place, and these very students have accepted the fullness of God's grace and have received the baptism in the Holy Spirit them-selves.

"One girl student from Manchuria was alarmed and disgusted with the volume of prayer which re-sounded through the chapel that first night of revival. She secretly prayed that God would make the students quieter. Instead, their voices gathered force as time went on and their hearts were poured out in worship to the Lord.

"Deep in her heart Kao Chu Ju truly desired the

presence of God but she was afraid to have any show made of herself, or for anyone to lay hands upon her. Suddenly she saw Jesus in a vision, and He graciously laid His own nail-pierced hands upon her. She fell to the floor under the power of the Spirit and soon was speaking rapturously in other tongues as the Spirit gave her utterance.

"A boy who had been antagonistic to the baptism in the Spirit was greatly moved, and several times felt tears running down his face. As he prayed there appeared before his eyes a great light, and it was not long before he fell under the power and began to speak in tongues.

"An unsaved girl visiting one of the teachers came into the meetings. Soon she was weeping before the Lord and, before the night was over, God met her hungry soul. She was saved, and gloriously filled with the Spirit.

"According to the Word of God, in the days of the Latter Rain His people should dream dreams and see visions concerning the things of God. One of our student girls lay prostrate on the floor beside Mrs. Hao, a student from Manchuria. Recently Mrs. Hao received news that her mother had gone on ahead to be with Jesus, and her heart was sad because she could not go home to pay her last respects.

"The girl near her was granted a wonderful vision of Christ and the land beyond the river. Joyfully she told Mrs. Hao she had seen her mother in that land of peace and happiness with the Saviour. Although she had never seen Mrs. Hao's mother, she recognized her as Peter, James, and John recognized Moses on the Mount of Transfiguration. Mrs. Hao's heart was comforted and she thanked Jesus for His gracious kindness and care for her in her sorrow.

"Mrs. Li, a day student in the Institute, related a remarkable dream the Lord had given her. She thought she was overtaken by robbers who were trying to force their mark or seal upon her. She felt it was

the mark of the beast whereby the enemy, who is
nothing but a thief and a robber, will seal the deceived inhabitants of the world. The robbers failed
in their purpose; and she awakened, greatly impressed
by the dream, and began to seek the Lord. Soon she
was sealed with the Holy Spirit of promise unto the
day of redemption.

"Later on in the meetings she came to the altar for
prayer that she might be healed. She saw fire coming
down out of heaven upon her head, and she was slain
under the power of God. The following day she testified that she was able to read her lesson sheets without
glasses. The Lord had healed her eyes, praise His
name forever!

"Praise God, not only the Bible school students
are receiving the blessings of heaven but Chinese belonging to other churches have been drawn to the meetings and have been filled with the Spirit. A visitor one
night saw a ball of fire coming down. He was slain
under the mighty power of God, and began to prophesy.

"Some prophetic utterances warned of impending
famines, earthquakes, and persecutions. In the face
of these words, came messages of comfort promising
the presence and grace of God to those who should not
fear but go out preaching the gospel to lost men.

"The children also are receiving a full measure of
God's treasures. One little boy belonging to a student
family saw Jesus moving in our midst. A small girl
who now attends Sunday school at the Bible Institute
came to one of the meetings and was slain under the
power of God, later speaking in tongues and prophesying. Our own boy, James, saw Jesus, His face all
radiantly beautiful, sitting beside him, and He said, 'If
you go with Me, I will go with you.' Our oldest boy
also saw the Lord, and received his Baptism, praise
God!"

In 1929 Martin Kvamme, together with a native
worker, entered Manchuria. A few years later he wrote:
"At that time our future workers for that field were

still in sin and darkness, some of them bound as slaves by evil habits. God brought them out one by one, and today we have in our Manchurian work in China proper more than forty evangelists, Bible women, and Christian workers giving all their (tme) to the work of the Lord. The majority of these workers have come from among our converts during these nine years. The Mukden station alone has produced sixteen full-time workers besides some students now in Bible school training.

"The Assemblies of God work in Manchuria has been blessed with the outpouring of the Holy Spirit from time to time. From among about eight hundred baptized Christians in our Manchurian churches a large percentage have received the baptism in the Holy Spirit.

"At the present time we have in the city of Mukden a beautiful brick tabernacle, three street chapels, and a large gospel tent. We also hold regular meetings in two large homes. Every day we carry on a good deal of house visitation work, besides holding regular meetings in gospel halls in the evenings, day meetings for Christians, and so on. Every morning we have Bible study for the workers and Christians who can come in. Whenever possible we have systematic Bible study, when we study the Bible book by book, going into it as deeply as we possibly can.

"During our terms of service in North China and Manchuria, we have been privileged to spread the Word of God. Some years we have sold as many as 100,000 portions, and the books generally go into the hands of people who have never read the Word of God before. One of our evangelists put in four months of street preaching in the city of Hsin King. The police gave him eight street corners where he could preach and sell Gospel portions. During one of the months, the cold month of December, he sold about 10,000 books in connection with his street meetings.

"Shortly after the Japanese army had brought

Manchuria under control, the Christian churches in Japan became stirred with love and compassion for the Manchurian people. They decided to send missionaries to this great field, and one of their pastors came to Mukden. He was a very active man, and in a very short time had blessed work for the Lord under way. The support of their missionaries, as well as for the engaged Manchurian evangelists and pastors in their work, is provided by the Christian churches of Japan."

An English missionary tells in the *Elim Evangel* the following incident in connection with the war in Manchuria: "In their invasion of China, the Japanese troops came to a mission station where there were a number of devout people, some of whom were rejoicing in the Pentecostal experience. The native Christians had barricaded themselves in their compound and soon there was a loud knocking on the gates as one of the Japanese officers sought immediate admission, calling upon them to open the door before they burst it in. Eventually the door was burst open, and in rushed the Japanese soldiers taking hold first of one of the company of Chinese, a native evangelist. He was about to kill him when the man burst into an utterance in tongues in the power of the Spirit. The soldier stopped and after a moment or two said: 'Why did you not tell me there were Japanese here?' He was told there were no Japanese in the compound, but he insisted that there were Japanese, and said this man had just told him in Japanese that if any harm were done to the compound or its inhabitants the judgment of God would fall upon him and his fellow soldiers. As a result of that incident none of the believers in the compound were harmed, and shortly afterward a revival broke out among the Chinese in the district and many were brought to Christ."

CHAPTER XIV

A Great Work in Egypt

A NATIVE of Egypt named Alexander Paul was in America in the year of 1907, and received the baptism in the Holy Ghost. He sent the news back to Egypt. The saints in the city of Assiout to whom he wrote were so stirred that they sent a cablegram to America to send them help. G. S. Brelsford, an evangelist, sent word that he and his family would come, although they did not arrive in Egypt until March, 1909. This brother labored faithfully in Egypt until his death in September, 1912.

In 1913 a number of new missionaries went out from America to Egypt, including C. W. Doney and his wife. A gracious work of the Spirit spread throughout Egypt. Several young men, saved and filled with the Holy Ghost, were raised up of the Lord as evangelists and pastors to devote their whole time to the preaching of the full-gospel message. In 1917 C. W. Doney wrote: "We now have ten preachers, ten mission stations, and several hundred people saved and baptized in the Holy Ghost. God has poured forth His Spirit in a marvelous way, and the work now extends from Alexandria in the north to beyond Assiout in the south."

At Assiout there is a large Pentecostal orphanage where some 1,000 children are housed. There are many destitute widows also in this orphanage. The founder of this work is Miss Lillian Trasher. Her story is a remarkable one: "I was reared a Catholic, and had never seen a Bible until I was sixteen years old. One day, in Atlanta, Georgia, I went to visit a friend. I saw a book on the table. I picked it up and read 'Holy Bible.' I said, 'Oh, this is a Bible; I have heard of the Bible.' I went home and told my mother that I had seen a Bible, and that I would very much like to have one to read. She promised me one for my birthday, which was some weeks off. I asked if I could have one to read. She promised me one for my birthday. She bought it for me. Oh, the wonder of reading for the first time the precious Word of God!

"On Christmas Day we had a few friends come to spend the evening with us. Our neighbor knew that we were Catholics but he let his light shine. He quietly began to tell the story of his life, how he was once very wicked but that God had saved him and changed his whole life. I got a little stool, drew it up by his side, and never missed a word he said. He remarked, 'We have a little prayer meeting in our house every Wednesday.' I asked mother if I could go. She agreed. The next day I went to see his wife and asked her to tell me some more of this good news. She said it was wash day and she was busy. I said, 'If you will tell me I will help you with the wash.'

"A few weeks after that I got down by a log in the bushes alone, and prayed until God wonderfully saved my soul. Later my dear mother was saved. She also left the Catholic Church and died a true Christian. After that, one day I went out and picked some wild flowers. I went to a quiet place and got down on my knees in the woods and said: 'Lord, I do wish I had something to give You, but I have nothing but these flowers.' I gave them to God as solemnly and as earnestly as I later gave my life and picked little Egyptian flowers for His kingdom. I am quite sure He accepted them."

When Lillian Trasher was twenty-three years of

age she was led to give her life to the Lord to be a missionary in Africa. She had only five dollars, for she had spent all her other money in arranging for her wedding which was to have taken place just ten days before that time. She knew the young man did not wish to go to Africa, and not daring to disobey the call of God, she determined to go to Africa by herself. At that time she was assisting Miss Mattie Perry in her orphanage in Marion, North Carolina.

When she started she had only enough to pay her fare to Washington, D. C. There she received enough to go to Pittsburg to meet some people she wanted to see. She landed there with twenty-five cents. As she was leaving Pittsburgh to go to Philadelphia she had no money, but one who took her to the station paid her fare. In Philadelphia she spoke at several missions and received forty dollars which she deposited at the shipping office towards her fare to Egypt. In New York City a sister gave her sixty dollars, which enabled her to pay the balance of her fare to Egypt. She was asked to speak one night in the Forty-Second Street Mission in New York City and received fifty dollars more.

She wrote: "We were having prayer in my cabin just before sailing and someone asked me to open my Bible and ask God to give me a verse. This I did, and noted the first verse that caught my eyes. It was Acts 7:34, a verse that I had never noticed before: 'I have seen, I have seen the affliction of My people which is in Egypt, and I have heard their groaning, and am come down to deliver them. And now come, I will send thee into Egypt.' In this unmistakable way God set His seal upon my call.

"I arrived in Assiout October 26, 1910, and went at once to Mr. Brelsford's Mission and began to study the language. After I had been in Egypt a little over three months I was asked to visit a dying woman. She had a baby about three months old, and it was being fed from a tin bottle. The milk had become caked and green and stringy, yet the baby was trying to drink it. Soon the mother died and the baby was given to me. I took it home. The child had never had a bath and its clothes were sewed to its little body. You cannot imagine the odors that came from that little creature. The little thing would cry and cry, making it hard for the missionaries to rest at night. They begged me to take her back, but I could not do that. So I went out and rented a house for $12.50 per month, spent my little all for a bit of furniture, and thus February 10, 1911, marked the opening of the Assiout Orphanage.

"My first donation to the work was thirty-five cents, and from that time to this our big family has never missed a meal, nor have we gone into debt for a single thing. When I opened the orphanage, *I made up my mind never to go into debt,* and decided that if the Lord wanted the orphanage, He would supply the needs. At one time our finances were very low, so I talked to the head teacher and said: 'The only thing we can do is to send home all who have a place to go to, until the Lord opens the way to bring them back again.' Then I called all the children into the prayer room, explained to them that we could never go into debt, and that since God was not providing the needed money, it was probably best for them to go to their relatives until the need was supplied. When I reached that point the children broke out in a wail such as I had never heard before. Unable to go on with my explanation, we got down to pray, and the noise was like that of a great camp meeting. The poor little boys, how they cried! After prayer I arose and told them I could never go into debt, and if God did not send in the money we would all suffer together. I was quite surprised when the next morning's mail brought a check from America for one hundred dollars. Before that was used up other money began to come in from Egypt.

"The children, in addition to their usual secular and

religious training, are receiving an unusual discipline in faith. Everything about our work has a tendency to stimulate simple trust in God for everything. At one time during the absence of 'Mama,' money was scarce and the daily menu consisted mainly of beans and lentils. This monotony in their fare aroused a protest. The children between the ages of four and five all marched into the kitchen and told the cook that they could not eat lentils any more, but wanted meat instead. The cook replied: 'My darlings, I cannot give you any meat, but if you want it you should ask the Lord and He will give it to you.' The baby deputation immediately retired to the nursery and began to pray, *Ya Rob, Yebart le hu lahn* (O Lord, send us some meat). While they were still praying a knock was heard at the door and someone came in bringing half a beef. 'Ask and ye shall receive.' "

On April 7, 1927, Sister Trasher wrote: "Today I witnessed the greatest revival I have ever seen in my life. Three days ago we started a revival meeting among the children. The Spirit was with us from the very first meeting, dozens getting saved and dozens seeking the Baptism. This afternoon I thought the children had better not have a night meeting as they had been praying and crying for hours; so I said that everyone was to go to bed early. I went to my room early also, but soon I heard such a noise coming from all sides that I sent a girl to see if there was a funeral passing by. She returned and said it was the children praying everywhere. I went first over to the widows and blind girls' department and found they were crying and praying. I went to the kitchen; they were praying, crying, and talking in tongues. I went to the big girls' room; they were all on their faces crying to God or shouting.

"But the most wonderful sight I ever saw in my life was when I followed the noise up to the housetop. There were dozens and dozens of little girls shouting, crying, talking in tongues, rejoicing, preaching, singing

—well, just everything you can think of, praising God. Several of the children saw visions. I have no idea of how many have received the Baptism. You cannot hear anything; it is as the roaring of mighty waters. Eternity alone can tell results. It is as if a mighty fire struck us. Nothing can stop it. It is as it was in the days of old when the Spirit of God fell upon the disciples. All school has been stopped. They pray in the fields, on the canal banks, and in all the rooms. The house and grounds have become a 'house of God.' God is doing wonderful things with these little orphans."

A week later she wrote: "The meetings are getting more wonderful. About fifty have received the Baptism in the Holy Ghost. Yesterday I sent for all of our big boys who had left the orphanage, who lived or worked near enough to come. Most of them came and we had a special altar call for all the big boys. It seems almost too wonderful for words, but God saved every one of them! Then we had a dedication service and they all came up on the platform and dedicated their lives to God. There were twenty-five of them. I do not mean the little boys, but our older boys, some in college, some married, others ready to be married.

"The revival struck the girls first, and all of the big girls were saved, then the widows, and now the boys! Oh, rejoice with me, rejoice with me! Can you imagine my joy? Seventeen years (and very dry years, too) of planting the seeds, then all at once to have such a wonderful harvest as this! Should I never see the real results, I knew that the Word of God was being given to them day after day and year after year, and I knew it would spring up sometime, somewhere. But I never dreamed there could be a revival anywhere such as God has given us.

"I mentioned the big boys and big girls. Needless to say, all the little boys and little girls gave themselves to God the first days of the revival. And now their faces shine with the glory as they dance and shout for joy.

"When I saw *all* of my big boys saved—well, my joy was past explaining. The only thing I could do was to weep and hold up my hands and cry out, 'Oh, people, look. God has saved my boys! God has saved my boys.' Just think of it; there was not one holding back, but each one was trying to speak, not being able to wait for the other to finish. Having spoken, they begged for a chance to speak again, all telling how they wanted to be lights in this dark land of Egypt."

Two months later Miss Trasher wrote: "Our revival is still as wonderful as it was during the first days. Sixty-nine have received the Baptism, and they are praying and singing and seeking all over the place."

Pastor H. E. Randall testified to what he personally saw in this revival: "The worst boy in the orphanage was Attila. He was angry about the revival and was going to scatter red pepper in the meeting. He got up in the night to go down to the yard for a drink of water. On the stairs he saw a shadow and went back. Then he started down again, meeting with the same thing. This time he went back and began to pray with a loud voice. Soon there were some around him to pray with him and help him get saved, because there were many who scarcely slept those nights for praying and praising. Attila was truly saved, and became an inspiration in the meetings.

"Another bad boy by the name of Habib, who was nearly grown up, was saved. His history is connected with a young man living in Assiout who was notorious for evil. His business was to sell cocaine in the villages beyond the orphanage. Then he would buy opium in these villages to sell in town, making about ten dollars per trip—illicit trade. He thought himself a great merchant. This young man, Fayheem by name, in passing the orphanage from time to time made the acquaintance of Habib, who got to thinking that he would like to be a merchant also. He had planned to run away just the night before he was saved. Then he wanted Fayheem to get saved and sent for him to come. Fayheem came to laugh at Habib and the rest, but was soon seized by a terrible conviction, and began to cry in distress. He himself was a slave to the co-caine habit, but was saved and delivered. The true ring of victory came into his voice and a shine upon his face.

"The widows of the orphanage, numbering over a dozen, are all saved, and nearly all baptized with the Holy Ghost. One morning I was taken to the kitchen door to have a look. Breakfast was in preparation, and the women were having a praise meeting while at work. Many of them had been praying all night. One of the most inspiring testimonies was given by a deaf and dumb woman. She would lift both hands, her face beaming with joy, and would make a joyful noise with her mouth. In one meeting many of the children were seen gazing up at the window over the platform, with a bright, astonished look on their faces. They said they saw a vision of the Lord Jesus."

It was not long before a number of the young men in the orphanage were going out to preach the gospel in many villages near the orphanage. Sister Trasher wrote in 1933: "Perhaps the work of all these years in the orphanage was just to get boys ready for the great work of getting the gospel to the dark villages, boys who are capable to read and explain The Way to these poor hungry hearts. To see my boys stand up and give out the gospel just fills me with joy. In our afternoon meeting today, one of my boys got up and preached for half an hour. He is now almost twenty years old, and as I looked at him and heard the sermon that I shall not forget soon, I thought of those days long ago when I took him as a baby four months old. Seeds planted years and years ago are beginning to bring forth fruit."

Another gracious revival came to the orphanage in May, 1936. Sister Trasher wrote: "For many months we have all been sad as we saw there was no spirit of revival among the children. It was a great burden to all of us. There seemed to be a spirit of carelessness and a great lack of spiritual interest. You cannot imagine how discouraging this has been to us who have given our lives, not to feed and clothe children, but to lead them and others to Christ. I felt led to have a special meeting in the church one night. I was not well, so I took a chair and sat on the platform and told how brokenhearted I was over their spiritual condition. I was so broken up that I could hardly talk. The Lord was with us, and the girls saw their condition and began to weep and cry. Oh, it was a wonderful sight—some of the worst girls rushed up to the altar, caught hold of my hand and asked for pardon, and some screamed out to the Lord for mercy. There was not a dry eye in the church and I cannot describe what it was like when we all got down to pray.

"This was all right for the girls, but there were the boys and the widows who also needed a reviving. A few days after the Lord touched the girls, our pastor came to me and said: 'There is going to be a three days' revival in the Pentecostal church in town. May the girls go?' I replied, 'No, it is too far for the girls to go at night, and the church would not hold half of the girls. Ask the ministers who are holding the meetings to come and have some meetings with us in the orphanage; then everyone can attend.' Well, they came, the time was ripe, and the Lord started working with everyone, boys, girls, women, and all. It has been wonderful! Last night, the meeting went on for hours. One of the older girls refused to leave the church until she had prayed through to God. At last we had to tell her to go to the other building so the thing could be closed up for the night. She went, and they started a meeting in the middle of the night. The boys did the same thing, and this morning the first I heard was the songs of joy from the boys' building.

"The power fell on the widows in a wonderful

way. One woman who lived near the orphanage, and has been considered a bad woman, got through to God and jumped up and down, dancing for joy, her face shining with glory. This started everyone. She was well known, and no one could doubt what she was doing was of God. A little boy, without anyone's knowing, sent a list of their names to the preacher saying that they wished to form a 'prayer army,' like the one they have in the Alexandria church. As I was going out of church last night, one of the worst girls I have, came up to me and said: 'Mama, I am going to start a prayer army among the girls, and I shall put my name the very first on the list.' Words cannot express my thankfulness to God.

"The revival has now been going on for several weeks. and many are getting through to God. Many of the little boys like to spend most of the day praying in the church. Prayers and songs can be heard in the dormitories until nearly morning."

For these many years God has supplied the needs of the orphans and widows. Miss Trasher wrote in February, 1939: "Our expenses last year were $21,-660.25. We started this year with a cash balance on hand of $1.05."

In June, 1939, there appeared in the *American Magazine* a remarkable article entitled "Nile Mother," written by Jerome Beatty, who told in a fascinating way the story of the orphanage, and how God had supplied the needs. He told of a British nobleman who, as a result of his visit to the orphanage at Assiout, has given to Miss Trasher more than $35,000, insisting that he remain anonymous. Mr. Beatty writes of the visit of this nobleman to the orphanage: "Jittery and embarrassed by her ignorance of the conventions, after Miss Trasher had shown him the orphanage she stammered, 'I—I—hope I haven't said anything I shouldn't. I mean. I don't know how to address nobility.' 'My dear lady,' he smiled, 'address me any way you like. Any titles I may have shrink to insignificance before the nobility of your character and your work.' "

On one occasion this nobleman gave the sum of $5,000. He said to her, "Miss Trasher, you have no idea what it has meant seeing your work. I went back to Scotland and opened a home for tiny infants after I saw all your little boys, and we now have thirty babies in the home." Miss Trasher says: "This nobleman holds some position in connection with an orphanage in Scotland where they have about 1,200 children. They have never accepted infants before. I was so thrilled to think of those thirty little Scotch babies in the home just because he had seen my work. Praise God for His wonderful ways, which are past understanding."

CHAPTER XV

A South African Glimpse

DAVID DU PLESSIS, the General Secretary of the Apostolic Faith Mission of South Africa, stated in an address that he gave at the Central Bible Institute, Springfield, Missouri: "In 1908 two brethren from the United States brought the first Pentecostal message to South Africa. These two men started off in a native church in Johannesburg and out of curiosity white folk went, but they stayed and received the Baptism. A tabernacle was offered in the center of Johannesburg. That place became a revival center. A thousand people crowded in and around it every night of the week. It stirred the city. Jews and Gentiles were saved, one the son of a Rabbi, who is still one of our best evangelists.

"We were not permitted to send missionaries into Rhodesia. But one brother had a real vision. He bought a 10,000 acre farm in Rhodesia, and we could do what we like there. We kept all the cattle and equipment on the farm that the regulations called for. The natives came to the farm and we preached to them, and when the government opened their eyes we had 6,000 members. It was more than the work of one missionary. It was the work of those who got saved, went back to their homes, and spread the gospel."

W. J. Kerr, a missionary, wrote of those early days in Johannesburg: "One night Maggie Truter came on the platform, feeling that the Lord would have her deliver a message. She lost courage when she saw the crowded hall and many of the scoffers. She retired to the vestry, taking a sister with her to pray. In about ten minutes she returned, spoke in the native tongue for a few minutes, then in High Dutch for about the same time, and then in English. While speaking in Dutch, the faces of the Dutch people clearly indicated that they were getting something unusual. When she spoke English—well, I have had the pleasure of listening to some of the world's greatest orators of the last century, but I can conscientiously say that I never listened to anything so fine for beauty, diction, and pathos. The subject was 'Jesus in Gethsemane' and the pleading with sinners to accept Him was irresistible. You could have heard a pin fall during the delivery of the English part, and for once the faces of the scoffers wore a sober aspect. A whole family, who had heard of the fine sport in the tabernacle, came to enjoy the fun, but were convicted and every one of them was brought to Christ. Several of the Dutch people told me that the Dutch spoken was a perfect rendering of the English, and some of the natives at the back told me that the native tongue was their language, and was the same as the Dutch. They, being Cape Colony natives, knew Dutch. Maggie knew nothing of the native language and very little High Dutch. It would be difficult to say how far-reaching the influence of that message has been to other souls besides the family brought to Christ that night.

"I have seen the blind receive their sight, the deaf hear, the dumb speak, the paralyzed rise up and walk; cases where death was inevitable, having been given up by as many as four of the leading doctors in Johannesburg; the most malignant cases of cancer healed, etc. I have seen these in abundance.

"Drunkards have been reclaimed, families (ruined and broken by drink and immorality) have been reunited and made happy; young people have been filled with an earnest desire to rescue souls, and spend all their spare time in this direction."

Brother du Plessis writes: "During the last twenty-five years the revival has continued unabated. Today, the Apostolic Faith Mission of South Africa has 150 established assemblies. Of these, there are about 100 who have their own church buildings. Properties of the missions throughout the country are valued at approximately half a million dollars. Together with the European work there also grew a native work. Today, praise God, we have 30 white missionaries in the field supervising about 1,000 native preachers, and a membership of about 60,000. We estimate that the Apostolic Faith Mission has over 31,000 white members. We have 80 full-time pastors and evangelists, besides the missionaries. Then we have about 250 lay preachers who assist the pastors or take charge of small assemblies that cannot support a full-time pastor."

At the beginning of 1940, David du Plessis reported that the work of the Apostolic Faith Mission in South Africa is going forward by leaps and bounds; their foreign missionary offerings for 1939 were double those of 1937; and their missionary forces have increased from 15 to 33. In the European section of the work in South Africa they now have about 150 assemblies, and have just built seven new churches, and enlarged several others.

Brother du Plessis mentions one outstanding and amazing incident in connection with their large native work: "It is very difficult to estimate the increase in our native work, but here is what happened in Rhodesia last year. One of our native evangelists in that territory had been grievously persecuted by the chief, and the tribe among whom he labored. Some time ago he decided to move away. Last year the chief sent for him, and he was asked to preach the gospel message

again. The Lord began to bless, and the fire fell.
Scores were saved and healed, until it seemed that the
whole neighborhood would turn to Christ. The native evangelist later reported: 'There were many people
healed and saved, and so I arranged for a baptismal
service in one of the pools in the river. I commenced
baptizing when the sun rose. I baptized until the water
in the pool became too little. Then I went to another
pool and baptized till the sun set. I had a good meeting that night, and next morning when the sun rose
I again began to baptize, and I carried on all through
the day to about 4:00 in the afternoon. And now, Sir,
please send me 2,624 baptismal certificates for all the
people I have baptized.' 'This,' says Brother du
Plessis, 'is almost equal to Pentecost.' "

L. Wesley Jaeger writes from Johannesburg, South
Africa: "It is a year since I left the U.S.A. and I have
had scarcely a day of rest since my arrival. The
meetings have been outstanding, and I can safely say
without exaggeration that over 1,000 people have given
their hearts to the Lord. In many meetings, in one
evening, between 25 and 30 have been converted. The
first camp meeting in South Africa was held in Johannesburg in March, and far exceeded expectations.
On the last Sunday there were between 3,000 and
4,000 people present, and the ten days were filled with
the glory and presence of the Lord."

In addition to the Apostolic Faith work there is a
work known as the Assemblies of God, affiliated with
the other Assemblies of God throughout the world.
John S. Richards writes us concerning this: "The
work of the Assemblies of God in South Africa was
begun by the late R. M. Turney, a former Baptist
minister in the United States, who came to South
Africa as a pioneer missionary thirty years ago. The
first mission station was at Doornkop, where the first
outpouring of the Holy Spirit upon the native people
in South Africa took place. From here the work
quickly spread, and various assemblies were started.

One of the evangelists found his way to Mapela (Potgietersrust), where he came into contact with a brother of the then reigning chief. This chief's brother with nine others had received the Baptism in the Holy Ghost while in a prayer meeting, while as yet none of them knew or had 'heard whether there be any Holy Ghost.' It was three months after this outpouring that the Doornkop evangelist came in contact with them and taught them the way more fully. Under the leadership of the chief's brother, the work quickly spread. The light was carried to the newer places including Houtboschrivier, where another outpouring of the Holy Ghost took place and a number received the Baptism in the Holy Spirit.

"On Brother Turney's arrival in Pretoria he found a group of believers who had received the Baptism. He formed the group into the first Pentecostal church in that capital. This he pastored until later he was succeeded by Archibald Cooper. From this assembly many workers were ordained and sent forth, including Brother Stoddart of India.

"The Assemblies of God fellowship now embraces missionaries from the United States of America, Canada, the British Isles, Switzerland, Norway, Sweden, Denmark, and Finland, who all work together in wonderful harmony. Today there are 177 assemblies (some of them white) besides a large number of preaching posts. There are over 150 native preachers, besides leaders in local assemblies and Bible women. There are 42 missionaries, 12 European pastors, and one working among the Indians. A Bible school is now maintained at Nelspruit where there are some fine students in training. A fine new modern printing house has been built at Nelspruit where Pentecostal papers are printed in the vernacular of the African continent."

Archibald H. Cooper, who has been identified with the Pentecostal work in South Africa from the early days, a few years ago held some tent services in Durban. Six or seven Zulus came to this meeting. One of the Zulus said to him: "Some months ago I was praying for God to reveal Himself and show me what I should be and do. As I continued in prayer, waiting for a revelation from God, He gave me a vision. In the vision I saw a man, and heard God say: 'That man I am sending to you. He will teach you the way. Listen to him. He will be your spiritual father and counselor.' So I waited for months and months for that man to come. When I entered this tent the other night, I knew I had seen you before. I was puzzled. I tried to think where I had seen you. Suddenly it flashed to me, 'This is the man you saw in the vision.'"

Brother Cooper says: "I did not know what the outcome of such an experience was to be, but I told him I would stand with him. He consecrated his life anew to God. We found a little hall and started to hold services. I paid the rent for it from my tithes and assisted him in the meeting when I could. God prospered the work and soon I had the pleasure of baptizing 14 Zulus. That was the beginning, small it is true, but today there is a mighty work, ever spreading and increasing. This Zulu brother became my right-hand man and is still such today. The work is considered by even missionaries of other denominations to be one of the most remarkable works in South Africa. Approximately 3,000 native believers are now in my division, and are out and out for the Lord Jesus. Of this company of 3,000 believers (now increased to 4,000) who gather in small and large meetings along the north and south coast of Natal and reaching to Pondoland, approximately ninety-five per cent are baptized in the Holy Ghost.

"This native work in recent years has grown without financial help from the white people. Their teachers (and I have at least 40 in my division) have faithfully taught the natives that they should tithe. Every Zulu Christian in the assembly is taught that it is not only his duty but his privilege to pay his tithe to God. So these Zulus are supporting their own pastors and teachers. Last year our native Zulu believers gave over $3,500 in tithes and offerings."

Brother Cooper vouches for the testimony of Mrs. Ivor Stevens, of Bloemfontein, who was raised from the dead on August 29, 1919. Sister Stevens testifies that after she passed over the river of death, she was escorted by an angel to heaven. But she was first given a sight of hell. She says: "Words fail me as I recall the horror and awfulness of it, and the anguish of the countless thousands which it engulfed. Then I was allowed to enter heaven; and oh, the brightness and splendor and glory of the place. . . . I at last arrived at a place where I beheld the Lord Jesus, who was surrounded by thousands and thousands of angels. Putting up His hand He kindly and tenderly said to me: 'Go back and work in My Vineyard.' He then showed me a multitude of people who are still in darkness."

Four who were present at the death, including her husband, and her pastor, F. M. J. Beetge, and were also present when the Lord raised Sister Stevens from her deathbed, testify to the reality of this miracle. One of these witnesses, S. M. Ulyate, says: "She was speaking in tongues and interpreting up to the last, and had hardly been brought back when she began again in the Spirit."

Brother Cooper writes: "One night (in 1908) a Chinaman came to the home and asked if he might attend the service. He was a native missionary who had come to preach to the thousands of Chinese who worked in the Johannesburg gold mines. With joy he was ushered in.

"After the meeting was over, John, the Chinese missionary, waited behind and quietly conversed with my father-in-law. My sister-in-law, Miss Gladys Schumann, was continuing in prayer. Suddenly John jumped up and went across to her, for she was speaking in Chinese, a language she had never known. John listened in amazement, then he began to converse with her, he talking in his native Chinese language and she speaking in the Spirit. Afterwards he explained that in answer to his questions God had said that this work was from Him, and that he must seek to be filled with the Holy Spirit for Jesus was coming soon. John returned home but before the week was over the Lord had mightily baptized him in the Holy Spirit in his own room. The following Sunday at service he told the congregation all he had experienced during that week, and the people were stirred in wonder. From time to time other similar experiences took place when Indians and South Africans heard the gospel in their own languages through the Holy Spirit."

A very gracious work has been accomplished in Mozambique, Southeast Africa. According to C. Austin Chawner, a missionary in this country, the work was started in this land by a young man of the Thonga tribe. This young man had labored in the gold-mining districts of Transvaal. While in Transvaal he had been saved and baptized in the Spirit. When he returned to his home in Mozambique, he told his three wives of his experience, sent two of them to their homes, and started to preach the gospel. Souls were saved and a Pentecostal work in Mozambique was started. For lack of support he had to go back to his work in the mines from time to time.

In 1929 Ingrid Lokken (now Mrs. C. Austin Chawner), a Norwegian missionary, entered this territory. She found two little groups of Pentecostal believers at Kamsoni and there was a gracious revival. About twenty were saved and baptized in water. One day the missionary thought she would start teaching them about the Baptism in the Spirit, but after the meeting the young leader of the group came to her and said, "Missionary, what you have taught us today in the meeting, we have already received." Everyone of those twenty had received the Baptism in the Spirit, although they had never heard about such an experience.

CHAPTER XVI

Great Outpouring in Central and West Africa

IN SEPTEMBER, 1915, two Spirit-filled young men, William Burton and James Salter, commenced work in Mwanza, a village in the heart of the Belgian Congo in Central Africa. They first had to learn the language. In twenty-five years they have been able to establish 500 assemblies.

From the very beginning the Word of God was confirmed with signs following. James Salter was raised up from a deathbed no less than six times. On the last occasion a sheet was laid over him and he was left for practically dead. He had arranged to start a convention with the natives that afternoon. He testifies that he felt, as it were, an electric shock touch him from the crown of his head to the sole of his feet. The Lord healed him perfectly and he was able to start his convention with the natives right on time.

For four years these two young men were faithful in preaching the gospel, and they won many souls for Christ. They prayed continually that they might see a real Pentecostal revival. This came with the dawn of 1920. We shall let Brother Burton describe this outpouring:

"We are in the habit of assembling our believers every three to six months for fellowship, teaching, and

conference. Those who at the last conference started
out to preach, returned to this one with a blessed harvest of believers. I started the first meeting at six
a. m. for our leaders, teachers, and evangelists, and
from that time on we did not have a moment to ourselves until late in the evening.

"On the fourth day of the convention, in our
morning meeting, there were about 160 persons present
when we spoke on Mark 16:15-18, 'These signs shall
follow them that believe...' There was a solemn,
heart-searching time. At the invitation to come forward to pray for, and to receive the Holy Spirit, almost
the whole congregation came forward. When the
angel came down and troubled the pool at Bethesda,
the first to enter the troubled water was healed, but at
Mwanza God Himself was troubling the waters, and all
who entered were blessed. Some strong men, with
earnestness, took a clean header; the youngsters, who
had only known Jesus within the last few weeks,
nevertheless scrambled in as best they knew how; while
some more dignified and aged elders of the community,
with still possibly some lingering hankering for the
fast-disappearing traditions of the past, had first to
try the water, and finding it not too cold to the toes,
managed ankle-deep, then knee-deep, waist-deep, and
finally—Oh, hallelujah!—the same results as with those
who took the first clean header. Waters to swim in, a
river that could not be passed over, bringing life and
healing to everything within its reach.

"It was not many minutes after we started praying
that the first few were filled with the Spirit, and then
they helped us by laying hands upon and praying with
others. It was only those on the outskirts of the crowd
that were within reach. The whole of those in the
center of the crush were out of our reach, but not out
of God's. Oh, how they cried, and groaned, as they
wrestled their way to victory. The news of this great
visitation was heard in the village one and a half
miles away. Truly the mountains of pride and self-

esteem were broken down, the valleys of fear and mistrust were filled up, and the crooked places of schism, quarrels, suspicion, and party spirit were made straight.

"That first wonderful meeting lasted from ten a. m. to three p. m. The whole place was swayed by God's Spirit. At least two cases occurred of those who praised God in beautiful English, and I also heard snatches of French, Dutch, or German. And almost all who spoke in tongues had languages with a beautiful clear "R" sound, which is significant since in the natural a Luban cannot pronounce this sound. When all was quiet of course I had to explain it all from Acts 2.

"Over 100 children were at the Sunday School on the middle Sunday of the conference. More than half of them were under the power of God, while quite a number were filled with the Spirit exactly as in Acts 2:4; 10:46; and 19:6.

"The hours between the meetings were fully occupied in answering questions, giving advice and encouragement, and listening to confessions of sin. This last is all the more wonderful since hitherto horses could not have drawn confession from a Luban. All their lives long they had lived in such deception and hypocrisy that to confess a sin, when they had not been caught red-handed, would appear to them the height of absurdity. But 'When He (the Spirit of truth) is come, He will reprove the world of sin.' John 16:8.

"During this convention the burdened ones ever forced themselves upon me. And, oh, what fearful tales of crime were unfolded. But against this hideous background of disgrace and shame, the cross of the Lord Jesus is all the more resplendent. How precious it was to kneel with these stricken, guilty lads, to hear them pour out their heart's burden to God, and then see them go away humbly, gratefully rejoicing, yet still amazed at the fact that 'the blood of Jesus Christ God's Son cleanseth us from all sin.'

"All our outstation teachers have gone back home today excepting one, and they are all baptized in the Spirit, as also are many chief carpenters, the three pupil teachers who help my wife in the school, etc. Last Thursday we baptized fifty-seven believers in water. In the case of several of these I had hesitated hitherto, but now 'can any man forbid water, that these should not be baptized, which have received the Holy Ghost as well as we?' Acts 10:47.

"Though many had already left for their homes, yet on the last Sunday, eighty-seven believers gathered around the Lord's table, to show forth His death in the emblems of His broken body and poured-out blood, 'till He come.' When it is remembered how less than four and a half years ago, I was stranded on this mission hill, with my companion and chum, Brother Salter, slowly coming back from the very gates of death, with fever; how we stood in the midst of the desolation of rocks, long grass, and forest, and looked across to the villages nestled among the trees; how having scarcely a word of the language we could only pray, pray, pray for those thousands who had never even heard Jesus' name; when you remember this, you can understand how our hearts nearly burst, and how often the well-springs of our being overflowed in boundless thankfulness to God, and how again and again when we sought words to praise Him for this band of rejoicing Christians, all that we could pour out at His feet were tears of gratitude."

After this outpouring the gospel soon spread to new districts. Brother Salter tells of one of their workers preaching in a certain village. There was a man there whose arms were set in such a way that he could not use them. He listened to the gospel message and came to the missionary at the close and said: "Could your Jesus do anything for me?" He pointed to the witch doctor and said he had given him his cattle, his chickens, and two of his wives, in order to get some relief, but no relief had come. He was prayed for and

the Lord miraculously healed him. His arms were
liberated and he was able to move them about as freely
as a child. As the missionary was traveling back to his
station, the native who was accompanying him, said,
"I want to leave you and go to my home. I had heard
the gospel preached, but today I have seen the power of
it, and I want to go and tell my people about the power
of the gospel." This native went back to his home, a
place that was so unhealthy that no white man could
possibly live there. It was practically a swamp for
four months of the year and the natives had to live
in their canoes. After some time the missionary visited this man's home and saw that on the one dry, el-
evated knoll of the village there was a Pentecostal
church with a fine crowd of saved people in it. A large
number of them had received the Baptism in the
Holy Spirit, and he heard them speaking in the most
perfect English (a language they had never learned)
under the power of the Spirit.

Again and again there have been repetitions of the
scenes of the 10th chapter of Acts when the Spirit of
God fell in the house of Cornelius and those who heard
the Word were filled with the Spirit and spoke in other
tongues and magnified God. Speaking of one of these
instances, Brother Burton wrote: "A few afternoons
back I was giving our young evangelists a Bible study
on Acts 2:42, when so sweetly and quietly the Spirit fell
and two young men received the Holy Spirit. We were
able to recognize several Welsh expressions. Now we
never use such expressions as 'Diolch Iddo' (anyone
who visited a Welsh revival will remember that this was
a common expression of praise upon the lips of the
converted Welshmen) and these lads never have heard
such sounds from us, so that it was a blessed confirma-
tion when we heard these expressions in tongues."

There was a gracious Pentecostal visitation in
another part of the Congo in 1938, when J. Roswell
Flower, General Secretary of the Assemblies of God in
the United States of America, together with Noel Per-

kin, Missionary Secretary, visited Central Africa.
Brother Perkin describes an altar service that he witnessed at Betongwe Mission Station: "Several wives
of the paramount chief are earnestly seeking the Baptism with the Spirit; one is already lost in praise and
prayer which pours forth in a tongue which she never
learned. Another woman (the wife of a young man
who for some time has felt God wanted him out in the
work of the ministry but who has been hindered because of the wife's opposition) finds herself shaking
under the power of God and soon is also speaking in
another language the wonderful works of God.

"Little fellows almost naked are kneeling on the
mud floor, crying and praying with tightly closed eyes
and uplifted faces. One little fellow begins speaking in
tongues. The missionaries near him say he is speaking
in English, yet he has not learned a word of English.
He says among other things, 'Jesus, you suffered so
much for me.'

"Here is a woman with tears trickling down her
cheeks and yet with the light of God on her countenance. We ask why she weeps. 'Oh, I have been such
a great sinner,' she says. 'But God has forgiven your
sins has He not?' 'Yes,' she replies, 'but I cannot help
crying for what I have done; I have been such a
wicked woman.'

"The meeting started at 9:30 in the morning and is
still going on without cessation as the evening shadows
begin to gather." Over 30 received the Baptism in this
meeting.

There has been a gracious work on the Ivory Coast,
in French West Africa, where a number of Assemblies
of God missionaries from the United States are laboring. It is entirely virgin territory. Writing of this
work Brother A. E. Wilson, one of the missionaries,
says: "We judge that altogether we have at least 1,000
Christians. Perhaps 150 or 200 of these have received
the Baptism in the Holy Spirit. We have a total of
some 50 native workers."

A most gracious outpouring of the Spirit has come to Nigeria, on the West Coast of Africa. It came through the sending of copies of the *Pentecostal Evangel* to some Christian workers in Nigeria. They sought and received the Baptism in the Spirit and the Lord baptized them in exactly the same way as He baptized the one hundred and twenty on the day of Pentecost, and they spoke in other tongues as the Spirit of God gave utterance. Lloyd Shirer, who visited the Nigerian work in 1939, describing this revival, says: "The Holy Spirit fell widely in all the province of Calabar. Thousands were filled. Pagans who were convicted by the Spirit rushed into the church and fell down before the baptized Christians, screaming and crying, 'Pray for me that God will have mercy on me. He has shown me my sins. I have seen hell.' Sinners were convicted without a preacher, and voluntarily destroyed their jujus.

"Pentecostal churches sprang up everywhere as a result of the manifestation of the power of God."

Brother Shirer and his wife visited many of the churches and found them in a most flourishing condition. While they were in Nigeria a convention was held and he says: "Not only was the church filled, but all around outside they had erected a large arbor, under which the greater number of the people sat to listen through doors and windows. Over 3,300 were counted present. Such singing! Such clapping! Such rejoicing! In spite of the large crowd there was no disorder, for the leaders kept the meeting well under control."

John M. Perkins and his wife were missionaries in Liberia under the board of the Methodist Episcopal Church. When they were filled with the Spirit they were refused another appointment. They returned to Liberia as Pentecostal missionaries on Christmas Day, 1908. While missionaries of the Methodist Episcopal Church they had had a faithful worker named Jasper K. Toe. Jasper dreamed that he saw eight white

missionaries getting into small boats and landing at
Garraway. He had never known of any missionaries
landing there, although Bishop Taylor and others had
landed there years before. Jasper told his dream,
and when the company of eight Pentecostal missionaries including Brother Perkins and his wife landed at
Garraway he declared: "This is just what I saw in my
dream." He felt called of God to help these new
workers, and became an earnest seeker for the Baptism in the Spirit.

One time he was praying for a sick woman who
had been given up to die. Her relatives said, "There is
no use praying, her time is past. She cannot live."
Jasper describes this incident in his own words: "I
took my Bible and took with me Mission Man Brown
and another man, and I said, 'Let us pray for this
woman. I can do nothing of myself, but God is great
and nothing is too hard for Him.' I read Mark 16:17,
18 and said to the man with me, 'Come, let us touch
this woman. God will heal her.' When I laid my
hand on the woman, God's great power came upon me
and I began to talk and cry in a very loud voice. I
talk in a tongue I do not know. Since my mother
conceive me I never talk in such loud voice. The next
morning the woman walk about by herself. She say,
'My sick leave me in night time. I can walk about
where I like.' She is fat this time. Other sick ones call
for prayer and are healed."

Brother Perkins writing of his experience as a
Pentecostal worker, says: "Shortly after the opening
of the station at Blebo, we experienced a real demonstration of the power of God. Many were prostrated
under the mighty power of God and quite a number of
the native schoolboys were baptized in the Holy Spirit.
Some of the heathen were struck down by the power
of God."

In 1916 there was a gracious outpouring of the
Holy Spirit in Liberia and over sixty men, women, and
children received the Baptism. "A visitation of the

Holy Spirit came to the girls' school which was then at Gropaka, and ten or more of the girls were mightily filled with the Spirit. At Newaka, where the boys' school was formerly located, a score or more of the boys in school were baptized with the Holy Ghost, and as many more were saved. The heathen town was stirred and some came forward boldly for God. Since the first outpouring of the Latter Rain, there have been times of revival at different stations. Revival fires were especially kindled in 1929 and 1930. During the years of 1929 to 1936, well over a thousand confessed Christ as their Saviour. Many were baptized with the Holy Ghost, and numbers of sick people have been healed through the prayer of faith. About fifty chapels were built by the people in as many different towns."

CHAPTER XVII

The Spirit Outpoured in Chile, South America

IN 1907, Miss Minnie Abrams sent to Mrs. W. C. Hoover, a Methodist missionary in Valparaiso, Chile (her former schoolmate in a Chicago Training School), a booklet giving an account of the wonderful outpouring of the Holy Spirit on the child widows at Mukti, in South India. This simple story awakened a deep hunger in the hearts of Dr. and Mrs. Hoover for a similar outpouring in Chile.

In February, 1908, Pastor F. Fransen, of the Swedish Church in Chicago, who was making a tour of missions, arrived in Valparaiso. He spent a number of days with great blessing in Dr. Hoover's church. Seated at table one day, Pastor Fransen recounted the experience of a friend who spoke in strange tongues. "While he was yet speaking," a letter was handed to Mrs. Hoover from an old friend in the home church, in which she recounted her experience in receiving the Baptism in the Holy Spirit, and speaking in other tongues while praying alone in her room. The remarkable coincidence of these two testimonies coming at the same moment seemed providential, and stimulated and confirmed the faith of both Dr. and Mrs. Hoover in the Scripturalness of the experience and manifestation.

That year Dr. Hoover was building a large church. He often prayed that the place when finished might be filled with the Holy Spirit and with people. The congregation entered into the new though unfinished church on the watchnight which ushered in the year 1909. This was followed by a week of prayer. On the first prayer night a strange thing happened. The whole congregation, numbering above 100 persons, broke forth simultaneously in audible prayer. It was a thing that had never happened before. The prayer lasted ten or fifteen minutes and was like the "sound of many waters." This same experience was repeated on several occasions.

One day in the month of January, a brother whose former besotted life had left him so incapacitated that he was unfit for labor, and was now a night watchman, came to Dr. Hoover and said: "Pastor, I was sleeping today at home, when the Lord came to me and said, 'Wake up, I want to talk with you.' 'Yes, Lord!' 'Go to your pastor and tell him to call some of the most spiritual brethren and tell them to pray every day, for I am going to baptize them with tongues of fire.' 'Yes, Lord, and may I be one of them?' 'Yes.' So I came at once." They had been praying for some time for a revival, and Dr. Hoover was greatly encouraged and formed a group of five persons who met every day at five o'clock, prayed in turn, and separated without any formality. This five o'clock meeting, after a month or so, was made general and became an important feature of the revival.

The annual Methodist conference was held early in February and the pulpit during the pastor's absence, was occupied by one of this group of five. One Sunday evening he called the members of the official board to occupy the front seats at the beginning of the service. Reading the second chapter of Joel, from the 12th verse and onward, he said: "You and I are responsible for the condition of this church and we must repent and get right with God if it takes all night." After a season of prayer at the altar he dismissed the congregation, asking the official board to remain with him all night, with any others who might desire to remain with them. Twenty or thirty remained. During the night

one saw a brazier of coals within the altar. Others felt
the hand of the Lord on their head as they prayed at
the altar; and such was the blessing received that they
asked this man to appoint another all-night meeting,
which he did, naming the following Saturday. By that
time the pastor returned from the conference and
attended the meeting himself, finding blessing in it.
These all-night prayer meetings continued week by
week. After a while they were held about once a
month, with an attendance which reached as high as
200, who spent all night in prayer. By these meetings
consciences were awakened and repentance, restitution and reconciliation became the order of the day.
Members went as far as Santiago and other points to
make peace, pay debts which they had forgotten or dis-
regarded, or to return goods or money stolen years
before.

Various manifestations began to occur. In a
testimony meeting a sister laughed for an hour, a delighted, half-quiet laughter which she was unable to
control, so she retired to a farther corner of the room
so as not to disturb anyone. Another fell and began to
sing most sweetly. She said the angels were teaching
her to sing. At an altar service, a brother who had
been many years in the church, but was wholly useless
as a Christian, arose and asked for prayer. He had
scarcely expressed the request when he fell as if
knocked down by a blow. Whereas formerly he was
unable to pray, now the words rushed from his mouth
in a torrent which he was unable to stem. Afterwards
he said he himself marveled where the words came
from. From that day forward he became a man of
prayer and power.

We shall let Dr. Hoover tell the story of this revival
in his own words: "The overwhelming flood came on
the 4th of July, 1909, which was Sunday. Saturday
night was an all night of prayer, during which four
vain young ladies (three of whom were in the choir)
fell to the floor under the power of the Spirit. One of

them, after lying a long time, arose and with remarkable power began to exhort, saying, 'The Lord is coming soon and commands us to get ready.' The effect produced was indescribable.

"The following morning, in Sunday School, at ten o'clock, a daze seemed to rest upon the people. Some were unable to rise after the opening prayer which had been like 'the sound of many waters,' and all were filled with wonder. It was impossible to separate into classes and study the lesson of the day. Praising, singing, exhortation by some under the power of the Spirit, surrounded by groups of wondering listeners, filled the hour, and at the close the people were loath to leave.

"From that time on the atmosphere seemed charged with the Holy Spirit, and people fell on the floor, or broke out speaking in other tongues, or singing in the Spirit, in a way impossible in their natural condition. On one occasion a woman, a young lady, and a girl of twelve were lying on the floor in different parts of the prayer room, with eyes closed and silent. Suddenly, as with one voice, they burst forth into a song in a familiar tune but in unknown tongues, all speaking the same words. After a verse or two they became silent; then again suddenly, another tune, a verse or two, and silence. This was repeated until they had sung ten tunes, always using the same words and keeping in perfect time together as if led by some invisible chorister.

"A lad stood with eyes closed giving a message of repentance, when suddenly he said, 'Oh, see what a lot of doves! Lord, send more than you did last Thursday. See, one fell upon a brother! I don't know him; he is new.' At the moment he spoke, a new brother began praying with cries and tears.

"Another lad, filled with the Spirit, said: 'See the Lord with His pierced hands! and His feet, too!' Then bursting into desolate weeping, he said, 'And yet people will not believe!'

"These are but illustrations of a multitude of marvels that kept us wondering. People began to fall under the power of the Spirit in their homes, or at work, on the street, anywhere. People looking at such in the church would be taken with a trembling and would hasten out lest they fall.

"These amazing scenes brought constantly increasing crowds of curious ones and the congregation grew by leaps and bounds, so that by September the congregation had reached the astonishing figure of 900 to 1,000, beginning with perhaps 300. In proof that not all were merely curious visitors, the attendance at the Sunday School, which had been about 250, reached the following average weekly attendance during the months named: July, 363; August, 425; September, 527.

"The 'yellow' press sent reporters who interviewed workers, examined the basement of the building to discover electric appliances that might be the cause of the inexplicable occurrences, and feigned repentance to discover the magic arts used. Then for two weeks a serial account, with headlines as alarming as those used in the World War, was run simultaneously with a criminal accusation which was instituted in court against the pastor, the gist of which was that 'he gave to people a pernicious beverage to drink called "the Blood of the Lamb" which produced a lethargy and the people fell on the floor.'

"The pastor appeared repeatedly before the judge (trials in Chile are not by jury) and thus was given an opportunity to testify to Jesus' power to save before various authorities who at different times sat with the judge. This trial was of course heralded by the press. The lurid accounts were used by the Lord to increase the attendance and interest of sinners, and by the devil to alarm saints. So the fearful and unbelieving, and the propriety-loving, began to write to the pastor urging caution, lamenting the 'scandal' of being painted in such colors before the public, and warning against fanaticism. They wrote to the bishop also, and so awakened similar fears in him, which resulted in his securing (unknown to and unasked by the pastor) a furlough for the pastor, to begin at the time of the following conference. Meanwhile, the work was moving grandly on.

"Those who came from far to see, carried home reports which awakened a deep hunger in the people for a similar visitation and they began to pray earnestly to the Lord. Now and then some baptized person in Valparaiso felt a call to go to some other place with the message. Such was eagerly received by the brethren, but sometimes with less cordiality by the pastors, who feared fanaticism. One such visited Santiago, and in the Methodist churches in that place there was an ardent desire for the Baptism in the Holy Spirit. This worker went to the Second church in the afternoon meeting and desired to speak while the offering was being taken. The pastor refused her permission. The people begged him to allow her to speak. He still refused. The people in a body went out of the church and gathered in the yard, where the assistant pastor, who was favorable to their desire, exhorted them to quiet and calmness. In the evening the messenger went to the First church. The pastor and the district superintendent, having heard of the disturbance of the day, dealt with brusqueness and arbitrariness. They promised the people that she might speak at the conclusion of the service; but when after the benediction the people sat down and she arose to speak, police in waiting were called to vacate the church and take the girl to the police station."

There was now a difficult situation. There were two congregations in Santiago who wanted to receive the Pentecostal experience, but they were opposed by their pastors. Dr. Hoover's colleagues and his bishop accused him of having caused this trouble, which was untrue except insofar as the revival in his church was the cause. In February, 1910, the Conference met. They felt they would settle the matter by sending Dr.

Hoover home on furlough. Two of the members of the Valparaiso church came to him and said, "Pastor, we are going to separate. The purpose of the conference is to scatter us and send you home, and the work will be destroyed. We are going out, and when they turn you off you can be our pastor."

Knowing the disposition of the bishop, the pastor resigned from the pastorate of the Methodist Episcopal church. He became pastor of the 440 who went out at that time. In all this, his wife was his able and wholly sympathetic companion.

Dr. Hoover says: "There was no grieving for the beautiful, commodious church building they were leaving. They said, 'God, who gave us this one, can give us another.' They had no fears because of having no missionary society to fall back on. They had no real animosity against those who had made this step a necessity. Of the numerous small meeting places which we had in the city, nearly all were in the homes of those who had separated, so we used them, and the official board arranged to rotate with the pastor in attending them. Sunday School teachers were appointed for them, and the work continued to prosper.

"As soon as the two churches in Santiago, who had separated previously, heard of the step taken in Valparaiso, they sent official letters to the pastor, asking him to be their superintendent. And so was formed an organization which soon took the name of the Methodist Pentecostal Church. The purpose in using the name 'Methodist' was to show that there would be no quarrel with Methodism. We were preaching the doctrines taught by Wesley and urging a life of perfect love. We declared that we were still truly Methodist —and those who criticized us were the ones who had departed from the old paths and from the old faith.

"Street preaching became an established practice, and the noise attending our meetings attracted crowds of the curious, among whom were always some hungry ones who found the Bread of Life. Praying for the sick became a blessing to many—to those who were healed and to those whose faith was awakened or strengthened by seeing the work of God in the body."

The work grew and expanded so that there were soon Pentecostal groups of various sizes in eighty cities and towns. There were two large congregations in Santiago, whose united membership in a short while reached 1,500. In a short time the membership of the church in Valparaiso reached 900. In the year 1919 the church in Valparaiso purchased a property and remodeled it into a church with a capacity of about 600. One of the churches in Santiago leased ground and built a church with a greater capacity. The work throughout Chile became wholly self - supporting and became the wonder and comment of the older denominations, who from the start had prophesied a disastrous end to the movement, believing it to be born of fanaticism and following a personality. Dr. Hoover says the utter mistakenness of their judgment has had a remarkable demonstration in the following. In the month of January, 1920, the pastor at Valparaiso was taken sick. His work as superintendent was carried on by one of the Santiago pastors, formerly a shoemaker. The work of the Valparaiso church was carried on by the official board. In June of that year, a remarkable revival broke out. The pastor was absent from the work one month less than two years, most of the time absent from the country, and when he returned he found the church filled to repletion, and more than 400 probationers added to the roll.

Dr. Hoover states that the secret of the marvelous revival was doubtless found in the words of an observer from another church, *"They honored the Holy Spirit."* Dr. Hoover adds: "This may be added—*They exalted the blood of Jesus Christ as the only and sufficient means of access to God and of reception of any and all blessings promised in the Word of God."* One chorus that was continually sung in this revival was given in the Spirit. Translated into English it would be this: "Glory to the blood of my Lord; it is that which washes the sinner."

Dr. Hoover testifies to the truth of the following remarkable miracles. Speaking of the one who gives the testimony that follows, he says: "Becerra is pastor of the church in Vina del Mar. He is a remarkably faithful man."

This is the testimony of Onofre Becerra: "Some ten years ago I went to lead a meeting in Caleta Abarca. There was a sick man there who had known the Lord but had fallen away. A brother asked me to go with him to pray for him, that the Lord would have mercy on him. My wife and others who were present accompanied us. When we arrived we found the man had been dead for half an hour, and his mother and family were gathered around him, weeping with despair. I have never seen a more horrible spectacle in a corpse, bristling hair and white eyes wide open. My heart was greatly moved for he had died without God. I told the family if they would repent that God was able to give them back their son. They assented. We all knelt down by the dead man. While we were praying there came over us such an atmosphere of demons that everyone but my wife left the room. Never had I prayed a prayer such as I then uttered, moved by the Holy Spirit. God gave me such a faith that I saw the man revive and live. When he returned to life I said to him, 'Brother, you were going to hell.' 'Yes,' he said, 'I was going down, down, to a great abyss of darkness and heat, but before I reached the place where I was going I was detained, and opening my eyes I found myself here.' We went to meeting and at its close we returned to the house and all saw the man. He is still living, but far from God."

Dr. Hoover himself gives the following testimony: "Corina was a dressmaker, abandoned by her husband, a Hollander. When she learned of Pentecost she decided she would not live by ministering to the vanity of women, and sought work as a nurse in a hospital where she spent some years. Then the doctors sought her for outside cases, and with her earnings she built a house with three rooms which she loaned freely for preaching services. Many were converted there. In her work she had such remarkable results praying for the sick that the doctors ceased employing her. The patients got well too soon, and on more than one occasion when the doctors were ready to operate they found nothing for which to operate. She herself was remarkably healed when she was expected to die at any moment. For months another person had a key to her house (she lived alone) and would come in in the morning half expecting to find her dead. For months she slept sitting in bed, resting her head on a stool. I went on a trip, leaving her in that condition. When I returned she was up and employed to care for a sick person. She is still living, but aged and somewhat frail.

"In the year 1912 or 1913 a North American lady who lived in Vina del Mar engaged our Sister Corina Schaap to care for her in confinement. After the birth the lady had fever, and it became necessary to maintain the child with artificial food. The child got on well for a short time, but later was taken sick with severe intestinal catarrh. It went from bad to worse in spite of all the doctor's efforts. It used as many as thirty cloths daily and was unable to take the bottle, or even cry. One morning while the doctor was there Corina asked, 'What do you think, doctor?' 'There is no longer any life,' he answered.

About eight o'clock the baby died. Sister Corina now continues the story: "With a strangeness I cannot explain I went to wash the diapers. But why should I when the baby was dead? Blanca (the servant girl) went to tell the mother and telephone the doctor. Then she brought clothes and water to wash the baby. But I kept on washing and praying at the same time, rather complaining to the Lord, 'Lord, I have been telling this lady about Thee. I have said that Thou answerest prayer—that what we ask we receive. How can I go and tell her that the baby is dead? Couldst not Thou, O Lord? Couldst not Thou, O Lord?'

"Blanca came and knelt near me, praying also, and I, washing and praying. About eleven o'clock we started to wash and dress the baby. When we went to take her up we saw her with her great eyes wide open, the little rosy face covered with perspiration, moving her little hands as a baby of a few weeks is wont to do. What joy and excitement there was. There was such a stir that the mother called from the next room, wanting to know what it was all about. We prepared a bottle and she took it all, when for so many days she had not been able to take anything. From that moment she was well. Blanca called the doctor and on seeing the baby he cried, 'This is a veritable miracle of God. Her life was gone, and now she is not even sick!' The mother tried to make out that the baby was only sleeping, but the doctor said, 'But Madam, the child had no life. It is a miracle.' Some days later I was out airing the baby in its carriage. The doctor came along and said, 'It is a miracle.' "

The following testimony of Gabriel Segundo Saurez was attested by Dr. Hoover: "In the year 1911 my mother, Martina Figueroa de Saurez, after a case of childbirth, was very ill. I was the eldest of five children. We were new converts. One night my father, wanting to go to the prayer meeting, left me in charge of the house. As I was sitting by mother's bedside I saw that she stopped breathing, and I did all I could to awaken her. I went to the meeting to tell my father that mother was dead. Several of the brethren and sisters accompanied us home. We knelt to pray and the brethren laid hands on her. The Spirit fell upon all, especially on my brothers. Carlos was on the floor under the table and Eulogio by the table, weeping and crying out to God. In a few minutes my mother sat up and said, 'Glory to God! I have been far away. There is no comparison in the other world with what passes here. I am very tired for I have walked so much.' We were all filled with joy and gladness, praising God and singing hymns. The next day my mother got up, entirely well, and that evening she went to the meeting."

Dr. Hoover and his wife, after many years of splendid service, have gone on to be with the Lord, but the work continues. "There are about 400 Pentecostal workers in Chile at the present time, including the newer works recently started in farm districts and mining regions. There are about 50,000 of the Pentecostal faith. Since the outpouring of the Holy Spirit in Chile in 1909 thousands of souls have accepted Christ as their personal Saviour, and thousands have received the Baptism in the Holy Spirit. The largest Pentecostal assembly in Santiago, Chile, has an attendance of 1,500 persons. Each afternoon at five o'clock several hundred Christians gather for prayer in the assembly hall, and wait on the Lord for a return of those times of refreshing from His Holy presence that are promised in His Word.

"Many unsaved are being reached through the ministry of open-air services in Chile. In the Pentecostal work in Chile today there is an excellent spirit of evangelism. An outstanding motto is 'Chile for Christ.' Groups of young men and women and even adults are going forth into the highways and byways to compel sinners to come to Christ."

Hugh Jeter, formerly a missionary to Peru (now in Cuba), after a visit to Chile, told us of this recent incident: "Arturo Espinoza weighed less than 100 pounds. The doctors had pronounced him in the last stages of tuberculosis, with only a piece of one lung left, and had told him he could not live more than five days. Instead of going right to bed as most of us might have done to conserve the remaining spark of life and perhaps live six days instead of five, Arturo immediately went to an open-air meeting and preached on the street corner. He then returned to the mission, knelt at the altar and told the Lord he was not going to give up till God healed him.

"Some visiting brethren at the church that night had a vision. They saw an angel with a basin in one hand and a surgical instrument in the other who approached Arturo as he knelt at the altar, opened up his back, took out the piece of a lung and put in two new lungs. When Arturo arose from his knees he was completely healed.

"About two days later he went back to the doctor who had previously examined him. The doctor was astonished to see a man walk in whom he expected to be in a dying condition by this time, and still more astonished to find after examining him that the lungs were perfectly well, with no trace of tuberculosis. The astonished physician called in ten other doctors who also examined Arturo and pronounced him absolutely well.

"Today that same man weighs over two hundred pounds. He is in perfect health, but the best part is that the Lord has used him to raise up an assembly in Chile which has about six hundred members."

CHAPTER XVIII

God's Visitation in Venezuela

A STUDENT of the Christian and Missionary Alliance Training School at Nyack, N. Y., G. F. Bender, received the Baptism in the Holy Spirit and was called of the Lord to preach the gospel in Venezuela. He was led to go to the city of Barquisimeto, a very strong Roman Catholic center. He and his good wife labored faithfully in that city for some years and many precious souls found salvation. They erected a chapel.

The following was told by Brother Bender when on furlough: "Our chapel was built with a seating capacity of three hundred, and God has worked marvelous things in that place. We preached about the outpouring of the Holy Spirit, and believed that God would one day confirm His Word with signs following. We kept seeking the Lord for revival. It was nearly five years before it came.

"The revival started with such deep conviction for sin that the people all thought they were lost. For almost a month they wept and cried to God, paid their debts, and got all grudges out of the way. I said, 'O Lord, this looks like the real thing!' In a Tuesday afternoon prayer meeting there fell on the audience such conviction, such weeping, moaning and crying out for sin, and we just let them cry on. Two of them wept their way through to God that afternoon, and when they came through they had the whole neighborhood together. The people came running to see

what was happening in the Protestant church. They
called us 'devils,' and they wanted to see what had
happened among the 'devils.'

"About that time, these two women that had broken
through, turned to the crowd, exalted Jesus Christ and
His Blood, and told them that the Virgin Mary could
not save them. How these two women preached that
afternoon! We could not close the meeting so we let
them go on, and we went about our work. And that
kept up until two days before our fifth anniversary.

"Three days before our anniversary, one young
man had a meeting in his home. Some friends were
coming from another town to visit, and in order for
them not to lose any time about hearing the gospel, he
organized a meeting in his own home. When the
prayer meeting started he was the first to receive the
blessing. As they went down to pray, the power of
God struck him, and in just a little while he was
speaking in another tongue. Hallelujah! What a
night that was! The effect of that boy's speaking in
tongues before them was so powerful that the children
and older people just cried out to God for mercy.
And these new ones from out of town got under such
conviction for sin that they too were included among
the seekers and were saved that night. There must
have been ten or twelve soundly converted, with the
glory of God on their faces.

"The next night was Friday, the regular meeting.
Suddenly, one jumped up and gave his testimony
about the prayer meeting the night before, and told all
about his salvation. One after another gave their
testimony. A young woman, a visitor from out of
town, got up to give her experience as to how God had
saved her. While she was telling it, oh such conviction
came over that audience! It was like a thunderbolt
out of a clear sky. People fell upon their knees and
there was confessing, and moaning, and groaning all
over that congregation of a hundred and twenty-five.
While the weeping and crying were going on, the whole

end of the town was stirred, and the running together reminded me of the day of Pentecost when the thing was noised abroad. The street and the court in front of the chapel were full of people, and the policeman had his hands full. The policeman had come to see what was going on and the crowd pressed him right inside the building. They did not know but that the 'devils' had gone crazy, and they wanted to see. The policeman was a friend of the gospel, because he was stationed on our corner and had heard it preached. A holy awe seized the policeman and the people. One would jump up and shout and praise God, with a shining face, another here, and another there; and the thing kept up and kept up. It was marvelous!

"The crowd was spellbound as they saw all these things happening. The policeman looked on for an hour or more, watching the workings of the mighty power of God. Then all of a sudden he took off his helmet, threw it down, and followed after it. He went down on his knees and began to cry for mercy. And if God ever touched a life, it was that policeman's. Now they call him the 'Protestant Policeman.' He has been accused of being a preacher and not a policeman. He does preach the gospel. He is all on fire and you may see him almost anywhere talking the gospel.

"From that time on, they began to get baptized in the Holy Ghost. At a prayer meeting we were singing, 'He was nailed to the cross for me.' All at once a young man with his arms up (we never told them to raise their arms, but they raised them spontaneously, inspired by the Holy Ghost—God had cleansed their hands and could accept them) started to pray, and everybody joined in that prayer. It seemed to me as though I had a company of angels before me, their faces all aglow. Before I knew it, that young man's language changed and he was speaking in new tongues.

"When the power of God struck him it seemed to affect everyone around. After some time the whole congregation dropped on their knees, and oh such praising! There was no weeping that night, it was all praising. God inhabits the praises of Israel, and God descended that night in those praises. Pretty soon a little fellow on my right (we called him Zacchaeus because he was so short) began to speak in tongues. I could not preach that night. All I could do was to sit back and look on. The Holy Ghost had begun to work, and from that time on, one after another came through to the Baptism in the Holy Ghost.

"Other missionaries had warned me, saying: 'You cannot let Latin people do what they do in North America.' Should a woman fall on the floor full length, I knew those wild people on the streets would rush right in and count it some immoral act. It would be a terrible disaster there to have a woman prostrated in a public chapel. I prayed, 'O God, save Your interests in Venezuela. The Latins must have the Baptism in the Holy Ghost, and I stand for it. Lord, give them Pentecost, and I will keep my hands off.' God adapted Himself to the circumstances of our land. Not one woman fell to the floor. They either received the Baptism on their knees with their hands up, or sitting on benches, or standing on their feet. Afraid to try God! Afraid to prove God! I was ashamed afterwards that I ever had a doubt.

"The only one that ever fell on the floor was a boy thirteen years old. The neighbors said, 'He fell on the floor. Some bad spirit must have got hold of him. He was too young to receive the Baptism.' I said, 'Where did you read he is too young?' I told them that even children could receive. Well, that was enough for those people. They scattered abroad the word that children could get the Baptism, and it was not long until nineteen of them had received.

"The year 1925 was ushered in with a mighty revival. On New Year's Day the elders of the church, a judge who had been saved in our meetings, and the judge's family went to a neighboring town to pray for a needy family that was sick. While they were praying, the Holy Ghost fell upon them and they were baptized in the Spirit and spoke in other tongues.

"A woman, who had been tormented for years with demons, heard about the power of God and came to Barquisimeto. She said, 'I have a tormenting spirit. I have come to be delivered, and I do not intend to go back until I am delivered.' Just as she was telling us, the spirit took hold of her, and I wish you could have seen that suffering. The beads of perspiration stood out on her, and in a few minutes her clothing was soaked, the agony from that driving demon was so terrible. We sat there helpless. We had no power to cast out the demon. The woman was staying in the home of a young man who had received the Baptism that afternoon. I said, 'We have power to stir up this demon, but not power to cast him out.' It drove us to our knees. Every time we went to the home where she was staying, those demons would writhe and stir her up, and she suffered terribly.

"It was all secretly arranged that on New Year's night, the church would gather and pray for her. Two of the elders were baptized in the Holy Ghost, one on New Year's Day and one before, and one elder was still unbaptized. The unbaptized one was not a convert of ours. He was saved in a neighboring State and brought lots of enmity right in his bones. While we were praying and speaking in tongues, he hardened his heart, and said it was not of God, and there was no need for such noise. They prayed and prayed, but got nowhere. There was an opposing power in that elder. But the church continued to pray until God broke that stiff man all to pieces and he humbled himself. He broke down, and in a few minutes he was speaking in other tongues and magnifying God. And when he broke through into the Pentecostal Baptism, he jumped up and rushed over to the woman, and in the name of Jesus Christ cast out the demon. And she is free today.

"The revival went on rapidly, until March 15, when

there was to be a baptismal service. There were
fourteen to be baptized. On the 14th the candidates
gathered in one of the homes to have what they called
a preparatory meeting. Many others gathered with the
candidates, and among the number was a young woman
who was sold to a life of shame. Her sister had talked
the gospel to her all that day, and had persuaded her
to attend the preparatory meeting. The power of God
was there and many were baptized in the Holy Ghost
that night. This girl was sold by her mother and
brother to a general of the Venezuelan army, and she
was to elope with him in two days. The wife of the
general was in that meeting, because she was a candi-
date for baptism.

"The power of God was there tremendously. The
girl sat there as long as she could stand it. When she
could endure it no longer, she got up and flung herself at the feet of the wife and confessed the whole
thing, confessed her sin, confessed that she was to run
away with her husband. The outcome was that the
girl got gloriously saved that night from a life of
shame; and not only saved but baptized in the Holy
Ghost. When she got home her mother said, 'I will
shake the Holy Ghost out of you,' and she grabbed
the girl by the hair and dragged her over the floor;
and while she was dragging the girl over the floor the
girl was speaking in other tongues. They tried to
force cigarettes into her mouth and to make her smoke.

"On the following day, her mother made her go
to a Catholic church and confess. When she got to
the confessional box she sat there. Pretty soon the
priest asked her if she was not going to confess. She
said she did not have anything to confess. She said,
'The Lord has forgiven me and baptized me with the
Holy Ghost.' Oh, but that priest was angry!

"Just before the preparatory meeting, when we had
a powerful meeting in the chapel, a woman whom we
knew to be the concubine of several men slipped into
the back seat. I remember seeing the tears run down

her face, washing off some of the red paint. But before anyone could get to her, she slipped out of the chapel and went away. The next day she took two of her illegitimate children, walked away out on the plains, hunted some shrubbery, and spent the afternoon in prayer and mourning before God. She did not break through and so decided to go to the preparatory meeting where the candidates were gathered. She was not in there long until she was gloriously saved. She took her handkerchief out and began to wipe the paint off. She threw off her bracelets and began to strip off her finery. Then she stood on her feet, raised her hands, and as tears of joy flowed down her face the Holy Ghost descended on her and she began to speak in other tongues and magnify God. If God can save a harlot and baptize her in the Holy Ghost in one night, what cannot He do?

"Those two little illegitimate children, one nine and one about eleven, got under such conviction when they saw their mother baptized, that they cried out to God for mercy; and it was not over half an hour until both of those girls were speaking in other tongues and magnifying God. There were seventeen baptized in the Holy Ghost that night, and the whole neighborhood ran together to look on. Some of the leading business men in that city were watching the power of God work.

"A large company of people watched the fourteen candidates go down into the watery grave, coming up with hands uplifted and speaking in other tongues and glorifying God. In the crowd that watched the service was a young druggist. He had lived with a woman for some years in the city of Barquisimeto, but this young woman had come into the light of the gospel and had discovered that she was living in sin with that man. She said, 'We cannot live together any longer. This gospel teaches me that we must separate.' He tried to persuade her, but she was determined to go through with God.

"Finally he wrote her a letter and said he would

marry her but it would have to be in a Catholic church. She sent word back, 'We will never marry until you accept my gospel and my Christ.' He came out one evening to the meetings, and in those days it was not hard to get sinners to the altar. Among those who came forward was this young fellow. He wanted that girl and so he went through the form of getting saved. I knew he had not touched God and so I said to her, 'That fellow is not real.' She said, 'Oh, I know him too well. I know that he is not real.' She was not to be deceived by any means.

"The following Sunday he came to watch the baptismal service. Just as I stepped out of the baptistry that fellow shrieked out, 'I am lost! I am lost!' And I knew that was a real shriek. The whole congregation gathered around that fellow and in less than half an hour they had prayed him through. He pulled out his cigarettes and threw them away, and said: 'I have no more use for that stuff.' That was Sunday morning. Before he came back into the evening service, he was baptized in the Spirit and speaking in other tongues.

"One night we were celebrating the Lord's Supper. I said, 'Any young man in the congregation that would dedicate his life to God for service, will you come forward?' There were four or five who responded, and among them was this young man. When the elders laid their hands on these young fellows and set them aside to help in the church, when we came to that young man I felt the power of God go through me, and the elders had such a witness that God seemed to open the heavens to us.

"On Wednesday all day long I felt in my soul I should call on him to give his testimony publicly. I asked him to give it. He walked right up and stood on the platform and gave his testimony, and it was a glowing one. When he got through he opened up his Bible to a text in Jeremiah and began to preach from the Word. I said, 'My God, where does all that come from?' I was overwhelmed, I did not know what to say. His message fed my poor soul. I said, 'Is it possible that a babe in Christ, not two months old, can feed me?' This young fellow went through a deep crisis. When his boss, who was a fanatical Catholic, found out he had turned to the gospel, he threw him out of the drug store. He went through a long, severe test, but God enabled him to get a good position.

"He came to me and said, 'Can you marry us now?' I said, 'Yes, indeed.' So they got ready for their wedding and they had it in our home. When people have lived in sin for a season, we do not have the ceremony in the chapel. We fixed palms and roses, and put benches in and invited all their relatives and friends to the wedding. If ever I saw a pretty sight, it was that night. And if ever I saw God's seal on a matrimony, it was on that one. What a time we had! There was that young couple with hands uplifted, speaking in other tongues and magnifying God, and all the people were on their feet magnifying God. It inspired our young people.

"It was on March 14 that we had our preparatory meeting, on a Saturday night; and from that Saturday night to the next Saturday night was the height of our revival. That week forty-two souls were baptized in the Holy Ghost and spoke with other tongues as the Spirit gave them utterance. Oh, that I could put into words the picture of the movement of the Holy Ghost that week. I had nothing to do with the revival. I would sit on the platform and laugh. I seemed to be on a vacation and God was working. Wherever you turned, there were prayer meetings. I remember going across the street to pray for a sick man, and one we call 'Zaccheus' was with me. As we came out there were five or six girls in the home and they said, 'Won't you lay hands on us that we may receive the Holy Ghost too?' I said, 'Kneel down here, and if there is a temple worthy, the peace of God will stay in it.' So Zaccheus and I went from one to another and laid hands on them, and in just a little while one of them began to speak in other tongues. No matter where you went you were met with the question, 'Will you pray for us?' "

The work continues. Brother Bender relates the following recent happening:

"Carmen Gonzales was educated in our school in Barquisimeto and also raised in our children's home. She afterwards returned home to Humo Caro Bajo where there was no gospel work. Having no spiritual help to speak of, Carmen grew cold in her spiritual life. A nice-looking young man began to pay attention to her, and while she was warned by her mother that there could be no alliance with the ungodly, yet the temptation was so great that she yielded and married this young man. He was very worldly and mistreated her many times. Her tribulation drove her into God. Her ungodly husband found her reading the Bible and strongly remonstrated with her. On another occasion he found her on her knees praying, and mocked and scorned.

"Carmen's sister visited us in Barquisimeto and we gave her some literature to take back with her. Among the things we sent was a book which contained many illustrations of the heart of man in sin and the heart of man when converted. Carmen's husband picked up this book and read it with interest. He asked Carmen to let him have her Bible. She gave it to him and he began to read the book of Job. He read this book through and was deeply impressed by the disease that the devil put on Job.

"One night he had a dream that Satan came to the outer court of his house. He noticed that the devil's limbs were diseased from the knees downward with a red fiery disease. He was continually scratching himself, and when he scratched himself there flew from his legs something like the scales of a fish and sparks of fire. When the man awoke in the morning he found he had the same disease from head to foot that he had seen on the devil's limbs. **For three days and three nights** he was so beset with the itch and high fever that on the third night he was given up to die.

"He was lying on his back, staring with glassy eyes at the ceiling. His wife sat by the side of the bed reading the Bible to him and praying with him. As he lay there he was given a vision. He saw the devil appear again unto him. He said to the sick man, 'If you will serve me I can remove that disease from you." The sick man answered, 'I will not serve you. Jesus Christ will heal me.' The devil said to him, 'If you will not scratch yourself,' and he specified a certain length of time 'you will belong to God, but if you scratch yourself in this length of time you will belong to me.' As he lay there his wife noticed that he just twitched and shrugged his shoulders as he suffered in agony, battling against scratching himself. And as he twitched the devil would laugh with glee into his face, believing that he had conquered. This lasted nearly all night long. Toward the morning the devil began to back out of the room. He backed out into the court and then suddenly disappeared. At this moment the man shouted with a loud voice, saying, 'I belong to God! I belong to God!'

"His wife, knowing nothing of what he had been passing through, and expecting his death at any moment, was surprised on examining him to find that he had been entirely healed. All trace of the disease had disappeared from his body and he was a new creature in Christ Jesus, saved and healed at the same moment. He is to this day a faithful witness in that town and in all the region round about, going everywhere and witnessing for the Lord, telling of His great power to save from vice and sin and to cleanse the sinner. I had the privilege of meeting him last August, when he came to Barquisimeto to attend the yearly convention."

CHAPTER XIX

Among the Latin Americans

THE STORY of the Pentecostal revival that came to the Latin Americans along the Mexican border is a glorious missionary romance.

H. C. Ball was born in Iowa, but because his lungs were affected the doctor told his mother to take him South to a different climate. The mother moved first to New Mexico and then to southern Texas, and there at the age of fourteen the lad found Christ as his personal Saviour. The night he was saved he felt a call to the ministry. With practically no knowledge of the Spanish language he began laboring among the Mexicans. He had the joy of seeing a number saved and in six months he had a church of twenty-two members. After four years the Pentecostal message came to this part of southern Texas and the young missionary received the Baptism in the Holy Spirit as they did at the beginning. He continued to labor among the Latin Americans and saw a number of them saved, but it was not until six months later that the Holy Spirit was poured out upon the Mexican believers.

Brother Ball states: "On July 4, 1915, I was to baptize thirteen in water. After the service we went back to the schoolhouse where I had been saved about four years before, and had the Lord's Supper. After giving out the emblems, the bread and the wine, the power of God began to fall. The first thing I knew, an old sister was receiving the Baptism in the Holy Spirit. I went to see, and noticed tears were rolling down her cheeks and she was speaking in an unknown tongue. I told the folk to come and see her. They had never seen anyone baptized in the Holy Spirit. The older son touched his mother's hands to see if she was all right. She said, 'All right. I am baptized in the Holy Spirit,' and she went on talking in tongues. This son threw up his hands and began to praise the Lord, and soon he was filled with the Holy Spirit. His wife was also shortly filled, and one after another were filled, until that afternoon nine were baptized with the Holy Spirit. Pentecost had come to the Latin-American people."

Miss Alice E. Luce, who labors among the Latin Americans, states: "As an illustration of the way in which the work spreads, I may mention the opening of the mission in Los Indios, on the Mexican border, not far from the mouth of the Rio Grande. A young Mexican was sent in his regular work to Kingsville, and, having a Sunday free there, he strolled into our church and for the first time heard the gospel preached. He was brightly saved and went back to Los Indios (more than one hundred miles south) with a burning desire in his heart to tell of his newly found Saviour. Before many days had passed we received a letter telling us that he had won six young men to Christ. Brother Ball was able to go down and visit them, took them Bibles, told them that whenever they were able to come to Kingsville they could be baptized in water, and that we would pray for them to receive the Baptism in the Holy Spirit.

"In a few weeks' time, three of them came, the leader and two of his converts. They spent one Sunday with us. In the afternoon they were all three baptized in water and in the evening one of them received the Baptism. On Monday another received the Baptism. On Tuesday morning they had to leave to return to their work, the leader not yet having received the Baptism though he was seeking very earnestly. The following Sunday one of these young converts said to two very godless friends of his: 'I do wish you would give up your sins and turn to Jesus.' They said nothing, and he, not knowing what else to say, remarked: 'I will read you a chapter out of the Bible.' This he did. The two lads, one aged eighteen and the other twenty, were confirmed drunkards and one was a notorious gambler. They said nothing but they went out of that house pricked to the heart.

"As they walked towards their own home, the younger one said to his brother: 'We ought to pray.' The older one replied: 'How can we, for we don't know Latin?' The younger one could not answer that, but made up his mind he was going to try. So when they reached their own little shack, the younger lad went down on his knees and began to cry to God for mercy. It was not long before the light broke in upon his soul. He realized that the burden of his sin had rolled away and he began praising his Saviour with all his might. In less than half an hour the Holy Spirit fell upon him and he began praising the Lord in other tongues. Nobody could be more surprised than he himself was, but he exclaimed to his brother: "Oh, this must be the Holy Spirit! Miguel said they had the Holy Spirit up at Kingsville!'

"He then begged his brother to go down on his knees and confess his sins, which he was only too ready to do; and in another half hour the elder brother also was saved and received the Holy Spirit. By this time they were both praising the Lord so lustily that the mother, who was making *tortillas* in the little kitchen at the back, rushed in, her hands all floury, to see what was the matter. She opened the door, exclaiming: 'What is the matter with you boys? Have you gone crazy?' To which the younger one replied: 'O Mother, the Holy Ghost has come. You must get down on your knees and confess your sins to Jesus.' The mother did so and the power of the Spirit was so mightily present that it was not long before she had the joy of salvation, and the Lord baptized her also with the Holy Ghost.

"By this time the sister, who had been helping her mother prepare the noonday meal, began to wonder why the mother did not come back, so she came in to see what it was all about. They called her also to get down on her knees and confess her sins to Jesus, and in a short while more the sister (a girl of about sixteen) was saved and baptized with the Holy Ghost. The shouts of rejoicing were now so loud that the Christians in some of the neighboring shacks heard of it and came rushing in. And they did indeed have a wonderful meeting all through the remainder of that Sunday. About twenty were saved that day and thirteen received the Baptism in the Holy Ghost; Miguel (the one who had first started the work) being among the number. By the time I first visited Los Indios, a few weeks later, there were sixty-four who had received the Baptism in the Holy Spirit.

"We have often seen tiny children in prayer, weeping their way to Jesus; one little mite only just able to toddle, when his parents were busy praying with seekers at the altar, used to go up to the sick ones and lay his tiny hands upon them, as if he knew all about them and was praying for them. A little girl of three used to pray for her grandmother every time she was sick, and many in that house were healed in answer to the prayers and faith of that little girl. Another little girl of four was taken into a cottage meeting in a new field. She asked if she might sing a hymn and on receiving permission, she climbed on a chair and sang with all her might, 'Jesus loves me, this I know,' etc. There was not a dry eye in the room, and two of the most hardened sinners broke down completely and were saved that night, as a result of the testimony in song of that little girl.

"In another city there was a large family who became interested in the gospel. The father and mother were saved and began to seek the Baptism in the Spirit,

but the two married daughters began to oppose it most
vigorously. The father had been a preacher for years,
but they could not bear to see him come into this
'despised way.' Their little boy of four was marvelously healed of infantile paralysis, and began to run
about with the other children, whereas before he had
had no use whatever of his legs; and then the little girl
of eight received the Baptism in the Spirit. This was
too much for the older sisters, and they came into
our meeting one night determined to see their little
sister in some 'extravagances,' as they termed it, and
then call in the police to put a stop to it all.

"While they sat there side by side, their hearts
filled with bitterness and anger, the power of the
Spirit fell on the little eight-year-old sister, and she
began to pray with tears for the salvation of her sisters.
Then, still under the power, she arose and went over to
where they sat, laying one little hand on each of their
heads, the tears streaming down her cheeks, pleading
with the Lord to soften their hearts and to save them.
Her prayer was heard, they went down in penitence
before Him, and before long both were gloriously
saved and received the Baptism in the Holy Spirit
themselves. There was great joy in that large family!

"In a bigoted Roman Catholic family, just over
the border in Mexico, the daughter heard of the Great
Physician, came to Him, and was healed of an incurable disease, her brother as a result being saved also.
This greatly incensed their father, and his fury knew
no bounds. The son finally said to him, 'Father, don't
you believe there will be a resurrection of the dead?'
'Oh, yes,' replied the old man, crossing himself very
devoutly. 'Then, father, if God is able to raise up a
dead body, is He not also able to heal a sick body
which is not yet dead? Surely He who is able to
perform the greater miracle can also perform the lesser
one.' The father saw the logic of the argument, his
heart was softened and ere long he and his whole family were rejoicing in Jesus as their Saviour.

"An old woman came into our meeting one afternoon with a stiff arm which she was unable to move. After prayer the Lord healed it perfectly, and she was overjoyed, raising it above her head and shouting the praises of her Great Physician. Another woman came to an evening meeting and asked prayer for internal trouble. (We afterwards learned it was appendicitis, and that the doctors were going to operate on her the next day.) The Lord healed her then and there, and as she rose to her feet with hands uplifted to praise Him, He baptized her with His Spirit and she began to speak with other tongues as the Spirit gave utterance.

"The very next night she was at the altar praying with other seekers like an old prayer warrior. A year later I visited that city again, and was called to go to a sick woman who was not yet saved. This woman who had been healed went with me, and it was blessed to hear her testimony to the sick one, telling of the awful pain she had suffered, how Jesus had taken it all away in a moment, and how she had been every whit whole from that day, living in the power of His Spirit. We found that the sick one to whom we were called had the same trouble—so her faith was strengthened by the testimony to believe for her own healing, and the Lord not only healed her but also saved her.

"In the early days of this outpouring, the Mexicans used to report in Kingsville that Brother Ball had an electric wire up his sleeve, and that he used to put his hands on people and then they talked in strange languages as a result of the electric shocks they got. In a very wonderful way God gave an object lesson to a group of unsaved young men that it was HE who was baptizing with the Holy Ghost and not any human being. We were holding our usual evening service, Brother Ball being at one end of the platform, the organ next, which I was playing, and the other side of me a group of women leading the singing. One of these testified how the Lord had saved her and how earnestly she desired the Baptism in the Spirit.

"Then we began to sing a hymn, and as we sang the power struck her and she went down on her knees right there on the platform, and the Lord baptized her in the Holy Ghost then and there, in full view of a number of sinners who were in the church; so that they could all see plainly that Brother Ball did not go near her, but that it was the Lord from heaven who had touched and filled her.

"A hardened infidel was won to Christ by the simple testimony of a humble little woman who was doing the cooking for him and a large band of men whom he was employing on a contract in the beet fields. One night he was going with a revolver in his pocket to kill another man, and was stopped by the Spirit of God, brought under conviction, and led to the Saviour by the ignorant, little cook woman. His wife was dead and he had two little children, a girl of eight and a boy of six. When their father came home saved, at the close of a meeting, he awoke them both and they screamed in terror, fearing he was going to kill them.

"But when they found he was a changed man, and had now nothing but words of love and tenderness for them, their delight knew no bounds, and they got down on their knees and asked God to give them what had made such a change in father. They afterwards told us about that wonderful night. The three of them were down under the power until seven in the morning, and the little girl told us she had seen Jesus, and He was holding a beautiful crown in His hand, and He told her she was to serve Him, and if she was faithful that beautiful crown should be hers.

"The boy said he saw a beautiful dove, oh, so white, he never had seen anything like it; and he ran to grasp it. Jesus told him that beautiful white dove was the Holy Spirit, and that He wanted to fill him with His Spirit. In a very short time the girl received the Baptism in the Spirit, but soon after they moved away and we did not see them for a number of years. But after that long absence the Lord brought

them in contact with us again, and we rejoiced to find
how the Lord had kept them witnessing for Him
wherever their work took them; and on the second
visit we had the joy of seeing the boy (now a big, tall
lad of fifteen) receive a glorious Baptism in the
Spirit. Oh, how the praises rolled from his lips! It
was just about this time when we heard a noted preacher say that praise was a lost art in the church, and we
said to one another how we wished he could have
heard the praises from the lips of that dear lad, as the
Spirit Himself took possession and praised Jesus
through him."

Looking back over the work during the years since
1915, Brother Ball says: "During these years God
has blessed us and given us an ever increasing
number of faithful ministers of the gospel among the
Latin-American people. At first only a few were
licensed to preach, but after a while a few were ordained and the work grew and grew and grew until at
the present time we have almost four hundred Mexican
ministers ministering on the border, and over in old
Mexico we have over two hundred at the present
time. How we thank God for these ministers who are
breaking the bread of life from Sunday to Sunday to
their people—ever growing in numbers and also growing in God's grace. We have our own Bible School,
and God has blessed us up to the present time with
one hundred and forty-seven students who have grad-
uated, and most of them are giving their lives to serv-
ing God.

"Recently we had the privilege of meeting a man
who has an independent Pentecostal church in the
city of Mexico. He told us there were as many as
nine hundred in attendance at the Sunday morning
services. In our own church in San Antonio, Texas,
we have something like five or six hundred present
in the Sunday services."

The work in Brazil was begun in 1910 by two
Swedish missionaries from the United States. Today,

according to the official organ of the Assemblies in
Brazil, there are about 650 churches with an approxi-
mate membership of 100,000.

Lester Sumrall writes: "Brother S. Hedlund, a
Swedish missionary, is called the pioneer, his special
work being to open up new works and then move
further afield. He assisted in opening the great church
in Recife, the capital of the State of Pernambuco. In
1921 it had eighteen members, and at present has well
over six thousand baptized believers. This makes it
the largest evangelical church in Brazil. It was interesting to learn that one third of all the streetcar opera-
tors in Recife are Pentecostal. Our brother was used
of the Lord to open up a fine work in Sao Paulo,
which is growing, similar to the first Pentecostal
church, having 'a daily addition.' "

Brother Sumrall tells of a Pentecostal work he
found in the Brazilian jungle among a colony of Lettish
people. Some years ago a sister living in this jungle
received from a cousin of hers in the United States a
copy of the *Pentecostal Evangel* published in Springfield, Missouri, and also a copy of a full-gospel magazine from England. This sister understood English
and read in these journals of marvelous revivals in
progress. Remarkable healings were described in a
manner that moved her soul. Then she read that God
was baptizing in the Holy Ghost today just as He did
in Jerusalem on the day of Pentecost. A tremendous
desire for more of God sprang up in her heart and she
began to pray earnestly for an infilling of the Holy
Spirit. Thereupon she was mightily empowered. As
she rejoiced in the blessing that she was receiving there
sprang from her lips words that were not intelligible
to her. She went to a neighbor woman and confiden-
tially told her about her experience. She and this
lady knelt in prayer and to the supreme joy of both,
the Lord baptized the neighbor in the Holy Ghost.
In the exuberance of their joy they went to another
neighbor and told their experience and asked if they

might pray with her. This neighbor received also. The strange news circulated about the colony from mouth to mouth and others received the Holy Spirit Baptism with great joy. The revival spread and the number increased until at present there are about one hundred and fifty believers filled with the Holy Spirit."

One brother, a pioneer worker, states: "We have seen what God can do in these last days since He has poured out an apostolic revival in Brazil. With unexpected rapidity the message has spread and whole towns are moved by the power of God. During 1938 missionaries and native evangelists have baptized about three thousand converts who have been gloriously saved from terrible witchcraft, demon power, horrible slavery in sin, and awful vices. I personally baptized 317 candidates in the southern provinces of Brazil during that year. The native helpers are baptizing every Sunday scores of saved Brazilians, going from town to town and village to village. In many villages and plantations of Brazil, where formerly strife and robbery, fighting and murder reigned, today big congregations of children of God are rejoicing in the glorious abundance of life in the Lord and Saviour Jesus Christ."

There has also been a gracious outpouring of the Spirit in Argentina. N. C. Sorenson, Superintendent of the work of the Canadian missionaries in Argentina, writes: "In the beginning things were hard and it seemed impossible to get much of a hold. The great indifference we encountered was our greatest enemy. However, we have had waves of blessing and revival fires burning here and there, and there has been a steady growth until at present we have 11 permanent assemblies, as well as some outstations, with a membership of about 800. The work was begun in 1921. Since that time some 2,000 have been saved and baptized, and many hundreds have received the Baptism of Holy Spirit according to Acts 2:4. All manner of diseases have been healed in answer to prayer. Our people have

been taught to trust in the Lord and use no other reme-
dies than James 5:14."

Miss Alice C. Wood, a pioneer missionary in
Argentina, stationed at 25 de Mayo, F. C. S., wrote of
a blessed visitation among the Indians: "The Holy
Spirit fell suddenly upon a hundred Indians who were
kneeling in prayer. First came a mighty shaking like
an earthquake, with wind and a sound like the firing of
cannon. Simultaneously the Indians arose to their
feet and began to clap their hands, shouting hallelujah,
and then broke out speaking in tongues. This brought
most of the town together until all the streets were
filled. A good neighbor living in front of the mission
brought out his great *machete* (knife) to defend the
missionaries for he thought the Indians had raised a
war whoop and were killing him and his family. As a
result of this outpouring of the Holy Spirit, many souls
are being saved."

A gracious pioneer work is also being carried on in
Peru where there are many hundreds of blood-washed
Peruvians who have been born into the kingdom of
God. They have their own Bible School where a
number of native young men are being trained to become evangelists and pastors, and a publishing house
has been established to supply gospel literature for many
parts of Latin America.

CHAPTER XX

The Work in Central America

WHEN Ralph D. Williams went to El Salvador in Central America, he found that a Pentecostal brother had visited this country in 1910, that he had preached in the power of the Spirit, and that as the result many hundreds had been saved and baptized and many had been wonderfully healed. The revival continued for several years, but because the Word of God had not been given its rightful place the spiritual side of the work suffered greatly. But through it all there was a group of people hungry to go on with the Lord.

Brother Williams called a conference, and about fourteen different groups were represented. These brethren continued five days in council, and this getting together proved to be a wonderful incentive to the growth of the work, and its continuance in harmony and in accordance with the Word of God. Provision was made for a Bible School, for fellowship meetings, and for an annual conference. The date was set for the opening of the Bible School and pastors were told to send in those who had already received their call to the ministry, and to do what they could to supply them with food and money.

About eighteen or twenty students came on the opening date. There were no funds with which to build a proper building. The first two or three days were spent in collecting packing cases, knocking them to pieces, and making desks and seats. Then they had three months of Bible School. It opened each morning at 6:15 with prayer, and the classes were from eight until noon. In the afternoon they studied the lessons assigned in the morning, and in the evenings there were evangelistic meetings.

Brother Williams says: "While we were having our first Bible School, we had a time of bitter persecution. We tried to hold street meetings, but after the first Sunday the whole town seemed to rise against us, so that on two occasions it was necessary for the mayor and captain of the town guard to protect us with soldiers from the fury of the mob. Sickness attacked the students and practically every one went down with fever at one time. But in spite of all the persecution and testing, the Lord blessed, and almost everyone who went to the Bible School at that time is preaching the gospel today. About thirty or forty were added to the church during that persecution, and two years later we were able to hold our annual conference at that same point with about three hundred brethren present.

"A young man named Moroy came with a dozen others, very drunk, to attack the little prayer meeting in the grass hut. Before they reached the hut they began to fight and quarrel among themselves, shooting and stabbing at each other with their knives. The next morning some were wounded, some were in jail, and others were missing. Moroy was impressed that God must have had His hand on the little prayer meeting, and later attended several times. One evening he was kneeling in the doorway of the meeting place. Some of his former companions, being the worse for drink, made for him to attack him. One was knocked over backwards. He got up and started for the young man, but again was knocked over. He accused his companions of knocking him over but they denied it. Then he ran over to Moroy, asking him if he had knocked him over. Moroy said he had not touched him. Then the man said, 'Surely the living God must have knocked me over.'

"Moroy was saved and began to read the Word constantly. He was avoided by his former companions. He tithed his income, and although he lost his occupation through envy, he bought a little coffee plantation and built a church on it. He went to Bible School and became a preacher. After a while he sold everything he had and started on an evangelistic mission around the villages where there were churches and in many others where there were no churches.

"A boy came to our Bible School but was unable to continue his studies because of sickness. He lived in a miserable little hovel. His name was Santos. He was suffering from various tropical diseases and intestinal parasites. It seemed that very soon he would leave us and go to a better land. The brethren came to me one night at about two or three a. m. and said, 'Santos is dying.' We went to the place where he lived and prayed for him. There seemed no miracle at the time, but in a few weeks he was up and rejoicing for he knew he had been healed. He had been almost dead. After his sickness he was greatly emaciated, but he soon picked up and it was not long before we learned he was having charge of a group of brethren, developing his ministry, and winning souls for the Master."

Brother Williams took a long trip to a place on the border of El Salvador, and as a result of his preaching a number received the Word. Eighteen months later he visited this place again and was delighted to find that instead of the six or eight who had received the Word, there were now thirty, and all of them zealous for God. They asked for a pastor and the Lord spoke to Brother Williams to send Santos. So he went up to minister to them. Brother Williams states: "The Lord has blessed his work, and instead of having one little church there the work has developed until there are now about six churches right on the border. Santos has gone over into Honduras, taking natives with him to preach and testify for Christ. Each time he goes he reaches further afield and as a result we have another section opened up in Honduras. There are about ten towns or villages where the gospel is now being preached."

The graduates of the Bible School are evangelizing not only throughout El Salvador but throughout the near-by republics.

The following story told by Melvin L. Hodges shows how the work grows: "I never shall forget the time I had the privilege of attending a little service in El Salvador. Back in the hills we went to visit this little church. When church time came people crowded in until there were perhaps 150 people gathered together and the place was filled to capacity. The pastor told me that before the gospel came, it was not safe for a man to go out in the country at night. People were being killed every week. But now even the women can walk down the street and not be molested. There are only two families in the whole community that are not Pentecostal Christians and these two families come to church.

"God's Spirit is moving in these days in a special way. We went into Honduras where we heard that God was blessing, although we had had no missionary there up to this time. About three years ago there had been a work there of another denomination, and a good work had been done. In a town where there was no established work there was a man who was a believer, and he was seeking the Lord. God laid it upon his heart to pray for a revival. He called in two others to pray with him and they prayed for several days. That man, although he had never been in a Pentecostal meeting or seen anyone baptized in the Holy Ghost, was filled with the Holy Spirit as at Pentecost. He called in others and God began to send a revival to that place.

"This man, after he had received the Baptism in the Spirit, got in touch with our workers in El Salvador. He wrote a letter to them and said, 'Could you send us someone to teach us about this way?' The

brethren prayed about it, and one native worker felt
led of God to go. He worked with them for two years.
At the end of that time thirteen people in the town
had received the Baptism in the Spirit. They said,
'This is a day of good tidings. If we hold our peace
we do not know what will happen to us. We had
better tell our brethren what God has been doing for
us.' And so, although they were not members of our
church, they explained to the members of their denominational church that was working in that part of
the country, and gave them an invitation to visit the
town. One pastor was particularly sympathetic because he had been in El Salvador some years before
and had heard something about this Pentecostal experience. He said, 'Come into my church and we will
put on a prayer meeting and ask God to bless us.' The
result was that in three months 150 people had received
the Baptism in the Holy Ghost, and God sent a gracious
revival to that section. When we were there about a
year ago, we counted 335 Pentecostal believers, without one missionary present, and only one native worker
laboring in the different towns.

"In one place the missionary of that denomination
felt called to oppose the work of God. He made the
biggest mistake possible. He said, 'I will take your
building away from you,' and tried to force them to
give up the place. They said just as sweetly as you
please, 'Take the building, praise the Lord!' They
left him with the empty building—absolutely empty.
They built another one in the town. In that community practically everyone is a Pentecostal believer."

CHAPTER XXI

The Isles of the Sea

GOD HAS graciously poured out His Spirit on a large number of the islands of the Sea. We regret that we have not space to tell of the revivals in Hawaii, Philippine Islands, Fiji Islands, and the West Indies.

There were many hungry souls in Australia who heard that God was pouring out His Spirit in Los Angeles in 1906. They waited on the Lord and asked that He would give them the Holy Spirit even as He was given to so many in the United States. The Lord graciously answered their prayers and many were filled with the Spirit. The news spread to many parts of this island continent and others received the Pentecostal experience.

In the early part of 1922 Smith Wigglesworth of Bradford, England, visited Australia and held meetings in a number of cities. Before us lies a report of a meeting held in Melbourne which says: "Tonight scores of anxious souls signified their desire to accept Jesus Christ as their personal Saviour. A young woman who had been suffering from consumption declared, 'I was brought to last Sunday's meeting, a poor dying woman with a disease that was eating into every part of my being. I was full of corruption outside as well as inside. But blessed be God, the Lord Jesus Christ came and loosed me and set me free. The whole thing dropped off, and I live to declare the works of the Lord.' To show that she was truly healed of her consumption, the woman sang a hymn before the congregation. Mrs. Buley said, 'I praise God. A few days ago I was deaf, and suffered from anemia and bad feet, but as soon as hands were laid upon me my ears were opened. I thank God for completely healing me.' Mrs. Witt of Box Hill, who had been twenty-two years in an invalid chair, arose and walked after Mr. Wigglesworth had ministered to her. Mr. Biret testified that a friend was healed the previous night of rheumatoid arthritis of four years' standing, and had discarded crutch and stick. A man arose in the auditorium declaring, 'I am the one.' Mr. Johnson, of Springdale, who had been deaf twenty years, came wheeling his wife, who had sat in a chair for six years. Both were healed immediately and the empty chair was wheeled to the railway station while the woman testified to all the bystanders of the great things the Lord had done for her. A handkerchief was taken to one who had broken two bones in his ankle. He was walking with two sticks. After the application of the handkerchief he threw away the sticks and walked with ease." (Many have been healed in this revival through the application of handkerchiefs according to Acts 19:12.)

In the city of Melbourne, C. L. Greenwood, an iron founder who had been baptized with the Spirit, began to have Pentecostal meetings in his own home. This home soon became too small and they purchased an old rifle range and did their best to turn it into a church. He testifies: "We had been praying and tarrying for about seven years, 'God, send a revival,' and every one who came to the prayer meeting seemed to catch the same vision. One week-end a man from a slum district where I had witnessed, came and gave his heart to the Lord, and later he asked me to baptize him in water. I did this the following Wednesday night. This was our very first baptismal service in that little hall. The man's wife was sitting in the front seat watching as I put him tenderly under the water. No one had said a word to him about Pentecost, but as he came up out of the water he was speaking in tongues. His wife rushed to him and said to me, 'You have driven him mad!' She wanted to take him home before he could even get dressed, but we shut her out of the room until he was ready. It was wonderful to think that the very first one to go into that water was baptized in the Spirit before we had even said anything to him about it."

A. C. Valdez visited Australia and was invited to preach at this mission hall. Brother Greenwood says: "On Friday night there were not many out, but as Brother Valdez gave a word of exhortation my sister-in-law slipped off her seat and the Lord saved her and baptized her in one operation. Right alongside her was an old lady, well over seventy, with her wrinkled face lifted up to heaven, and she burst out speaking in other tongues. Beside this woman was another old lady, and she too burst out in other tongues, and before we knew it five had received the Baptism in the Holy Spirit. As we closed the meeting that night everyone of us felt the hush of God on our souls.

"The next night the campaign opened and then began one of the greatest revivals I have ever heard of outside of the Bible. From that day on, the place was packed and God poured out His Spirit in great and mighty power. One day when I opened the nine o'clock morning prayer service, I noticed a lady who had come to pray. That night when I went into the prayer room at nine o'clock I found her in the same place, still praying. Somewhere about 9:30 that night she was filled with the Holy Ghost—the eighteenth one that day.

"We soon found that our little hall was too small, so we secured the large town hall and the attendance quickly grew to five hundred. The news of the outpouring reached one of the local Bible institutes, but the students were forbidden to attend. However, that did not stop them from coming. First one and then another came, until the school took a real stand and

told them if they continued to attend these meetings
they would have to leave the institute. As far as I
remember, about twelve students left the institute at
once. The secretary to the principal came to us and
said, 'I believe that one can get the Baptism in the
Holy Spirit gradually.' I replied, 'Now, listen. You
are a student of the Bible. Show me one gradual
Baptism with the Spirit in the Bible.' He started to
open his Bible but soon closed it again, saying, 'No, it
is not there.' I said, 'I can take you to the Old Testament and to the New, and in every instance you will
find that the Holy Ghost came suddenly. "The Lord,
whom ye seek, shall suddenly come to His temple."
The Holy Ghost fell suddenly on the day of Pentecost,
and when Paul laid his hands on the people the Holy
Ghost fell upon them. Every time there was a visitation from God the Holy Ghost came suddenly.' That
young man attended the next meeting and he with many
of the other students, came through to the Pentecostal
Baptism.

"Week after week, and day after day, a continuous
stream of people came through to the Baptism until
hundreds had received. Time fails to tell of some
of the wonderful scenes that took place during that
revival. It was not long until we were able to secure
a building costing $40,000, which after much prayer
we were allowed to purchase for $20,000."

Smith Wigglesworth visited New Zealand in 1922.
Mr. E. Pennington, chairman of the New Zealand
Evangelical Mission, states: "Mr. Smith Wigglesworth
came to Wellington little known to any of us. There
was no flourish of trumpets to herald his advent. A
few small advertisements in the local press announced
his meetings. About 100 attended his first meeting
on Sunday evening, and the night following this number was increased by 500 to 600. From then on it
was impossible to secure buildings large enough to
accommodate the crowds, and the large town hall,
seating 3,000, was packed every evening. On some

occasions the crowd waited for hours by the doors before the commencement of the meetings. Never had the writer witnessed such scenes as followed the presentation of the Word of God by this Spirit-filled man, although he had been associated with mighty evangelists in other campaigns. On every occasion when an appeal was made for the unconverted to decide for Christ, the response was immediate, sometimes as many as 400 or 500 responding in a meeting. Over 2,000 'made the great decision during the mission in Wellington. In some cases whole families entered the kingdom of God." There were many miracles of healing in this campaign and many were filled with the Holy Ghost.

Writing concerning this same revival, Harry Roberts says: "The Pentecostal church here sprang into existence through the coming of Brother Smith Wigglesworth. The town hall in Wellington, seating 3,000, was engaged and the scenes that occurred nightly will long remain in our memories. The crowds were so great that the staff of the town hall were on duty, also the police, to keep order. Not only were the seats occupied, but the passages were crowded, and over 1,000 were addressed by Brother Lovelock and others outside. Many were saved outside, and a number healed on the town-hall steps. The sick and diseased came from all over the Dominion, and many remarkable cases of healing took place—in fact, all manner of sickness and disease was healed. In one meeting a call for the unsaved to stand and surrender to Christ and receive Him as their personal Saviour, resulted in about 500 rising to their feet to signify their acceptance of Him."

One of those who received the Baptism in the Spirit was John A. D. Adams, a barrister of the Supreme Court of New Zealand, the author of the well-known book, "The Voice of God Unheard, and the Reason Why." This barrister wrote an excellent book on the Baptism in the Holy Spirit.

Lester Sumrall in his book, "Adventuring with Christ," tells of a visit he made to Java. When Howard Carter and he arrived here they were first taken to Sourabaya where they found a Pentecostal church built to seat 1,200. There were 2,000 present at their meetings. They found in various parts of Java strong Pentecostal assemblies had been raised up of God.

Mr. Sumrall tells the story of a village that is entirely Pentecostal: "While visiting the village of Gambang Walla, the mayor of this hundred per cent Christian village gave his testimony. He was so enthusiastic that I asked our interpreter to translate it to me. The story is as follows.

"Many years ago, when he was just a boy, he came in contact with Black Magic and desired to have the power. Therefore he went into the bush and fasted and prayed for ten days and nights, begging spirits to inhabit his body. At the end of this time a power gripped his body that threw him over and over on the ground, making him foam at the mouth like a mad dog. From this time, he had remarkable power and was recognized as a doctor of black art. Some of the things he says he did, and all the people in the village verified it, are too weird for description.

"Years later a missionary woman appeared in the village and began teaching about Jesus, and healing the sick. The natives began flocking after her, and this made the witch-doctor angry. He came to the meetings and sat and tried to throw his devilish influence over the missionary, so that she could not talk. He failed, although it did greatly disturb her.

"He came a number of times until at last one night in a fury he challenged the young lady, saying that if she had more power he would leave the village, but if he had more power she must leave. The missionary said, 'Well, do something.'

"He walked to the front of the church before all the people and he lay down on the dirt floor, and was perfectly motionless for a few moments. He became

stiff; one could hardly see him breathe. Then he began
to move; his feet, head, body, all on a level, gradually
ascended. He floated knee high, waist high. This
was the power of levitation being demonstrated.

"'What can I do?' said the missionary girl. 'I know
I cannot float in the atmosphere.' The natives were
nearly hysterical seeing their master float. A thought
came to the missionary that all she could do was to get
him down. She reached and caught him in the chest,
and shouted, 'Come down, in Jesus' Name.' Down he
came, but started up again. Then she held him down.

"The anointing of the Lord came upon her. The
Apostolic ministry of Mark 16:17 became hers. She
began to rebuke the vile, unclean spirits, commanding
them to loose their victim in the Name of the Prince of
Peace. The witch-doctor went into convulsions, but
she held him down. He choked and foamed at the
mouth, his stomach moved on the inside as if something was coming out. The girl, trembling under the
holy unction of God, bound those filthy demons and
delivered him of them. The missionary prayed that
God would sweep and clean the temple and come in to
dwell.

"The witch-doctor stood up. He felt himself all
over, then looked at the people and then at the missionary. He said, 'Something has happened; my power
is gone; but I am happy in my heart.' Praise God for
a work that was done that night that has not ended yet.

"Before the missionary would let the former witch-
doctor leave the church, she laid hands on him and
prayed for him to receive the Holy Spirit. He received that night, and has since become a leading native preacher in that part of the country. He is now
the Honorable Mayor of Gambang Walla, the hundred
per cent Christian village."

For more than 25 years before the attack on Pearl
Harbor there was a Pentecostal testimony in Japan. Mr.
and Mrs. C. F. Juergensen, together with their son and
two faithful daughters, labored for many years in Tokyo.

Both father and son laid down their lives laboring in that field. As a result of their street meetings, many were drawn into their mission and saved, and a number were filled with the Spirit. A Bible school was established for the training of native workers.

Other missionaries also labored in Japan before the war, and as a result of their work quite a number of churches were established in various cities. When the United States declared war on Japan Miss Jesssie Wengler was our only missionary remaining in that land. For nearly four years our Missions Department received no word concerning her. It was not even known whether she was still alive. In January, 1946, we had the joy of hearing from her lips the story of how God had permitted her to dwell safely in her own house in the suburbs of Tokyo throughout most of the war. For nine months they experienced bombing raids every day and every night; for a whole year she kept her clothes on constantly, never going to bed, but ready to run for her life in case the house should be destroyed.

She said: "As far as I was able to find out before I left Japan, the Assemblies of God churches were intact, with the exception of the Hachioji church which was totally destroyed.

"The Kofu church is safe. The city of Kofu was more than two thirds destroyed and the fire came within a few houses of the church, but miraculously the church was left intact. The Christians also escaped, but many of them lost all they had. I was permitted to visit Kofu before leaving Japan in October. I saw that the fire had roared all around a large gasoline tank that was quite near the church. The flames had come to the very base of that tank; had it exploded or caught fire, our church would have been destroyed, but God took care of it. I had the pleasure of meeting with some of our Christian people there in Kofu.

"In Takinogawa also only a small district was saved from fire but the church was preserved. I saw Mr. Yumiyama, the pastor, and he reported all his flock safe, although many had lost all by fire and bombing.

"The Yokohama church and pastor are safe. That district was untouched. Some of the Christians there came through the war in a way that was truly miraculous.

"Some Christians said to me before I left: 'We want you to come back. We want you to tell the Christians in America that we are humiliated and need to repent before God. We want to have peace and friendship built up. We want to see the mighty power of God move in Japan.' "

There are thousands of Pentecostal assemblies on the earth today. We have never known of a Modernist among them. All believe in the plenary verbal inspiration of the Bible. All teach repentance toward God and faith in the Lord Jesus Christ, and salvation from sin through the all-blotting-out blood of Jesus Christ. All believe there is healing through the stripes of the Crucified one, and it is a general custom for them to obey the definite instructions concerning sickness in James 5:14-16. Everywhere a life of practical holiness is taught. All are looking for the near and premillennial coming of the Lord Jesus Christ and, needless to say, they all believe in receiving the Holy Ghost just as He was originally received on the day of Pentecost.

Some may question, "But have there been no regrettable things in this revival?" Yes, there have been. There are in every revival. We only have to read the Acts and the New Testament Epistles to see the continual failure of the human element. The words of Paul to the elders of Ephesus have doubtless been necessary in every subsequent revival: "Take heed therefore unto yourselves, and to all the flock, over which the Holy Ghost hath made you overseers, to feed the church of God, which He hath purchased with His own blood. For I know this, that after my departing shall grievous wolves enter in among you, not sparing the flock. Also of your own selves shall men arise, speaking perverse things, to draw away disciples after them." Acts 20:28-30. Satan has still plenty of wolves to destroy the flock, and there is always the need of watchfulness on the part of God's shepherds.

We are conscious of the need of constant prayer for more and yet more of the Holy Spirit's presence and power. But as we give ourselves yet more and more to prayer, we shall see greater and more glorious revivals.

The Apostles said, "We will give ourselves continually to prayer, and to the ministry of the word." Acts 6:4. Can we not definitely pray that the Lord will raise up at least 3,000 in these days, that will follow this apostolic example? Will you be one of these? If so, get alone before God and ask Him to take you into this truly sacrificial ministry, a ministry that will bind you in closest intimacy with Him who ever liveth to make intercession. Write your prayer promise out, put the date on it, and then day by day make this ministry first and foremost. Sacrifice even good and legitimate things to perform it. And as you are faithful this one thing is certain, the Lord will show you great and mighty things that you know not now.

But remember this word: "When thou vowest a vow unto God, defer not to pay it ... pay that which thou hast vowed. Better is it that thou shouldest not vow, than that thou shouldest vow and not pay." Eccles. 5:4, 5.

CHAPTER XXII

A Sign to Them That Believe Not

PAUL says: "In the law it is written, With men of other tongues and other lips will I speak unto this people; and yet for all that they will not hear Me, saith the Lord. Wherefore tongues are for a sign, not to them that believe, but to them that believe not." 1 Cor. 14:21, 22.

God has been speaking throughout the Pentecostal outpouring, but, alas, many stop their ears and will not heed His last-day message. But there are instances of some being arrested as on the day of Pentecost, through hearing the speaking in tongues. The speaking in tongues has proved a sign to them that signified the presence of God. In response to the question, "What is the use of tongues?" Mrs. G. R. Polman of Holland says: "I could fill the whole day in reporting what they have done for us in Amsterdam. The first time I spoke in tongues it brought the whole congregation to the dust, for sin was revealed. Men and women, whom we held in high esteem, found themselves out to be abominable sinners. Interpretation often was given to help sinners to fear God and to cry for salvation. Many have been saved, cleansed and sanctified in this way."

The following incident took place in the early days of the revival: Lewis Rudner, a Jew born in Austria, twenty-six years of age, related these facts to the editor of the *Household of God* in April, 1907, in the city of Oakland, California:

"I was born in Austria, of Jewish parents, and spoke the Hebrew language from childhood. I have been in America about six years. A rich uncle in Seattle, Washington, wrote to me to come and clerk in his pawn shop. I went, and was working for him.

"On a Thursday last winter I was passing a mission building on Seventh Avenue, in that city, on a rainy day. I saw a sign *'Welcome'* over the door, and entered to get out of the rain, not knowing what was being done inside. All were kneeling in prayer. Shortly I heard a man (Brother Junk, a preacher) repeating the fifty-third chapter of Isaiah in the Hebrew language. A woman (Brother Junk's wife) was singing a song in Hebrew, which Jews sing on their New Year's Day. A little girl, twelve years old, on her knees, was repeating the twelfth Psalm in Hebrew Then she repeated the sixth Psalm. A colored woman (Mrs. Miller of Los Angeles) commenced repeating part of the thirty-third chapter of Jeremiah in Hebrew. A Scandinavian woman (Mrs. Olson) spoke in Hebrew pointing at me, telling me that I was lost, and urging me to turn to God.

"All this was during the prayer service, and I found tears flowing down my cheeks. After prayer they all commenced singing the song, 'The Old Fountain,' which broke my heart. Hearing all this Hebrew talk, I commenced to wonder where I was. I saw I was not in a synagogue and the people were not Jews.

"Then Brother Junk preached in English from the text: 'His blood be upon us and upon our children,' and said that great darkness fell on the earth when Jesus died on the cross, that Jerusalem was destroyed soon after, and the Jews scattered throughout the world, and have had no rest since.

"After the preaching Mrs. Olson testified in Hebrew and told me to read Luke 14, Romans 5:8 and Romans 3:26. The twelve-year-old girl testified in Hebrew and asked me again and again where I would spend eternity. This brought me into great concern about my soul. The altar call was made and Brother Junk came to me and taking me by the hand, urged me to come and be saved.

"I asked Junk if he were a Hebrew, to which he replied, 'I am a German.' I asked Junk if he had studied Hebrew, and he replied 'No.' 'How then can you speak Hebrew?' I asked. Junk asked, 'Did I speak Hebrew?' 'Yes,' I said, 'just such Hebrew as persons speak who are born and raised among the Hebrews in my country.'

"Then Junk told me that it was God who was speaking to me and saying just what He wanted to say without the speaker knowing what was said. I asked him who these other persons were who had spoken in Hebrew, pointing them out. I asked if the girl were his daughter and desired to speak with them. Brother Junk called the woman to come and sit down by me, and immediately the Spirit of the Lord was upon them and they all began to speak in Hebrew, urging me to give my heart to God and be saved.

"This sudden outburst startled me. They urged me to kneel down and pray, but all spoke in Hebrew, not knowing a word they spoke. They dropped on their knees and all commenced to pray in Hebrew. Then I fell down and commenced praying in Hebrew, crying to God for mercy. This lasted over an hour; I was crying so loud I could be heard a block away. All were praying in Hebrew. I was converted to God and am now a happy Christian."

Another instance of a Hebrew being saved through the ministry of speaking in tongues is that of Dr. Florence Murcutt, an Australian Jewess who was brought up in the Jewish faith. She was taught by her mother that she must never believe that Jesus was the Son of God. Having an inquiring mind, on the death of her mother, she read through the whole Word of God from cover to cover in six weeks. She first came in contact with the Pentecostal people in Vancouver, British Columbia, and heard Mrs. Lillian Garr speak in tongues and interpret the message. She was convinced that there was something very real about this manifestation of the Spirit.

She came in contact with some Christians and asked them why the signs that were promised were not following in these days. She was told, "These are different days to the apostolic days. The signs do not follow today." She would invariably reply, "You speak like my Jewish mother. When I would ask her why we did not have sacrifices today as in days of old, she would tell me that the times have changed and that I must not speak of these things. And when I speak to Christians about these things that happened in apostolic days, I am told the same thing—that times are changed. What am I to believe?"

There was a desire for the truth in Dr. Murcutt's heart and she would attend different churches. She even went to Oberammergau to see the Passion Play. She states, however, that the very moment she heard the speaking in tongues she was convinced it was of God.

She was traveling down from Vancouver to Los Angeles and stopped off at Portland, Oregon, where there was a Pentecostal camp meeting. She saw the signs following. There were many saved and healed and filled in this meeting. One night she stood close by the tent where there were ten Canadians. She was conversing with them when one Canadian brother, who was under the anointing of God, began to speak to her, addressing her in the purest Parisian French, a language with which she was familiar. Dr. Murcutt says: "He told me I was a sinner and that I could be saved only one way, and that was through Jesus Christ who is the Way, the Truth, and the Life. He told me that Jesus was the Door and that I would have to enter by that door. He told me that He is the Bread of life and that I would have to be sustained by Him. As he spoke he urged me to yield to God. This brother was absolutely unfamiliar with Parisian French but was speaking entirely under the anointing of God. He told me that this Pentecostal outpouring was of God and that it was the Latter Rain which God had promised to send in the last days. The Spirit through him gave me a full revelation of the truth concerning the Trinity.

"The power of God was so heavy that it was felt by those who were worshiping in the tent. We talked for over an hour in Parisian French. When I said anything that tallied with the Word of God, the Spirit of God in this brother rejoiced. When I said anything contrary to the Word of God, the Spirit of God in him would moan. As a result of this manifestation of God's presence, I went on my knees and yielded to God." Dr. Murcutt after a short while gave up her practice and devoted the remainder of her life to missionary work.

The following incident is told by Maurice Kullman, a Hebrew who was formerly a Baptist minister. He says: "Wife and I were conducting a mission among the Jews of St. Louis, Missouri. We were backed by some wealthy people in whose eyes Pentecost was a shame and disgrace. Wife, like most women, was more susceptible to spiritual things than I was, and so in course of time she received the precious Baptism in the Holy Spirit. I thought she had lost her mind and I became bitterly opposed to the precious truth. She conducted prayer meetings at our home and I remember how I used to walk out of the house in anger over her inviting Pentecostal workers into our home.

"One night I thought I would stay to hear them pray and try to pray with them. Now my wife is a converted Roman Catholic. I have thanked the Lord many times for inducing me to stay at home that night. As my wife prayed she began to lose her natural language and began to speak in the pure Hebrew tongue. She quoted Deuteronomy 6:5, 6: 'Thou shalt love the Lord thy God with all thine heart, and with all thy soul, and with all thy might. And these words,

which I command thee this day, shall be in thine heart.'
I thought that she had picked up the quotation. Later I
asked her to repeat it, but try as she would she couldn't
repeat those two verses in Hebrew. I asked her if she
knew what she said, and she replied, 'No.' I quoted it
for her and have asked her to repeat it a hundred times
or more since then and she has never been able to say
it after me till this day.

"I remember as she quoted it she emphasized the
Hebrew word 'bekol' which means 'all' in our English
language, just as if she were giving me an admonition
for not loving the Lord as I should. She articulated
the Hebrew guttural sounds perfectly which none but
a Hebrew can.

"This heavenly message convinced me, a converted
Jew and a Baptist preacher, that God was still doing
the supernatural in this day and time. Not very long
after that I also spoke in tongues when I received
the Baptism in the Holy Spirit, and many are the
times that the Spirit has spoken through me in the
same marvelous manner as He did through my wife
that night."

The following testimony is given by Mrs. Carrie
Judd Montgomery, editor of *Triumphs of Faith*.
"Soon after receiving the fullness of the Holy Spirit
in June, 1908, I was filled with a remarkable love for
the Chinese people. There has been in my heart a great
interest in them for many years, but this was something
different—an outgoing of the Spirit in divine love
toward them, and intercession which was wonderful.
I had been speaking in several different 'tongues,' some
of which sounded like the languages of India, but about
this time I was conscious of speaking another language,
which seemed like Chinese. As time went on a number
of different Chinese people who heard me speaking
assured me that I was talking in Chinese. I was led
to ask the Lord to raise up a credible witness, for the
glory of God, to verify this Chinese language, if such
it were.

"At Beulah Park, Ohio, I met Mrs. Harriette Shimer, a missionary of the Society of Friends, who had been working in China for the past seven years. This dear sister did not know much about the Pentecostal work and was opposed to what she had heard of it. She was interested, however, after I told her of my personal experience. I invited her to stay that evening to a little meeting in an upper room, where we had arranged to pray for some hungry souls. She accepted this invitation. The meeting was very quiet and the power and presence of God pervaded the room in a wonderful way. Presently Mrs. Shimer heard someone singing in Chinese and opened her eyes to see who it could be. She was amazed to find it was I through whom the Spirit was giving utterance in this way. I perceived upon her countenance conflicting emotions, great awe, consternation, and bewilderment. So troubled did she look that in the midst of the singing I smiled at her to make her know that all was well. She said afterwards that this smile did much to reassure her, for she saw I was not unconscious or in a trance, but in perfect possession of all my senses.

"As it was too late after the meeting for Mrs. Shimer to return to her home in Cleveland, I offered to share my room and bed with her. We slept quietly for three or four hours, then both became wide awake. The sweet melting power of the Lord was upon me, and His music was in my innermost soul, and it welled up in song (not loud enough to disturb other sleepers near) in a language that did not sound to me like the Chinese. Mrs. Shimer, however, assured me that I was singing another Chinese dialect to one of the tunes often heard in China. The manifestation again seemed so marvelous as to produce a degree of fear in this dear sister and she asked if she could light the lamp to look at me, to which I consented. She placed her hand upon me and made the remark that my flesh was soft and warm and not rigid and cold, as she supposed it might be under such extraordinary manifestations.

As soon as her fear was removed this dear one (who had been sweetly taught of God in the past) began to recognize the presence and power of God which brooded over us both, and to yield to it herself, so that her own soul began to receive great blessing. The rest of the night at intervals I sang and talked Chinese in different dialects which she recognized, but toward morning she said, 'You have not yet spoken in Mandarin, which is my dialect.' I replied, 'I will ask the Lord to let me speak in the Mandarin,' to which she answered, 'No, I have had all I can stand for one night.'

"The next morning we were gathered again in a precious little meeting, when I began to sing in the Mandarin, at which Mrs. Shimer interrupted me with: 'Do you know what you are saying?' and gave the translation. After this, again and again the Spirit gave utterance in the Mandarin, which of course, was always easily translated by Mrs. Shimer, as she said I spoke it much more perfectly than she could, although she had been in the country seven years. Sometimes the most difficult Chinese songs were reproduced note by note with mighty ascriptions of praise to God. Sometimes the soul of this dear sister was so melted by the power of the message that she wept, and sometimes she was so filled with heavenly joy that she laughed with delight. Twice the Lord gave me interpretation before she could translate it, and in each instance the interpretation was verified by Mrs. Shimer. It is impossible for me to describe the great joy and the adoration to God which accompanies these manifestations of the Spirit's indwelling. When so many are yielding themselves to the enemy that he may use their lives and their lips to carry out his evil purposes, how blessed it is to feel one's self a channel for the divine Spirit to flow through and speak through as He will."

Mrs. Shimer has written the following corroboration of the above: "I desire to testify to what I have witnessed of the wonderful power of God as manifested in the gift of tongues. At a Christian Alliance convention I met some Spirit-filled women who had received this gift, and in a prayer meeting which was held for the healing of some sick ones, I heard Mrs. Carrie Judd Montgomery of Oakland, California, praying in the Chinese language. I could understand her, because of my years of mission work in China. Some weeks following this convention it was my privilege to be much associated with Mrs. Montgomery, and she repeatedly prayed and sang in Chinese, the tunes themselves sometimes being distinctly Chinese. My astonishment at this marvelous working of God was greater than the joy that came to me at the quickening of my own spiritual life through this experience. Previous to this I had been much prejudiced against what is known as the Pentecostal movement, but through God's direct teaching and leading I cannot but believe that God is ready to bestow the fullness of His Holy Spirit, and this Pentecostal gift of tongues upon His wholly surrendered children. So I am constrained by my love and loyalty to Him to give this testimony, that others prejudiced as I was may be encouraged to take God at His Word and press on to receive all of His fullness.—(Signed) Harriette M. T. Shimer."

Mrs. Montgomery further writes: "The Holy Spirit has spoken several languages through me which have been understood by people who are acquainted with those languages." We give one instance of this. In the year 1916, Mrs. Mary Norton of Benares, India, was in America on furlough. She was sick in body and Mrs. Montgomery prayed for her. While she was praying she began to speak in tongues and Mrs. Norton said, "Oh, you are speaking a language of India and you are saying: 'Take, my little one; take.'" Mrs. Norton heeded the message and began to "take" from the Lord and was soon restored to perfect health.

Mrs. Montgomery writes: "At one time in Mexico Mr. Montgomery and Mrs. C. Nuzum saw a young Yaqui Indian girl converted and filled with the Spirit

and heard her talk in English and in French, although
she knew not a word of either language. Although
she had been entirely ignorant of salvation previous
to that time, and had known nothing about the coming
of the Lord, yet they heard her giving a wonderful
prophetic message in English and she was speaking
about the soon coming of the Lord."

Frank Trevitt, an English missionary to China, told
of a similar instance where the Spirit of God fell upon
a Chinese girl. She began to speak in English and
gave a remarkable prophetic message on the soon
coming of our Lord Jesus Christ. This girl was
absolutely ignorant of the English language.

Pastor T. B. Barratt of Norway writes: "I could
relate numerous instances of the speaking in known
tongues through the Holy Spirit. Take that in India,
which was related by several missionaries, and about
which I obtained a written statement from the missionary on the station where it took place. Two native
women, one deaf and dumb from childhood, had often
spoken in the Hindustani language perfectly as the
Spirit gave utterance, although they were absolutely
unacquainted with that language.

"A Baptist preacher in my hearing related in a
meeting in Norway, that a lady, not knowing English,
had spoken perfectly in this language, and given a clear
translation of what she had been speaking. In Copenhagen, Denmark, a man who opposed this movement
was convinced that God was in it, when he one day heard
his sister praise God in the Spanish language and give
a correct interpretation of what she was speaking, although she did not know the language. He himself
had been in Spain and knew Spanish. He gave himself fully to God.

"Mr. Gilbert E. Farr relates that when he attended
a mission in Houston, Texas, a young man spoke for
five minutes or more in a foreign language, under the
power of the Spirit. When the invitation was given
for seekers to come forward to the altar, a Mexican

came forward, weeping and in broken English, said: 'I sinner, I Catholic, I no Christian ... Woman spoke Spanish, said I sinner, no Christian, God said I repent. Pray I be saved.' They prayed with the man and he became happy, and gave good evidence of salvation.

"Mr. Farr states furthermore that he, in Pueblo, Colorado, saw more forcibly the value of tongues in foreign languages than in any other mission visited. At the Bessemer Steel Mills several thousand men are employed, and more than twenty nationalities are represented among them. As most of them are Roman Catholics, the priests forbid them to attend the meetings. But they will stand on the street and listen to the workers as they sing and speak in tongues. There were Greeks, Poles, Russians, Chinese, etc., and to each of these groups messages were given in tongues, perfectly understood by them so that it was here as in Jerusalem on the day of Pentecost. These different nationalities heard the messages of God in their own language wherein they were born.

"Dr. A. B. Simpson of New York related a case in his paper, of a lady, the wife of a Baptist pastor, who under power of the Spirit was able to converse in the German language, although she had not known that language before.

"In Sweden a Lutheran pastor lectured on his visit to Christiania, after the outbreak of the revival there. He stated that he personally heard a young woman speak the Finnish language perfectly, when she was under the power of the Spirit. He asked her several questions in that language afterwards, but she could not answer a word, only when the power of the Holy Spirit was upon her. He had labored several years in Finland and knew the language well."

The following is taken from the *Chicago Inter-Ocean:* "Irene Piper, only ten years old, converses with a Chinaman, and he understands her. The mother of the youthful prodigy also talks in an unknown tongue, and a friend is able to translate the words. The first manifestation the little girl had of her remarkable gift was on November 4, 1907, when she suddenly spoke to those about her in a strange language, and cried out: 'Jesus is coming soon.'

"Mrs. Jennie Willie, at whose house the little girl was visiting, took her to a Chinese laundry, and she immediately entered into conversation with the China-man, asking him to come to her church and accept sal-vation. Moy Lee, to whom the child talked, declared that her accent was perfect, and that her forms of speech were so exact that ten years' study would not give the average Occidental such knowledge of the language."

The following incident is taken from the *Bride-groom's Messenger:* "During a New York convention a former student of the Missionary Institute, now the wife of a Baptist minister, and herself a useful evan-gelist, was present throughout the services. During the second week of the convention she was confined to her room for a short time with illness, and sent for Pastor E. D. Whiteside and another Alliance friend to pray with her. After prayer, while thanking the Lord for her healing, she was suddenly prostrated for a few moments with the power of the Holy Spirit, and be-came apparently lost in God for a short time. Im-mediately afterwards she began to praise God with great fervor in the German language which she never had spoken or understood. Writing from Newark, N. J., she says:

"'I want to tell you something for the glory of God. When I got to Newark, Tuesday morning, my sister-in-law said: "Come into the kitchen and let me introduce you to my washwoman. She is a German and a Christian." When I went in she spoke to me in German. I understood at once, and answered her in German. She said, "Oh, can you speak German?" and I told her I could. You don't know how strange this seems to me. It humbles me in spirit.'"

In 1907, Charles S. Leonard, a Baptist minister of

Springfield, Massachusetts, received the Baptism in the Holy Ghost. In *Word and Work* of May, 1907, we read: "Brother Leonard has spoken in tongues in several places and interpreted. He has spoken in several languages but usually in Chinese or Hebrew. Someone suggested that he should go to a Chinaman and see if he could understand. So taking a witness along with him, he went to his laundryman, Chin Toy, and talked, asking if he understood, and Chin Toy nodded assent. As Brother Leonard waxed eloquent, Chin Toy looked at him in amazement, unable to comprehend by what power he had come into possession of his language."

Mrs. Woodbury, of the Christian and Missionary Alliance, in her report of the work in Shanghai, tells of the following miraculous answer to prayer: "A substitute worker in Beulah chapel has been provided. A handsome, cultured student, related to a Mandarin in Szechuen, was taking a holiday stroll in Shanghai. Way down the road he came upon a party of Pentecostal missionaries, Mr. and Mrs. Hansen and others, who were speaking and singing on a street corner. Mrs. Hansen spoke in Chinese, yet did not know her own message. The astonished student, drawing near, heard his own Mandarin tongue, and was filled with wonder that the lady did not do this by her own power but by the power of God. He yielded himself to God and in due course was baptized. At just the right time he suddenly appeared in Beulah chapel. As Mr. Wanghow Chang told his story, after the meeting on Sunday, we felt that he was the one God had sent to teach a part of each day in Leigh's place, and leave Dr. Wong free for translation. So it proved. He is in the vacant place and divides his time between Mr. Hansen as interpreter and Beulah chapel."

Speaking of how the Lord gave her the Chinese language, Mrs. Sophie Hansen of Shanghai, referred to above, who has since gone to be with the Lord, said: "Before I received the Baptism in the Holy

Spirit, the Lord told me that I should ask Him for the Chinese language to be given me through the Holy Ghost. We then had the call to China for three years. When I received the Baptism in Chicago, I spoke in Chinese, and it was understood by a returned missionary. We were sent to China the same year. When we had been there six months, one Sunday morning, in 1908, I was moved by the power of the Holy Ghost to speak to the Chinese in their own language. This was outside of the door, on the street. We had a wonderful time. Some who listened had tears in their eyes; it was spoken to them with such love and tenderness of the Spirit. Crowds came to see what had happened, because they knew I could not speak Chinese. Students from schools near by came to investigate, and were heart-broken when the Lord spoke to them. I was afterwards led to go from street to street, into their houses and opium dens and idol temples. I also went up the river, where thousands live in small boats. God was with us in power. Souls have been brought into the kingdom through this gift, and it remains just as bright today, and there is discerning with it. Whenever evildoers or hypocrites come around, the Lord lets us know what is going on, and points out the person. I can speak it at any time, but the gospel only. It is not given me to speak earthly things, and I cannot read or write it."

The following is the testimony of Pastor A. G. Ward. These instances took place in the city of Toronto while he was pastor of the Christian Workers' Pentecostal church. He says: "A lady living out of town heard that her sister was attending our services, and having learned that the Pentecostal people were a very fanatical company, she felt bad to think her sister had gotten in among them. Later she came to Toronto to visit her sister and on Sunday morning decided she would come to our church to see for herself what the Pentecostal folk were like. During the services I spoke at some length in other tongues, not understanding what

I said. But this lady at the close of the service informed her sister that she had understood the message in tongues, the preacher having spoken in the Scandinavian language. This was so convincing to the lady that she no longer felt bad that her sister was attending our church."

Pastor Ward further states: "Some years later a German lady, who had recently come from the old country to visit her son, and who was a Roman Catholic, came to our church because she wished to see where her son worshiped. Poor old soul, I felt sorry for her for she did not understand the service at all. But the Lord accommodated Himself to that lady and let the preacher speak in tongues. When the service was over she seemed so happy. She said: 'My boy, the preacher talked this morning in German and told me about the coming of Jesus and said He would be back soon.'"

Arthur W. Frodsham states: "Some Persians came into my office and I spoke in tongues before them. One said I was speaking their ancient language. He said I was speaking the ancient Chaldean or Syrian Chaldean and he could understand me. It was their religious language. Later on, visiting this Persian when he was sick, I was praying in a general way and then went off into tongues. At the close I asked him if he understood and he smilingly replied: 'Yes. You were praying for me, that I might be more true to God, more faithful in reading the Bible and praying.'

"At another time in conversation with this Persian, I spoke in tongues. He understood what was said and interpreted it into modern Persian to his companion who was sitting close by. He tells me that probably the language I am speaking is that which was spoken by Abraham.

"I talked in Hebrew to some Jews in Toronto and Chinese to a Chinaman in Ottawa. I spoke to several Persians in Chicago and elsewhere and they understood. In conversation in English with a Persian brother I asked him how he came to be converted and in this way of faith. He said: 'Because I heard a message in tongues telling me to repent. I didn't. I came back again and heard a message to the same effect in tongues; then I repented and got saved.' "

The following instances are related by Mrs. W. D. Yerger of Los Angeles, California: "In a campaign at Phoenix, Arizona, only a few remained till the midnight hour. The evangelist was dealing at the altar with a notorious character of the town. Suddenly a Swedish woman on the front seat jumped up under the power of the Holy Spirit and walking across the front space gave a message in tongues, and returned to her seat.

"There were three Apache Indian girls in the back. One of them pricked up her ears on hearing the woman talk. A second time the Swedish sister was impelled to jump up and give a message. This time the Indian girl came half way up the aisle, her eyes wide open with wonder. A third time the woman jumped up and repeated the message. The Indian girl came to the front and in awe-stricken tones said: 'This woman speaks my language. She says Jesus is coming soon. Indian girl better get ready.' She did, and helped to get the other two ready also.

"A friend of mine, recently baptized, answered a knock at the door. It was a foreign peddler, Russian Jew I believe. Opening her mouth to speak, she was amazed to hear a strange language pour forth. The man looked in startled wonder and said in broken English, 'Where did you learn that language?' She said, 'I don't know what language that was. I never learned it.' He said, 'That is my language. God is speaking to me,' and he walked slowly away.

"A friend in Los Angeles told me that when he was receiving the Baptism, the Holy Spirit was speaking very fluently. There were three young men in an adjoining room with the door open. One of them rushed in and at the conclusion said, 'Do you know what you are speaking?' 'No,' he replied. 'You were talking in my language, Hindustani. It was a message to me.' Shortly after this the young man went to the mission fields.

"Brother Anglin of the House of Onesiphorus, China, told me when in my home a few years ago, that many of the Chinese children who do not know a word of English, when receiving the Baptism, say in perfect English, 'Jesus is coming soon.' He said it always rejoices his heart to hear this in English."

Howard Carter, the principal of the Bible and Missionary Training School of London, England, relates the following: "In the People's Hall, Lee, in the southeast of London, where my brother and I have ministered the Word of life for some years, I had a remarkable experience when praying for the sick. A Welshman, with many others, had come to the front for healing. I prayed with two or three, and then laid my hands upon this young man. He was suffering from deafness, and after prayer I asked him if he could hear any better, and he replied that he could not. I prayed with some others, and returned to this young man, and waited for some moments until the power of the Spirit came upon me. Then I laid my hands upon him and was moved to speak in tongues while doing so. Immediately his ear opened, and he could hear the faintest whisper, and the ticking of my clock. With tears streaming down his face, he gave testimony to the gracious healing.

"The details are briefly these: While praying with him I had spoken in the Welsh language through the Spirit and uttered the words, 'It shall be done tonight.' Immediately his ear opened. I did not know that I had spoken in Welsh, not knowing that language, until he bore testimony to the fact. How wonderful are God's ways!

"One time at a convention in Sunderland, a brother under the power of the Spirit gave a peculiar cry and then shortly afterwards gave a message in tongues. Mrs. Crisp interpreted the message. It happened that in that convention there was a missionary from the Congo, Alma Doering. She testified that the language spoken was that of the Kifioti tribe of the Congo. She said that in the Congo sentries were put at certain places and when an important message was to be sent from one tribe to another they would send out a warning note. It was a call to attention. This brother under the power of the Spirit had given the call to attention before the message came forth. She further stated that the interpretation embodied the message that he had given in this language of the Congo."

Mr. Carter relates an incident concerning a sister whom he met at a convention in Birmingham, England. She was called to visit a dying Chinaman, who was absolutely friendless. She came under the power of the Spirit and prayed for him in the Chinese language and he perfectly understood. As a result of her ministration to him in the Chinese language this man was blessedly converted. She further told of speaking to two Japanese infidels under the power of the Spirit in their language. One became broken and yielded to the Lord but the other did not yield.

Miss Jessie C. Burgess of Bushey, Herts, England, relates the following incident that took place while she was living in the city of Toronto, Canada. At the time Mr. and Mrs. George A. Murray were in charge of a Pentecostal assembly in Toronto. Brother and Sister Murray had spent eleven years in Palestine and had learned to speak Arabic. One day Mrs. Murray prayed: "Lord, if You would only let someone speak in Arabic a little, I should be able to interpret what they say!" That evening, when they were gathered at the altar, they sang a song about Calvary. Miss Burgess was then under the power of the Spirit and talking in tongues which she did not understand. Suddenly there came a cry in the Arabic language, "They crucified Him! They crucified Him!" Mrs. Murray recognized it at once. After a little she cried out again, "They crucified Him and He died." **Once** more, after an interval she cried, "They crucified Him and He died, but He liveth!" Mrs. Murray translated these messages from Arabic to English.

The following incident is related by Miss Zelma Argue after a campaign in Cleveland, Ohio. "The meeting was held in a theater; at the back of the stage the seekers for the Baptism tarried. Miss Willa Lowther from China was attending the meeting and was in the tarrying room. Over in China she had heard a young man, who could not speak or pronounce any words in the English language, speaking in a clear English tongue and saying, 'Jesus is coming soon, get ready.' Miss Lowther wanted to hear someone in America, when receiving the Baptism, speak the Cantonese tongue. At this meeting one woman at the back of the stage began to speak plainly in the Cantonese dialect with which Miss Lowther was familiar. She was saying, 'Flee from sin. Sin is separating you from God.' This sister was evidently preaching in Chinese in the Spirit."

The following incident is given by Miss Mollie Cressey of New Zealand: "For some months there has been a deep cry in my soul for the Maoris of New Zealand, and I believe God will shortly open the way for me to devote all my time to the natives. God assured and encouraged me in this by wonderfully blessing the efforts of myself and companion when we visited them at Wairaupah. We found these dear Maori people very receptive to the Word, and most reverent where spiritual things are concerned, and they never tire of our singing hymns to them. God gave me wonderful liberty in the first meeting we held there. The power was mightily upon me, and I knew the Spirit was trying to speak through me in tongues; but fearing lest these people would not understand, I tried to resist and hold back the message. But God dealt with me in such a way that I had to yield, with the result that God spoke through me a message in their own language. The effect of this was apparent at once upon the people, although I had given no interpretation.

"After this incident I yielded to the prompting of the Holy Spirit through me in the following services, and each time God manifested Himself and spoke more deliberately to them in their own language. At our last service of this first visit, most of the message was delivered to them in the Maori tongue, and the moment God spoke in this way, one fine Maori man, who had been earnestly drinking in the message, was seen with tears streaming down his face, and was so broken down that he went out. We felt led to give an altar call on this occasion, with the result that five hands were immediately raised to accept our Jesus as their own personal Saviour, and eight stood up to reconsecrate themselves to God. While speaking in the Maori in tongues, the blessing in my own soul was joy unspeakable and full of glory."

W. F. P. Burton, one of the founders of the Congo Evangelistic Mission, tells how on one occasion during an open-air meeting at Lytham in Lancashire, the power of God fell on one of the company and she began to speak in a strange language. As she spoke he found he could understand all she was saying. A solemn silence fell on the crowd as the woman spoke with other tongues and Mr. Burton followed with the interpretation in English. Directly the speakers had finished, a big middle-aged man stepped into the ring of listeners and, falling on his knees, cried mightily to God to save him. He had been a prominent tailor in Lytham, but had lost practically everything through drink, but here he was down at the foot of the Cross seeking mercy as the result of that message, every word of which, he afterwards stated, went straight to his heart.

Another instance is given of a meeting in Preston, again in an open-air meeting. Mr. Burton was the one who spoke with other tongues and the interpretation was given by P. N. Corry. The unction of the Spirit was upon the speakers, and the crowd was hushed to silence as God spoke. When the speakers had finished, a woman instantly pushed her way through the crowd into the center of the ring where she fell on her knees sobbing for forgiveness.

Instances of dual interpretation illustrate the supernatural working of the Holy Spirit in this revival. Mr. Heitrarchy of Ceylon went to Germany to hold some campaigns, but not knowing the German language, he asked Mr. Arthur Booth-Clibborn to accompany him to translate the messages from English to German. At one meeting a German brother spoke in tongues under the anointing of the Spirit and Mr. Heitrarchy, having the gift of interpretation, gave the interpretation in English. At the same time one of the German brethren gave the interpretation in German. The two interpretations were identical.

We heard Miss Minnie Abrams relate the following. She was in a meeting at Mukti, India, in the early days of this outpouring and heard a message given in tongues. Immediately the Spirit of God gave her the interpretation in English. She waited for a minute and one of the Indian girls arose and gave the interpretation in Marathi, word for word as she herself had been given it by the Spirit of God.

Mrs. Harry Hulbert of New York City states: "I was one night in the prayer room at Glad Tidings Church in this city. A message was given in tongues. I was in the center of the prayer room and was interested to hear one at one end of the room and another at the other end giving an identical interpretation."

We take the following report from the *Latter Rain Evangel:* "When Dr. Price was speaking on one occasion in Spokane, Washington, the power of the Spirit came upon him and he began to speak in Chinese. For nearly half an hour the message poured forth. Sitting on the platform was a Presbyterian missionary returned from China who arose and gave the interpretation, but from his knowledge of the Chinese language. There were eleven ministers present and he convinced them that the message was from God. He said he had never heard such pure Chinese spoken as was given under the anointing of the Spirit."

John H. Carter wrote to us early in 1927: "We had a blessed New Year's convention at Edinburgh. Mr. Burton was there from the Congo. Suddenly, while Donald Gee was praying with a brother seeking the Holy Spirit, Mr. Burton heard Mr. Gee say, in pure Kiluba, 'O this is good food.' He said that a native could not have said it better."

Clinton H. Patterson of Pomona, California, states: "In one local, midweek service at which I was present, a stranger entered the room. His hair was disheveled. He seemed restless and out of place. Near the close of the meeting, the pastor gave a message in tongues. I do not remember that the message was interpreted. When the invitation was given this man was persuaded to go forward and give his heart to God. In a few minutes he was speaking in tongues.

"Service ended, he asked the pastor if he understood the Russian language and was told that he did not. The stranger then told the pastor that his message was in the Russian language and was a warning to him to be reconciled to God. He was a member of a gang that had come to the city for the purpose of robbing a bank that night. He came into the church to escape the police until time to begin their operations.

"The next night he came again to the church and we had never before seen so great a change in a man in one day. His hair was combed, he was smiling; a new creature in Christ Jesus. Shall we say that this work of grace and miracle of salvation was of the devil if the message in tongues was not interpreted? The fact that the message was given in the Russian tongue was doubtless the thing that convinced the man that God was speaking to him."

Bert Webb, now Superintendent of our Southern

Missouri District, received the Baptism in a meeting at Wellston, Oklahoma. He spoke in tongues at length, and a Pole the following day went to the pastor and said: "I would like to get in touch with that Polish lad who spoke in Polish for so long last night. He spoke of the wonderful works of God and gave a special message to me." The pastor assured him that the young man did not know a word of Polish, that he had been reared in Fayetteville, Arkansas, and that what he spoke must have been the result of the anointing of the Holy Spirit. This miracle had such an effect on that Pole that he yielded his life to God.

Alma Ware Crosby, pastor of Magnolia Park Assembly of God, Beaumont, Texas, writes: "There is a Jewish woman in the hospital, very sick with diabetes. This woman called for me and for prayer, and she professed Christ with her lips, but I was fearful she had not been born again. She was suffering so and would say, 'I am a good woman. Always have been; and I believe Jesus Christ is the Son of God.'

"In my earnest pleading with her about her soul (as it seemed she couldn't forget her foot to think of her soul) I began suddenly speaking in another language. She looked at me surprised and said, 'I understand you. That's the language I spoke back in Rumania, in the old country.' I asked her what I had said and she replied that I had said for her to get her sins forgiven. She called on the Lord then to forgive her sins, and afterwards I began speaking again and she said it was a prayer for God to have mercy on this poor, sick woman.

"You can imagine how real this made the Lord seem to me. He, in His great compassion to win this Jewish woman's soul, used me to speak to her in her mother tongue that she had used as a child. She wanted to know where I learned it and I explained to her that God was performing a miracle to get her sins forgiven."

We could multiply instances of this kind, but we believe we have given sufficient for unprejudiced ones to see that the prophecy of Isaiah, quoted by Paul and referred to in the beginning of this chapter, has been fulfilled; and that with stammering lips and another tongue *God is speaking to His people.* Will you close your ears to His message, or will you give heed?

CHAPTER **XXIII**

Pentecostal Outpourings in History

DURING the past nineteen centuries, in times when the spiritual life ran high, the Holy Spirit has been received just as at Pentecost, with the accompanying manifestation of speaking in tongues.

Irenaeus, who lived from 115 to 202 A. D., was a pupil of Polycarp, who was a disciple of the Apostle John. He wrote (A. D. V. Her. 6, page 6), "We hear many brethren in the Church having prophetic gifts, and speaking in all sorts of languages through the Spirit."

Tertullian, who lived from 160 to 220 A. D., speaks of the spiritual gifts, including the gift of tongues, as being manifested in his day. See Smith's *Dictionary of the Bible,* vol. 4, page 3310.

Justin Martyr, who lived in the same century, writes how in his time the spiritual gifts were active in the Church.

Origen, who lived from 185 to 254 A. D., wrote of the speaking in tongues in his time: "I suppose that he (St. Paul) was made debtor to different nations, because through the grace of the Holy Spirit, he had received the gift of speaking in the languages of all nations; as he himself also saith, 'I speak in tongues more than you all.' Since then anyone receives the knowledge of languages, not for himself but for their sake to whom the gospel is to be preached, he is made debtor to all those of whose language he received the knowledge from God."

According to A. Butler, in his book entitled *Lives of the Saints,* published in 1756, St. Pachomius, who lived 292 to 348 A. D. after seasons of special prayer was able to speak the Greek and Latin languages, which he had never learned, under the power of the Spirit.

Dean Farrar in his book, *Darkness to Dawn,* in which he states: "Even for the minutest allusions and particulars I have contemporary authority," refers to the persecuted Christians in Rome singing and speaking in unknown tongues.

The following is attributed to Augustine in the fourth century: "We still do what the apostles did when they laid hands on the Samaritans and called down the Holy Spirit on them by the laying on of hands. It is expected that converts should speak with new tongues."

Chrysostom, who lived during a part of the fourth and fifth centuries, wrote: "Whoever was baptized in apostolic days, he straightway spake with tongues ... and one straightway spake in the Persian language, another in the Roman, another in the Indian, another in some other tongue, and this made manifest to them that were without that it was the Spirit in the very person speaking." See Smith's *Dictionary of the Bible,* vol. 4, page 3309.

Even in the "dark ages" God gave some gracious revivals. From the twelfth to the fifteenth century there were revivals in Southern Europe in which many spoke in other tongues. Foremost among these revivalists were the Waldenses and Albigenses.

The Encyclopedia Britannica states that the glossolalia (or speaking in tongues) "recurs in Christian revivals of every age, e. g., among the mendicant friars of the thirteenth century, among the Jensenists and early Quakers, the converts of Wesley and Whitefield, the persecuted Protestants of the Cevennes, and the Irvingites" (vol. 27, pages 9 and 10, 11th edition).

In the history of the Christian church by Phillip Schaff, Vol. 1, page 237 of the edition of 1882, he shows that the phenomenon of speaking in tongues reappeared from time to time in seasons of special religious revival, "as among the Camisards and the prophets of the Cevennes in France, among the early Quakers and Methodists, the Readers (followers of Lasare) in Sweden in 1841-1843, in the Irish revivals of 1859, and especially in the 'Catholic Apostolic church,' commonly called Irvingites, from 1831 to 1833, and even to this day."

In this church history it says of Vincent Ferrer who died in 1419, "Spondamus and many others say, this saint was honored with the gift of tongues." This work also tells of Francis Xavier, who died in 1552, that he "is said to have made himself understood by the Hindus without knowing their language." *The Catholic Enclyclopedia* also speaks of his preaching in tongues unknown to him. Xavier was a truly converted man and a most remarkable missionary.

Writing of the revivals among the Huguenots, Pastor A. A. Boddy states: "When Louis XIV of France in 1685 revoked the Edict of Nantes which had given religious liberty, he strove by dragonades to drive Protestants into the Roman Catholic church. The Huguenots were led by John Cavalier, a farmer, into inaccessible mountains. Among these persecuted people were those who spoke in tongues. There are records both by enemies and by friends as to their prophetic gifts.

"Prophets came from the Cevennes to Holland, and on to Germany. At that time among professors and students there was a great receptivity to God's power. In 1714 they brought the gift of tongues and prophecy to Wetterau, near Frankfort-on-Main. Their leaders were an ejected Wurtemburg pastor named Gruber and a Brother Rock, a saddler. They and their 'gifted' followers were called 'the inspired ones of the Wetterau.' "

J. J. Gorres wrote in 1862: "This gift, which the apostles received at the day of Pentecost, we find again later among the hermits of the desert. Thus it is related of St. Pachomius who, wishing to speak with a brother who knew only the Roman language, of which he himself was ignorant, received the power after having prayed three hours. This gift is reproduced often in modern times, though many times a supernatural gift has been confounded with that which was only the effect of a natural aptitude.... But it is impossible to attribute to a natural aptitude that which is told of Ange Clarenus, who received in 1300, during Christmas night, knowledge of the Greek language. It is related in Chapter II of the second book of the *Life of St. Dominick* that this saint, going from Toulon to Paris and having arrived at Pierre d'Amont, passed the night in prayer in the Notre Dame Church of the place with the brother Bertrand, his traveling companion. The next morning as they went on their way together, they encountered some Germans who were traveling like them.... He set himself then to prayers, and commenced immediately to speak German to the great astonishment of these strangers; and for four days more he discoursed with them concerning the Lord Jesus. When they arrived at Orleans, the Germans, quitting them, commended themselves to their prayers. The same thing came to the saint at another time under similar circumstances.

"We have above stated the proofs of this same gift in St. Vincent Ferrier.... St. Francis Xavier spoke the languages of people to whom he announced the gospel as easily as if he was born among them. Often when he preached at the same time to men of different nations, each understood in his language that which caused veneration for him, and gave a singular authority to his work. The same thing is told of St. Louis Bertrand and of Martin Valentine. Jean of St. Francis also obtained from God in prayer the knowledge of the Mexican tongue, and immediately set himself to preaching in this language, to the great astonishment of all hearers.

"This gift was also accorded to St. Stephen in his missions in Georgia; so that he spoke Greek, Turkish, and Armenian so fluently that natives held him in admiration. It is also said of St. Colette that she had the gift of tongues; and among those which she learned in this manner Latin and German are cited. The Abbe Tritheme reports the same thing of the Abbess Elizabeth. A French woman named Marguerite came one day to see St. Claire of Monte Falcone, who spoke French with her a long time, although she had never learned this language. The blessed Jeanne of the Cross had the gift when she was in ecstasy; and she was able to communicate in different languages, according to the needs of her auditors, the light which she received from on High. Two Mohammedans who could not decide to embrace Christianity were brought to her one day. She had an ecstasy, and spoke Arabic with them; so that they finished by demanding baptism. Jeanne instructed them later in her ecstasy of the truths of the faith."

In this same book we read that God first communicated the gift of tongues to Francis Xavier when preaching in Travancore. "He spoke very well the language of those barbarians without having learned it. . . . At Amanguchi, God restored to St. Francis the gift of tongues; for he preached often to the Chinese merchants, who traded there, in their mother tongue, which he had never learned."

In this same book we read of Louis Bertrand, who lived from 1526 to 1581, that he was the recipient of the gifts of tongues, of prophecy, and of miracles. "He is said in three years to have converted 30,000 Indians, of various tribes and dialects, in South America."

At the time when the Huguenots were suffering great persecutions in France, many of them were filled with the Spirit, and the gifts of the Spirit were in manifestation including the gift of tongues. A book was issued in 1749 by the learned Dr. Middleton who discredited the miraculous powers, especially speaking in tongues. He said, "After the apostolic times, there is not, in all history, one instance, either well attested, or even so much as mentioned, of any particular person who had ever exercised that gift (of tongues), or pretended to exercise it in any age or country whatever."

It was left to John Wesley to make a protest against this statement. He wrote: "Sir, your memory fails you again.... It has been heard of more than once, no further off than the valleys of Dauphiny."

In the diary of Thomas Walsh, one of Wesley's foremost preachers, March 8, 1750, the record stands: "This morning the Lord gave me language that I knew not of, raising my soul to Him in a wonderful manner."

In the year 1800, at Saltcoats, on the west coast of Scotland, twin brothers were born, James and George MacDonald. The life story of these brothers was written in a book by Robert Norton, M. D., published in 1840. In the year 1830 both of these brothers were filled with the Holy Ghost. James was the first to receive the Baptism in the Holy Spirit. His sister was apparently in a dying condition, yet so filled at times with the glory of God that "it was as if her own weakness had been altogether lost in the strength of the Holy Ghost. It was while she was in this condition that she prayed that James might be endowed with the power of the Holy Ghost. Almost instantly James calmly said, 'I have it.' The first thing he did was to bid his sister rise from her bed; which she did, being instantly healed. A few evenings after the above occurrence, during a prayer meeting, George, in whom nothing supernatural had ever previously appeared and whose natural caution had made him the last of the family to welcome the supernatural manifestations in others, began suddenly to speak in an unknown tongue. James followed him; and thus commenced that speaking in tongues and prophesying which never afterwards wholly ceased."

At the time that these brothers received the Baptism in the Holy Spirit with signs following, others in Scotland received a like experience. In the *Religious Anecdotes of Scotland,* edited by Wm. Adamson, published in 1893, we read the following: "The intensely devoted and pious Mary Campbell of Gareloch fame, lived at Fernicarry, and was the subject, about the year 1830, of peculiar experiences regarding which there was very great interest excited at the time in the west of Scotland. She with many others believed that the gift of tongues and other special gifts were vouchsafed to the church. On a Sunday evening in the month of March, Mary, in the presence of a few friends, began to utter sounds to them incomprehensible, and believed by her to be tongues such as of old might have been spoken on the day of Pentecost or among the Christians of Corinth."

The following is an account of a miraculous healing of the same woman: "On the Saturday previous to my restoration to health I was very ill, suffering from pain in my chest, and breathless. On the Sabbath I was very ill and lay for several hours in a state of insensibility. Next day I was worse than I had been for several weeks previous, the agony of Saturday excepted. On Tuesday I was no better. On Wednesday I did not feel quite so languid but was suffering from pain from breathing and palpitation of my heart. Two individuals who saw me about four hours before my recovery said that I would never be strong—that I was not to expect a miracle to be wrought upon me. It was not long after until I received dear Brother James MacDonald's letter, giving an account of his sister's being miraculously raised up as in New Testament times; and in which he similarly commanded me to rise and walk also. I had scarcely read the first page when I became quite overpowered, and laid it aside for a few minutes; but I had no rest in my mind until I took it up again and began to read. As I read, every word came home with power, and when I came to the command to arise, it came home with a power which no words can describe; it was to me, indeed, the voice of Christ; it was such a voice as could not be resisted. A mighty power was instantaneously exerted upon me. I felt as if I had been lifted from off the earth, and all my diseases taken from off me at the voice of Christ. I was verily made in a moment to stand upon my feet, leap and walk, sing and rejoice."

Mr. Adamson writes: "Mary Campbell, who before this time had been confined to bed, from this moment without any interval, returned to active life, became, as was natural, the center of double curiosity and interest, speaking, expounding, and giving forth utterances of her power in crowded assemblies, and entering into the full career of a prophetess and gifted person. The MacDonalds, less demonstrative and more homely, went on in their modest way, attracting crowds of observers without being thereby withdrawn from the composed and sober course of their existence; and thus a new miraculous dispensation was to the belief of many inaugurated in all the power of apostolic times by these waters of the west."

The MacDonalds were contemporaries of Edward Irving. In the year 1834, at a time when the Edward Irving church was moving away from its original moorings, George MacDonald wrote to a friend: "At its commencement the work bore every Scriptural mark which could be desired as far as we know, and the Spirit of God among ourselves bore abundant testimony to their having really received the Holy Ghost among them." This is a worth-while testimony to the fact that originally Mr. Irving's church in London was endowed with the miraculous power of the Holy Ghost. The MacDonalds protested that they felt that in Mr. Irving's church "the wrong place was given to the word of prophecy." In making his protest, George MacDonald said, "Is it because I think lightly of the precious gifts of the Holy Ghost? By no means. They are His most precious treasures which He says are for the perfecting of His saints and the edifying of His body; but precious as they are, they can never be to us in the place of His Word."

At an international conference held in England in 1885, Mrs. Michael Baxter, the widow of the late Michael Baxter, the founder of the *Christian Herald* of London and the *Christian Herald* of New York, told of being able to preach for thirty-five minutes in German when she was almost entirely unfamiliar with the language. She was well understood and one soul was converted. She stated, "After that He led me to speak almost every day, and often twice a day to hundreds of people, although when I went into a shop I could not make myself understood, nor could I understand the people."

Some years ago Dr. F. B. Meyer visited Esthonia, one of the Baltic provinces of Russia, where he found some simple peasant congregations of Baptists. He wrote to the *London Christian* of the wonderful work of the Holy Ghost that he saw among them. He stated, "It is very remarkable, at a time when the Lutheran church of this land has lost its evangelistic fervor, and is inclined to substitute forms and rites for the living power of Christ, that God raised up a devoted nobleman, Baron Uxhull, to preach the gospel in all its simplicity, and is renewing among the peasantry those marvelous manifestations which attended the first preaching of the gospel when God bore witness to the message of salvation 'with signs and wonders and gifts of the Holy Ghost.' To have come across a movement like this is intensely interesting. The gift of tongues is heard quite often in the meetings, especially in the villages, but also in the towns. Here at Reval, the pastor of the Baptist church tells me that they often break out in his meetings. They are most often uttered by young women, less frequently by men. When they are interpreted they are found to mean,

'Jesus is coming soon; Jesus is near. Be ready; be
not idle.' When they are heard, unbelievers who may
be in the audience are greatly awed. A gentleman who
was present on one occasion was deeply impressed by
the fact that those who spoke were quite ordinary people until they were uplifted as it were by a trance and
then they spoke with so much fluency and refinement."

H. L. Christopher of New Britain, Connecticut,
writes of a remarkable revival that the Lord gave in
Oslo, Norway, in 1899, in which many Norwegian
people were filled with the Spirit and spoke in tongues
as the Spirit gave them utterance.

CHAPTER XXIV

Is This a Scriptural Revival?

THOSE who have read this book thus far must have been struck with the fact that in the revivals in every country of which we have spoken, the speaking in tongues has been an accompanying phenomenon. Two questions will arise in the hearts of many: First, Is this scriptural? Secondly, What is the use of speaking in tongues?

We shall go to the Word of God for our answer to these questions. In Isaiah 28:11 we read, "For with stammering lips and another tongue will He speak to this people." The question arises, Who is this one referred to here as "He"? The answer will be found in 1 Cor. 14:21 where Paul writes, "In the law it is written, With men of other tongues and other lips will I speak unto this people; and yet for all that will they not hear Me, *saith the Lord.*" This scripture shows us that it is the Lord Himself who is using this means of speaking with other tongues and other lips. This is confirmed by the record of what happened on the day of Pentecost when the hundred and twenty spoke in other tongues *"as the Spirit gave them utterance."* God was speaking through lips of clay by the power of the Holy Ghost in a manner wholly supernatural.

When our Lord Jesus Christ came to this earth, men refused to recognize Him as the Son of God. They closed their eyes to the divine, and only saw the natural, and so they questioned, "Is not this the carpenter's son?" And they rejected and at last crucified the

only begotten Son of God. ⌈Today when the Lord by
the Holy Spirit speaks through human lips, men do
not recognize Him; many go so far as to attribute the
speaking in other tongues entirely to the devil. This
should not surprise us, for did they not call the Master
of the house Beelzebub (Matt. 10:25), and is it any
wonder that they declare that the manifestation of the
Holy Spirit is from the devil? Scripture was fulfilled
when they despised and rejected the Son (Isa. 53:3),
and Scripture is being fulfilled today as men close
their ears to the Lord when He speaks by means of
the Holy Ghost through stammering lips and another
tongue⌉ "yet for all that will they not hear Me, saith
the Lord." 1 Cor. 14:21. It is the day of the rejection
of the Third Person of the blessed Trinity. There were
a few, however, who recognized the Son of God and
believed in Him. And happy is that little flock who
today recognize and welcome the Holy Spirit in His
divers manifestations.

But what is the value of these stammering lips and
other tongues by means of which the Lord declares He
will speak? Isa. 28:11; 1 Cor. 14:21. The Scriptures
themselves answer this question. "To whom He said,
*This is the rest wherewith ye may cause the weary to
rest; and this is the refreshing."* Isa. 28:12. Ruskin
once asked, "What is the greatest need of the people
today?" He answered his own question by declaring
"rest." It is the rest that the Master promised to give
to the weary and heavy laden, and to those who would
take His yoke upon them and learn of Him. Those
who receive the Comforter that He promised to send,
enter into this rest and receive this glorious refreshing.
Take special note that it is the Lord who declares:
"This is the rest ... *this* is the refreshing." This is a
plain statement from God Himself and it should be
sufficient for all.

In the second chapter of Joel there is given the
prediction of a great outpouring of the Spirit of God,
and when the Holy Spirit came upon the waiting hun-

dred and twenty on the day of Pentecost and they were all filled with the Holy Ghost and began to speak in other tongues as the Spirit gave them utterance, Peter declared: *"This is that which was spoken by the prophet Joel; And it shall come to pass in the last days, saith God, I will pour out of My Spirit upon all flesh."* Acts 2:16, 17. Here we learn that in addition to the speaking in tongues being evidence that those who have received the same have entered into God's rest and the refreshing spoken of by Isaiah, it is also the fulfilling of Joel's prophecy of the Spirit's being poured out upon all flesh in the last days. Many have eyes to recognize the very significant evidence forthcoming concerning the restoration of Israel at this time, but how few recognize that at the same time God is bringing about the restoration of His true church, giving to her in these last days what she had at the beginning?

In the record of the outpouring of God's Spirit upon the household of Cornelius, in the tenth chapter of Acts, the Jews, who accompanied Peter to Caesarea were astonished "because that on the Gentiles also was poured out the gift of the Holy Ghost." How did they know that the Holy Ghost had been poured out on these Gentiles? The Scriptures give the answer, *"For* they heard them speak with tongues, and magnify God." The speaking in tongues was conclusive evidence to these Jews that the Holy Ghost had been poured out on the Gentiles.

In the nineteenth chapter of Acts, we read of some disciples at Ephesus who had received partial instructions as to divine things from the lips of Apollos. When Paul visited them he must have been conscious that something was wrong, and so he questioned them: "Have ye received the Holy Ghost since ye believed?" or as the Revised Version has it: **"Did ye receive the Holy Ghost when ye believed?"** They did not start to argue with the Apostle that every disciple has the Holy Ghost as soon as he believes, nor did they endeavor to persuade Paul that what he himself had received was of the devil. They simply declared: "We have not so much as heard whether there be any Holy Ghost." After they were baptized in water, Paul laid his hands on them, and "the Holy Ghost came on them; and they spake with tongues, and prophesied." Acts 19:6. They had the speaking in tongues, and prophecy in addition, when they received the Holy Ghost. This was ample evidence to the Apostle that the Holy Ghost had come to these Ephesians.

Lieutenant Colonel G. MacKinlay has recently written a remarkable book entitled, *Recent Discoveries in St. Luke's Writings,* to show that there is a significant law in Luke's writings, *the law of a threefold mention.* We see this law in the Acts when Luke gives three instances (Acts, 2, 10, and 19) to show when the Holy Ghost came at the beginning He manifested Himself in the speaking in tongues. This threefold witness is sufficient.

After His resurrection, the Lord Jesus Christ appeared unto the eleven and gave them this commandment: "Go ye into all the world, and preach the gospel to every creature. He that believeth and is baptized shall be saved; but he that believeth not shall be damned. And these signs shall follow them that believe; In My name shall they cast out devils; they shall speak with new tongues, etc." We know that this scripture is questioned by some who state very positively that the last part of the sixteenth chapter of Mark is not inspired. God knew that this scripture would be challenged in the last days, and so He let there be a remarkable discovery to confirm the inspiration of this chapter.

Early in the century, a wealthy Detroit merchant, Mr. C. L. Freer, was in Cairo, Egypt, and purchased from an Arab dealer a quantity of Greek manuscript. It was not the tattered fragment of a papyrus roll from the rubbish heap of a lost town, but a volume on vellum that must have been kept intact in a monastery or a tomb. This volume proved to be an ancient copy of the New Testament in Greek. On his return to America, Mr. Freer arranged that at his own expense a sumptuous reproduction of this volume should be gotten out by the University of Michigan, so that he could present an exact copy in facsimile to each of the leading museums in Europe. These copies were sent and one reached the authorities of the British Museum in London, who are custodians of the Codex Alexandrinus, from which the Authorized Version of the Scriptures was translated, and they state that the manuscript purchased by Mr. Freer is as old as or older than the three oldest manuscripts known.

The three oldest manuscripts of the New Testament are the Codex Vaticanus, which is preserved in the Vatican at Rome; the Codex Sinaiticus, which was discovered in the last century and preserved in the Russian capital until it was recently purchased by the British government and taken to England (both of which are supposed to belong to the fourth or fifth centuries); and the Codex Alexandrinus, which was discovered in the early part of the fifth century. The first two codices do not contain verses nine to twenty of Mark 16, but the Codex Alexandrinus does. These words, however, are found in most of the subsequent manuscripts. The Codex Freer contains Mark sixteen, nine to twenty, in full, and also some further words of Christ's which are found in no other known manuscripts of the New Testament, though they were known to the early Father, Jerome, who quoted part of them. Moffatt's translation of the New Testament has these words in full.

So it will be seen that when the words of His Son were being fulfilled, and at the same time challenged by some, it pleased God to let one of the best and oldest manuscripts of the New Testament be discovered, in which these important words of Christ are confirmed. As one has said, "To now question the authority of the last part of Mark sixteen is to be out of date; not to believe these words is to be out of blessing."

In 1 Corinthians 12 we have some instructions concerning the spiritual gifts or "spirituals" of which we should not be in ignorance. We learn here that "the manifestation of the Spirit is given to every man to profit withal." Where the Spirit of God is, He will surely manifest Himself and such manifestations will be given for profit. The nine manifestations of the Spirit's presence, or gifts of the Spirit, are recounted, and we see plainly that the Spirit gives "divers kinds of tongues." Later on we read, "God hath *set* some in the church, first apostles, secondarily prophets, thirdly teachers, after that miracles, then gifts of healings, helps, governments, diversities of tongues." 1 Cor. 12:28. Those who want to eliminate the speaking in tongues would unset and upset what God has *set* in the church.

Later in the chapter the question is put: "Do all speak with tongues?" The inference is that a negative answer is required here. It is perfectly true that all are not endowed with the *gift* of tongues, or the other gifts about which the Apostle is here speaking. But we must remember in this connection the positive declaration of the Lord Jesus Christ when He Himself said concerning the *sign* of speaking in tongues, "These signs shall follow them that believe ... they shall speak with new tongues." Mark 16:17. There is a clear distinction here between a sign that follows them that believe when the Holy Ghost comes in as described in the Acts, and the permanent gift described in this twelfth chapter of First Corinthians.

In the fourteenth chapter of First Corinthians, Paul recounts to us some of the benefits from the speaking in tongues. He says: "He that speaketh in an unknown tongue speaketh not unto men, but unto God: for no man understandeth him; howbeit in the spirit he speaketh mysteries." 1 Cor. 14:2. The child of God is privileged to have speech with God and no man understands this secret speech, for the saint is allowed to speak in the language of divinity—a language unknown to humanity. There is prayer unto God and also speech unto God. When he speaks in an unknown tongue he converses with God Himself. After God created the world we see that He came in the cool of the evening to hold converse with the one He had created. The work of Satan was to stop this converse. Sin was introduced and communion was broken. But God sent His Son and He went to Calvary to bear man's sin. After He died, was buried, rose again and ascended on high He sent the Holy Ghost on the waiting disciples and once more communion was restored. And today those who are cleansed from sin and filled with the Holy Ghost can have part in this restored communion and have converse with God Himself. Our communion with God can be in the "unknown tongue" or can be "with the understanding." 1 Cor. 14:13-15. Men consider it a great honor to speak with kings or presidents, and it is a very difficult matter to secure audiences with them; but the humblest saint can enjoy supernatural converse with Him who made the worlds, in a language not understood by man, or by the devil either.

Paul further declares: "He that speaketh in an unknown tongue edifieth himself." 1 Cor. 14:4. These are days when there is much wear and tear on the spiritual life, but God has given in the speaking in tongues a supernatural means for the saint to be built up. Men, when they are below normal in their bodies, go to a doctor and he prescribes a tonic for their rundown condition. God has here provided a spiritual tonic for the building up of the tried and tested saint. Paul wrote to the Corinthians: "I thank my God, I speak with tongues more than ye all," and he must, therefore, have been the most edified; but since in the church he preferred to speak five words with his understanding rather than ten thousand words in a tongue, he must have used this means of spiritual edification in his private devotions, and being thus edified personally, he could go to the church and edify others. And the whole church of Christ has been permanently edified by the writings of this man who declares that he spoke in tongues more than they all.

Paul wrote further, "I would that ye all spake with tongues." v. 5. Was he speaking out of his own heart when he made this statement? No, later in the chapter he declares: "If any man think himself to be a prophet, or spiritual, let him acknowledge that the things that I write unto you are the commandments of the Lord." v. 37. He says also: "He that is spiritual judgeth all things," and so it is clear that any spiritual person will discern that this saying of his, "I would that ye all spake with tongues," is not a mere opinion of the Apostle's but it is an injunction of the Lord. It is a dangerous thing to try to explain it away. It is better to acknowledge in time that the things which Paul wrote are the commandments of the Lord and profit thereby, than to deny the same now and lose thereby in eternity.

The inspired Apostle further states: "Tongues are for a sign, not to them that believe, but to them that believe not." v. 22. Are signs needed? This country is full of signs to the auto driver directing him from one city to another. Take down the signs and you have confusion and many are in perplexity. It is an illegal act to remove the landmarks, and men who do so must suffer a heavy punishment; and yet today men want to remove this sign. Religious leaders have conferences on how to reach the unsaved, and yet many of them are seeking to remove one of the signs, one of God's signs, that He Himself says is a means of reaching the unbeliever. Some argue, "But does not Paul tell us that tongues shall cease?" Yes, but since the speaking in tongues is a sign to them that believe not, we cannot expect it to cease until unbelief has ceased.

In the thirty-ninth verse of this chapter, Paul says, "Forbid not to speak with tongues." It is a very serious matter to forbid the speaking with tongues since, "He that speaketh in an unknown tongue speaketh not unto men, but unto God." A hundred and twenty persons tried to prevent Daniel's speaking unto God. They got a temporary favor, but they had a permanent disfavor.

For himself, Paul declared, "I thank my God, I speak with tongues more than ye all." The Apostle was very thankful to God for the copiousness of this remarkable gift. Some will argue, however, "Yes, it was for Paul's day, but it is not for today." His writings are for today, and he wrote at length concerning this manifestation of the Spirit, declaring, "I would that ye all spake with tongues." If you want to get rid of Paul's experience, you will have to get rid of his writings which tell of his experience. Paul was in the Spirit, and in the Spirit wrote of the operation of the Spirit, and those who profess to be born of the Spirit cannot afford to set aside the experiences of this Spirit-filled man.

Summing up what the Scriptures show concerning the speaking in tongues, we see:

1. That God Himself would speak with the people by this means, to whom He said, "This is the rest wherewith ye may cause the weary to rest; and this is the refreshing: yet they would not hear." Isa. 28:11, 12.

2. That "this is that" prophesied by Joel concerning the outpouring of the Spirit in the last days. Joel 2:28-32; Acts 2:16-20.

3. That it is one of the five signs the Lord Himself declared should follow them that believe. Mark 16: 16-18.

4. That all the Apostles and the women and others with them spoke in other tongues when they were filled with the Holy Ghost on the day of Pentecost (Acts 2:4) according to the promise of Christ. Acts 1:5, 8.

5. That the Gentiles both in Cesarea and Ephesus also spoke in tongues when they received the like gift. Acts 10:46; 19:6.

6. That it is described in 1 Corinthians as one of the manifestations of the Spirit given for profit.

7. That he that has this gift speaks, converses, or communes with God in a language no man can understand. 1 Cor. 14:2.

8. That he that speaketh in an unknown tongue edifieth himself. 1 Cor. 14:4.

9. That the Apostle, speaking at the commandment of the Lord, declares, "I would that ye all spake with tongues." 1 Cor. 14:5, 37.

10. That the peer of Apostles speaks in definite gratitude concerning his speaking in tongues more than all the voluble Corinthians. 1 Cor. 14:18.

11. That it is a sign to them that believe not that God Himself uses. 1 Cor. 14:21, 22.

12. That the Apostle gives the final injunction, "Forbid not to speak with tongues." 1 Cor. 14:39.

But the speaking with tongues has not been the principal feature of this revival. By no means. Our Lord and Saviour Jesus Christ has been exalted as the One altogether lovely and as the chiefest among ten thousand, yea, as all in all. The first and foremost thing in this outpouring has been *the magnifying of the person of the Lord Jesus Christ.*

We heard Pastor Jonathan Paul of Berlin, an acknowledged Pentecostal leader in Germany, say, "I have not put the word 'Pentecost' on my banner. I have the word 'Jesus' on it and expect to keep it there." And the rest of us say, "Amen."

A well-known religious paper published an article speaking very scathingly of what the writer called "the Tongues Movement." The late Dr. W. S. Manners of San Leandro, California, a physician who belonged to the Plymouth Brethren, sent in a protest, and although they did not publish this letter, he was kind enough to send us a copy from which we quote. This doctor wrote: "Dr. K.'s article is all a criticism of this movement and is in keeping with many other articles of a similar nature that I have seen from time to time. As far as I can remember, I have never seen a word of praise of the Pentecostals in any paper or journal that I take. I am wondering just how much these writers really know at first hand as to the Pentecostal people anyway. The criticism reminds me of the harsh things that were said and written of the Brethren fifty years or more ago. I have been with the Brethren for over fifty years. I remember that Dr. Brooks of St. Louis, that great Bible teacher of those good old days, who knew the Brethren from the ground up, made the remark, 'Well, the Brethren have at least one earmark of the early church—they are "the sect that is everywhere spoken against." ' Acts 28:22. The Pentecostals today are receiving the same kind of treatment that the Brethren received in those early days. Needless to say, most of the strictures heaped upon Brethren then were just as unjust as the criticisms meted out to our Pentecostal friends today.

"Any fool can criticize. Personally I am *for* all who stand squarely by the Old Book and the Old Gospel, and I am *against* all who are trying to pull the Word of God to pieces, and repudiate all that the Cross stands for. I may not see all that our Pentecostal folks stand for, but I know more about these people than those who are criticizing them, for I have attended scores of their meetings, and can bless God for their zeal and loyalty to God and to His Word—and rejoice in the results they get. In conclusion let me say that I think I have heard more of the great Bible men of America than 99 per cent of your readers—Brooks, Parsons, Erdman, Hudson Taylor, Moody, Whittle, and scores of others, not to mention all the best teachers among Brethren, and I think I know the gospel when I hear it, and I want to say that time and again I have heard as clear a presentation of the gospel in Pentecostal meetings as I ever heard among the Brethren, and if any class know the Old Book better than Brethren do, I would thank you to name that class for me."

A young evangelist of the Assemblies of God
(Lester Sumrall) and the president of a large section
of the Lutheran Church in the U. S. A. recently met
together on the same train. The young man asked this
official what he thought of the modern revival popularly
called "The Pentecostal Movement."

The Lutheran minister stated that he believed that
God had sent this revival to fill a great need in the
world today. This need he felt was to touch the non-
church-going masses. He believed that Methodism was
primarily sent for the same purpose, and that when they
ceased to reach the poorer masses the Lord sent the
Salvation Army to meet the need. His expressed conviction is that the present revival is, in the purpose of
God, filling this great mission.

The Lutheran minister said the *universal* growth of
this revival was amazing to him. In his visits to Norway and Sweden he had found a great work. He knew
the late T. B. Barratt of Oslo, who expressed the belief
of the Pentecostal people: "As regards salvation by
justification, we are Lutherans. In baptismal formula,
we are Baptists. As regards sanctification, we are
Methodists. In aggressive evangelism we are as the
Salvation Army. But as regards the Baptism in the
Holy Spirit, we are *Pentecostal!*" These tenets of
faith brought people from all denominations to the Pentecostal Church.

This Lutheran elder spoke of the rapid growth of
the Pentecostal revival in America. He felt that each of
the Pentecostal tabernacles dotting the countryside like
mushrooms was "a rebuke to them." The young
evangelist said, "Is it not rather *a challenge?*"

At the beginning of the dispensation the church
of Christ was not divided, but *of one accord*. Surely
this is how God purposes us to be in the last days. Our
Lord Jesus Christ prayed the Father concerning those
that were His: "That they all may be one ... that the
world may believe that Thou hast sent me." In a report
just received from China we see how God is answering

this prayer of His Son.   A convention was called to meet in Kalgan for six days—April 19-26, 1941, but it lasted for nearly 50.   Horace S. Williams, Chairman of the Mengchiang Christian Council, writes of "the new thing" the Lord did in those days:

"During the early days of the Convention it was revealed to us in a new way that we were all members of the one body of Christ. For the most part we were well acquainted with each other before and naturally there were many lovely friendships. But now the Spirit showed that we were members of His body and that He would have the whole body fitly joined together and compacted by that which every joint supplieth, according to the effectual working in the measure of each part, making increase of the body unto the edifying of itself in love.

"When we consider that during these nearly 50 days together about 90 different missionaries have participated for longer or shorter periods; that we have represented some 10 nationalities and some 15 denominations or Mission societies and that practically 100 per cent of those who have been here, have felt this bond of oneness and love without any sense of compromise or urge outside the conviction of the Holy Spirit, it becomes apparent to us all that God is in our midst of a truth.

"The messages from the Lord have truly been remarkable. Each person assembled stood on an equality as to opportunity to speak or participate in the meetings, yet each meeting has been a complete unit, and these units have been one complete whole. Some messages came by songs, some by exposition of the Scriptures, some by tongues with interpretation, some by gift of prophecy and some through testimonies. But it was the one, same Holy Spirit speaking to the churches. The burden of the messages can be summed up as follows:

"The time is short; the coming of the Lord is near; the present opportunities of evangelism will not last long; the Lord longs to work in a new, glorious, and mighty way to show forth His glory and save souls; the only hindrance is that the people of the Lord will not permit Him to cause them to be prepared as His glorious vessels and channels; 'O that there were such an heart in them that they would fear Me, and keep all My commandments always, that it might be well with them.' 'Ye have not chosen Me but I have chosen you, and ordained you, that ye should go and bring forth fruit, and that your fruit should remain, that whatsoever ye shall ask of the Father in My name, He may give you. These things I command you, that ye love one another. Every branch in Me that beareth not fruit He taketh away, and every branch that beareth fruit He purgeth it, that it may bring forth more fruit. Now ye are clean through the word which I have spoken unto you.' 'And behold I send the promise of My Father upon you; but tarry ye in the city of Jesrusalem until ye be endued with power from on high. All power is given unto Me. Go ye therefore ... I am with you alway.'

"The deepening of our spiritual life during these weeks of listening to what the Spirit has said to the churches, and to us as individuals, has been amazing. The meetings opened in a blaze of glory and great joy. Then, little by little, we went into the valley as sins of various kinds were revealed to hearts, and then the battle with the powers of darkness and victory. The altar was the scene of operation in each service as we sought Him whom our souls loved, and whom we had grieved. With tears we opened our hearts to Him, and received again the peace and joy which had been ours. There was a cry unto Him also, that He should baptize us in the Holy Spirit and those who were already baptized in the Spirit sought to be filled anew. Many who in days past had had gifts of the Spirit, but on account of disobedience, or other causes had lost these gifts, prayed and received again. Those of our number—and they were few—who had grievances one with another, were gloriously united in loving embrace and all were given new love, and came to cherish each other as never before. Truly these have been days of heaven upon earth. Our cups run over. The joybells have rung day and night.

"Many came to the meetings with physical weaknesses and in some cases with some disease. According to James 5:14, 15, where the sick children of God are enjoined to call the elders of the church and be anointed in the name of the Lord, here we too have prayed for all who requested it. A large number availed themselves of this fountain of healing and already the large majority of those prayed for have been completely healed. The others are definitely improving. We are glad also to testify to the healing of a two-months-old baby brought five times for prayer, whom the Lord graciously, completely healed of epilepsy. And this paragraph is not complete without reference to the sister who was instantly healed in her room in another part of the city at the exact minute friends here —without her knowledge—prayed for her at the breakfast table. Thus by many infallible proofs our Lord has showed us that He is alive today.

"Finally we mention the burden of evangelism and revival which has been given us. We believe greater things are just ahead, and that this revival will spread far and wide. This hope is based on the fact that what has taken place here is so evidently the work of God. Furthermore, it has been shown us so often during these days that He is working a new thing, not because we are worthy—for we each feel ourselves to be great sinners and so often disobedient to our Lord—but for His own Name's sake, for Jesus' sake, and for the sake of His promises. Therefore we believe it is merely incidental and entirely His grace that this work should begin here. Perhaps just now similar revivals have begun in various parts of the earth without our knowledge. If not, we have a charge exceeding what we could ask or think. Surely God's time has come to revive His children and reach the lost with the gospel, —yes, that every creature should hear. 'For this gospel of the kingdom shall be preached in all the world for a witness, and then shall the end come.' "

In this book we have told of a few things which have happened in the last few years, and we leave it to the readers to judge whether they are of God or not. In every revival some things happen which are regrettable. The story of the early church is no exception, but who would dare to say that the revival described in the Acts of the Apostles was not of God because of the failure of Ananias and Sapphira, and because in the revival at Samaria Peter and John found a real counterfeit in a supposed convert, Simon Magus. It is very clear that Paul had to correct many errors that arose in the church, and it is clear that in the first council held at Jerusalem there was no small disputation because many were not prepared to walk entirely in the way of grace. Practically all of Paul's Epistles are corrective because there were many things that needed correction in the assemblies. Paul even had to correct Peter for his dissembling. But despite all this we must confess that God mightily poured out His Spirit at the beginning of the church period.

And thank God, He is mightily pouring out His Spirit in the last days, at what is surely the end of the church period. There is no doubt that the enemy of souls today hates this revival which is taking away so many from his kingdom, and is seeking to destroy the work in every way, to belittle it, and to bring it injury. But the more the enemy seeks to destroy the more the Lord pours out His Spirit and continues to bless. We are often reminded of that lesson that Bunyan let Christian learn in the House of the Interpreter. Christian saw a fire burning which continued to burn despite the devil's constantly throwing water upon it. The Interpreter showed him the cause. He was taken to the other side of the wall and there he saw Christ continually pouring oil upon that fire.

Christ is pouring the oil and the fire still blazes, and we all believe it will blaze until that glad day when the Lord Jesus Christ shall descend from heaven and take His church to be with Him forevermore.

As I close may I ask two simple questions of my reader. Do you personally know the power of the precious blood of Christ to cleanse from all sin? And, if so, have you received the Holy Ghost since ye believed?—the oil upon the blood. If not, you can ask the Lord now, and He declares: "Everyone that asketh receiveth."

011803